Television and
its Audience

SAGE Communications in Society Series
Edited by Jeremy Tunstall

Already published

New Communication Technologies and the Public Interest,
edited by Marjorie Ferguson

New Media Politics, *by the Euromedia Research Group,*
edited by Denis McQuail and Karen Siune

The Myth of the Information Revolution,
edited by Michael Traber

Pressure Sensitive: Popular Musicians under Stress
Geoff Wills and Cary L. Cooper

Television and its Audience

Patrick Barwise
and
Andrew Ehrenberg

 SAGE Publications
London • Newbury Park • Beverly Hills • New Delhi

First published 1988

Reprinted 1990, 1992

SAGE Publications Ltd
28 Banner Street
London EC1Y 8QE

SAGE Publications Inc
2111 West Hillcrest Drive
Newbury Park, California 91320

SAGE Publications Inc
275 South Beverly Drive
Beverly Hills, California 90212

SAGE Publications India Pvt Ltd
32, M-Block Market
Greater Kailash – I
New Delhi 110 048

British Library Cataloguing in Publication data

Barwise, Patrick.
  Television and its audience. – (Sage communications in society series)
  1. Society. Effects of television.
  I. Title II. Ehrenberg, Andrew.
  302.2'345

ISBN 0–8039–8154–6
ISBN 0–8039–8155–4 Pbk

Library of Congress catalog card number 88–062287

Typeset by System 4 Associates Limited
Farnham Common, Buckinghamshire
Printed in Great Britain by Billing and Sons Ltd, Worcester

Contents

Preface

Television as a medium is rarely considered in the light of how we as viewers actually use it. Discussions of the effects of television, its funding, its future, or its programs are seldom related to any real and detailed knowledge of people's patterns of viewing and program choice. Nonetheless, implicit assumptions are often made about how people watch. For instance, it is widely thought that programs and channels each have their regular viewers, that people mainly want to watch the most popular programs, that public service channels appeal to only a small or elitist minority, and that people want their television to be free of charge. Such views are formed on the basis of an often totally mistaken understanding of market demand as revealed by the audience's actual viewing behavior and willingness to pay. This lack of understanding matters particularly in the current context of deregulation, of the 'video revolution', and of worldwide funding crises for television.

There is thus a need for a book that makes sense of the nature of television and its problems in terms of the audience's viewing patterns and of the economics of the market. *Television and its Audience* aims to do this for students, teachers, practitioners, and interested members of the public. It draws mostly on research from the USA and Britain, with some results from other countries. The book summarizes technical work in a non-technical style. References and background material are given at the end of each chapter and there is a glossary at the end of the book.

ACKNOWLEDGMENTS

The preparation of this book has been supported by a generous grant from the Markle Foundation of New York to the London Business School (LBS). Completion of the book has also been part of a program of work at the LBS Centre for Marketing and Communication, which is supported by thirty-five leading companies.

The research background comprises more than one hundred reports prepared over more than twenty years: in the USA mainly for Arbitron and the Markle Foundation, and in Britain mainly for the Independent Broadcasting Authority, 1967–84, and more recently for the BBC. Much of this work on audiences was carried out with our colleagues, Professors Gerald Goodhardt and Martin Collins, and was summarized in *The Television Audience: Patterns of Viewing* (Goodhardt et al., 1975, 1987). Our emphasis here is much broader.

Of the many people to whom we are indebted for support and discussion, we single out particularly Lloyd Morrisett, President of the Markle Foundation, and William Phillips, for his informed and painstaking help during the draft stages.

The book has benefited greatly from constructive criticisms and comments, especially those given by:

Lord Annan	Peter Meneer
Guy Aston	Pam Mills
Dr Neil Barnard	Professor Bill Motes
Professor Jay Blumler	Gerard O'Neill
John Bound	Rip Ridgeway
Richard Brooks	Professor Tom Robertson
Mary Campbell	Harold Vogel
Katrina Ellis	Dr Dan Van Vuuren
Len England	Dr Jacob Wakshlag
Stephen Hearst	Alan Ward
Clay Herrick	Professor Jim Watt
John Howkins	David Webster
Dr Heikki Kasari	Professor Jim Webster

and, above all, Helen Bloom Lewis.

T. P. Barwise
A.S.C. Ehrenberg
London Business School

Detailed Contents

PART ONE
THE GIANT MEDIUM

By any measure, television today is the giant among media. The amount of time that people give to it, and how and why they do so, throws light on the many practical and ethical concerns surrounding television. In Chapter 1 we stress the need to link our thinking about these concerns with how the audience actually uses television. The chapter also gives an overview of how we address this in the five parts of the book.

Chapter 2 looks at how much time people spend in front of their television sets, how this amount varies among individuals, and how people spread their viewing across different times of the day and week. Whereas overall viewing levels follow regular patterns and are fairly steady from week to week, an individual's viewing is typically much more irregular.

Chapter 1
Introduction and Overview

Watching television is a major feature of modern life in developed countries and, increasingly, in developing countries. The 'box' is a frequent topic of conversation although, as viewers, we usually seem to have little to show for the hours that we spend in front of it. Television is also a significant industry in its own right and is a major advertising medium in most countries.

For these reasons, television has always attracted a lot of 'punditry'. Debates rage about whether it is a waste of time; about whether it has to be run in the way that it is or if it might be organized better; about its coverage of sex, violence, profanity, politics, and social issues; about its stereotyping of minority or underprivileged groups; its role in education and cultural improvement; about the effects of television advertising; and so on. These questions also arise in the context of other mass media but the ubiquity, immediacy and vividness of television put it in the center of all these debates. The fact that fairly little is known objectively about the issues has not reduced the amount that is said and written.

The past few years have also seen an intensified commercial and political focus on television. The growing interest in market forces and deregulation, which often implies that television should increasingly be funded by advertising (as traditionally in the USA), has recently brought advertising into many previously non-commercial television systems from Italy to India. In addition there is the impact or potential of the new video technologies, especially cable, satellites, and video cassette recorders, with the promise of more to come. Some enthusiasts are already proclaiming a new age of television, with untold program choice that is controlled by the viewer rather than by channel schedulers.

What often seems to be missing from these debates is any real reference to the *audience*, other than perhaps a mention of the ratings – the numbers of people who watch a program. How the viewers actually consume television throws light not only on the practical policy issues but also on the overall nature of the medium. That is the focus of this book.

As we will describe, there are predictable patterns in the way that people

watch television: the range and variety of different types of program
that people choose to watch, the extent to which viewers watch a series
regularly, their loyalty to a channel, and so on. These patterns can affect
how programs are produced, how they might be scheduled across the
evening, and how television can be funded.

Would starting each episode of a series with a recap of the story so far
be tiresome or useful? Can schedulers 'catch the audience young' early
in the evening and keep them watching their channel all evening? Does
concentrating on programs that attract the highest ratings really give
viewers what they want? What is the impact of television violence? Are
the more highbrow programs watched merely by some elitist minority?
What is the best way to position the programming of a new television
channel – to capture high ratings and revenues or to give viewers more
effective or satisfying choices?

In addressing such issues, perhaps the most important background
knowledge that is needed is the overall picture of how people watch
television. We watch a lot but it is mostly at a fairly low level of involvement, often at a lower level of attention than in a cinema or theater, at
a live concert or sporting contest, or for most books or magazines. We
are not even always watching the screen when the set is on. Yet many
participants in debates about the effects, the organization, and the future of
television seem implicitly to assume a continuously *high* level of audience
involvement.

Some enthusiasts of new technology have, for instance, described a
future world of individuals who start every evening actively designing their
own tailored viewing schedule by searching through a limitless cornucopia
of program information. Another widespread belief is that, by at least the
year 2020, the patterns of distribution, production, and consumption of
television or video will be much the same as those of the print media today.
It is thought that today's mass audience channels will be supplemented
or even supplanted by a flowering of highly targeted 'narrowcast' channels
analogous to books and to specialist or local print media. These narrowcast
channels are expected to reach small, well-defined, and highly involved
audiences and to be profitable because, compared with today's few mass
channels, they will be able to earn much more revenue per viewer from
relevant advertisers or from direct pay-TV subscriptions or indeed from
both.

Such scenarios seem to us unlikely to occur on anything like the scale
that is often assumed. We do expect that more new channels will evolve but
also that the total time spent watching them will be fairly small compared

with the vast amount of time that people spend viewing television as a whole. The main reason is that watchable new programming is unlikely to become available on a sufficiently dramatic scale. For the more revolutionary scenarios to occur, there would also have to be big changes in the patterns of viewing seen to date, in how television acts as a communication medium, in the costs of program production, and in how revenues are generated. Yet no such big changes have been predicted by anyone involved. Nor do we ourselves regard them as at all likely, with the possible exception of marked increases in what we pay.

There will be change, but we think it will have only a limited impact on the bulk of future viewing. Because of this difference of opinions about the future, we present here the existing evidence about the present and past so that readers may judge for themselves.

AN OVERVIEW

The book is divided into five main parts. The first three are concerned with people's viewing behavior: how we use television.

The second chapter in Part One describes how much and when we watch television. Most people watch a lot, often more than twenty hours per week, although some of us watch less. There are many regular patterns in this, the most obvious being that peak viewing or 'prime time' is always in mid-evening. However, as individuals we are often very irregular from day to day or week to week as regards when we watch. Viewing mostly seems to occur when we have nothing more compelling to do.

Part Two deals with people's choice of programs. Most people watch a wide variety of different types of program, as discussed in Chapter 3. This is so for viewers of all kinds. There is no special tendency for viewers of a particular program to choose other programs of the same type. Perhaps surprisingly, viewers of *Dallas* are no more likely to watch *Dynasty* than are viewers who do not watch *Dallas*. The audience of *Dallas* is not a collection of soap opera addicts, nor is that of *Dynasty*.

Each of us cares enough about some programs to make some effort to see them. But in Chapter 4 we note how (as with television generally) our viewing of specific television series is mostly rather erratic; only about *half* of those who watch a peak-time program this week will have seen last week's episode. The proportion for lower-rating programs is even smaller. Hence very few viewers watch all of even a limited-run serial.

The converse is that many people will get to know some part of it. For example, half of the UK population saw at least one episode of the acclaimed weekly series, *Jewel in the Crown*. But despite each episode being shown twice per week, only two in a hundred saw all fourteen episodes, and not very many more saw twelve or thirteen. Such irregular viewing is typical for all regular series. It is predictable in detail and is little affected by having a VCR.

These two patterns in people's viewing – spreading across different types of program and rarely watching any one of them very regularly – do not mean that their viewing is just random or that they do not care what they see. People have real preferences. But watching a particular program right then is not always enormously important to them, so long as there is a good degree of choice available over the week. In Chapter 5, we explore this in terms of audiences' expressed appreciation of television programs. The evidence is that people mostly quite like what they watch, enough to go on watching the program in question, and definitely more than they like the programs that they know about but do *not* choose to watch. There are some programs that some of the viewers like especially, but this differs greatly from person to person; while one person's meat may not be another's poison (otherwise they would hardly watch the program), it may well not be as palatable. So the average viewer of a program typically only *quite* likes it rather than regarding it as a preferred favorite. Television is a mass medium because it is so widely watched, not because everyone likes or watches the same thing.

Low-rating programs, those that are watched by few people, tend if anything to be liked *less* by their few viewers than are high-rating programs by their many viewers. A partial but important exception to this pattern occurs for programs which are emotionally or intellectually more demanding and not classifiable as 'mere entertainment'. These are usually watched by fewer (although often numerous) people than the top-rating entertainment shows but tend to be appreciated just about as highly as the latter.

There is, however, almost no evidence to back up the commonly held expectations about true 'minority interest' programs: that programs exist which have very few viewers but are liked exceptionally well by most of these. Television programs do not appear to work like that. This matters when we are concerned with the range of programs that might be produced or with alternative ways of paying for programs or with the possible 'segmentation' of the mass audience.

In Part Three (Chapters 6 and 7) we turn from program choice to the distribution channels through which programs reach us. We usually choose to watch programs, not channels, and we are not always very aware of which channel we are watching. We are not glued to one channel if there is choice.

Even on a single day, the average viewer tunes in for significant periods to almost three channels in the UK or four in the USA, and this pattern predates the advent of remote switches. There is a degree of channel preference or loyalty but this is weak and divided: most viewers watch all or most of the larger channels.

The 1980s have seen a proliferation of distribution channels based on new technologies, as we review in Chapter 7. Many homes now have more than one television set. Large numbers of people have video cassette recorders (VCRs), a very different kind of channel for distributing, or redistributing, programs. Cable television is widespread in some countries such as the USA, Canada and Belgium, either to replace over-air transmissions for better quality pictures or to give additional choice, but it is hardly used at all in most other countries. VCRs and cable-only programming are each viewed for several hours per week by their users, which makes them significant leisure activities in absolute terms, but this is relatively small *compared with the 20-plus hours per week* that people watch programs available over the air via traditional broadcast channels.

The new distribution channels are mostly used to give us some extra freedom of choice over and above the main channels. This extra choice is largely a question of timing: users of the new channels tend to watch a rather similar range of programs, or even re-runs of the same programs, as are on the over-air channels. The new channels are therefore not revolutionizing our viewing choices or our viewing behavior: television is still television.

In summary, Parts One to Three focus on how we watch television and on our choices of particular programs and channels. Parts Four and Five then deal with the economics of television and with the nature of the medium more generally.

Part Four discusses what television costs and how we pay for it. Making watchable programs is very expensive and Chapter 8 explains why this is so. Paradoxically, *watching* television (i.e. receiving programs) is mostly very cheap. It costs only a few pennies per viewing hour for channels funded by taxes or license fees, such as most European channels, or is even apparently free if funded by advertising. It may seem odd to spend over $1 million on making one episode of *Dallas* but, if some 100 million people around the world see it, that amounts to only one cent per viewer –some of the cheapest television there is.

The way that television is paid for, together with both the good and bad effects of competition, influences the kind of programming that is produced and watched in different countries. Under the right conditions, competition can greatly enliven the programs that are offered. However, if it means that channels have to depend on achieving the highest possible ratings all the time, competition can also stifle initiative and risk-taking and can limit the diversity of choice available to the viewer.

Advertising is often an important part of television. It can be the main source of funding for the general run of program material. It also provides its own program material, the commercials, for us to watch and listen to and it can influence our attitudes and behavior as consumers of goods and services. Thus advertising, as part of the television scene, is touched on at various stages in the book. As it is also a communication service in its own right, the general role of advertising and how it works is reviewed separately in Appendix A.

Part Five of the book gives our view of some of the broader implications of television. First, how watching television is such a compelling pastime and yet seems to be done at such a low level of involvement most of the time. We look at how television differs in this and other respects from other media such as radio and print.

We also discuss how and why television raises a great many concerns and ask if these are perhaps often overstated. Three special features of television are that the set is in the home, that nearly everybody can therefore watch it so much, and that moving pictures can be so vivid. It might therefore be thought that television must have a big effect on people. However, when we take account of how many programs, newscasts and commercials people actually watch, viewing any one of them can hardly ever be a very significant event. The possibility of longer-term or 'drip' effects of television is not so clear cut and raises technical questions of evidence and ethical questions of the burden of proof, which we also briefly review.

As for the future, nobody has yet spelt out why people's viewing patterns or the economics of providing watchable television programs will or should radically change. Some of the new technologies will affect program distribution methods but, as explained in the final chapter, we doubt whether they will dramatically change how much, what or how viewers watch.

DATA AND SOURCES

The discussion in this book centers on the USA and Britain, two countries which have been extensively researched and which are also especially familiar to us as authors. They differ markedly in how television is organized and should provide a range of background knowledge and understanding for other countries.

Insofar as the book is about audience behavior, it is based on millions of dollars' worth of audience data and numerous research projects, (although we hope that it does not read like that). The basic data about people's viewing of programs and commercial breaks are collected every week by leading marketing research operators, the ratings services, in most developed countries. The measurement techniques used are outlined in Appendix B.

Most of the data referred to in this book measure whether people are in a room with the television set on and to which program the set is tuned. But we all know that those in the room are not always paying attention to the set. Some of them are also doing other things or may even be asleep. The audience's level of attention can be measured fairly accurately but largely for reasons of cost this is not done routinely.

In Britain, for example, it has been known for many years that, at commercial breaks in the evening, about 20 percent of those present in the room during the surrounding quarter hour are momentarily absent for any given commercial; some 10 percent are present but not viewing; 30 percent are viewing but otherwise also active (e.g. reading, talking); roughly 40 percent are 'viewing only'. There is evidence that the breakdown of the US audience during commercial breaks is fairly similar.

During program transmissions these other activities tend to occur less but, of those people normally measured as viewing at any time (i.e. being in the room with the set on), typically some 60 percent are then 'viewing only' and 40 percent are giving the set less than their full attention. The 60 percent figure is a good guideline for the evening but for day-time the ambiguities over just what is implied by 'viewing' are even more marked. The 60/40 percent breakdown is a very substantial factor and is essential background to the figures in this book. Nonetheless, the amount of attentive viewing that people do remains very large. No-one denies that *other* people watch a lot of television.

The various findings on people's viewing referred to in Parts One to Three are largely based on analyses of the above kinds of audience data over many years. Accounts of the analyses have often been published and others are available, as noted at the end of each Chapter.

For example, the finding that, for a regular program series, at least half of the current week's audience will usually not have seen the previous week's episode is based on some fifty research studies, ranging from an initial report twenty years ago to current updates. These analyses have covered different programs and types of program, different days of the week and times of day, consecutive and non-consecutive weeks, high- and low-rating levels, different channels, different population subgroups, different years and countries, and different measurement techniques and data sources. The work has also sought to pin down exceptions or sub-patterns, for instance that repeat-viewing levels for some soap operas are a few percentage points higher than for other drama series. Few of the other results in this book have been established as comprehensively but they have been confirmed widely, in particular for the USA and Britain, at different times and under a range of different programming and viewing conditions.

The interpretation of such research findings is another matter. The book therefore sets out both what we know and what we think. We trust that the difference will always be clear.

NOTES

Further Reading

For US television, two introductions are Comstock's (1980) short textbook and Cole's (1981) selection of articles from *TV Guide*. A useful source is Brown's (1982) *Encyclopedia of Television*, which includes some data for other countries. Articles on the structure and finance of broadcasting in Europe, North America, Japan, and Australasia are in Blumler and Nossiter (1988). A shorter account of television in Europe is Pragnall (1985).

Williams (1974) gives a brief, well-written comparison of network television in the USA and Britain focusing on programs. Wheen (1985), based on a TV series, illustrates program types. CPB (1978) and Taylor and Mullan (1986) describe how viewers in the USA and the UK talk about television in group discussions.

On television's role in people's lives, an innovative step was Steiner's (1963) survey of US viewers, updated by Bower (1973, 1985) who discusses trends over the twenty years. See also Lo Sciuto (1972). Much wider ranging is Comstock et al.'s (1978) summary of the literature on television and human behavior. This built on earlier work for the US *Surgeon-General's Scientific Advisory Committee* (1972). A follow-up investigation was published by the National Institute of Mental Health (NIMH 1982), which has a 90-page summary volume. Blumler and Katz (1974) brought together research on the 'uses and gratifications' of watching television. A useful recent summary of television's role in family life is Gunter and Svennevig (1987). Standard texts such as De Fleur and Ball-Rokeach (1982) and McQuail (1987) set television in the context of mass-communication theory.

On the financial and commercial aspects of television, there are official and trade sources in addition to the annual reports of the broadcasting organizations in different countries. Vogel (1986) includes references to other sources in his excellent account of the financial side of TV in the USA. A detailed description of US commercial television is given by Poltrack (1983); one can also refer to the main texts on advertising, such as Kleppner (1986). Numerous research and consultancy services monitor the US new media industry, the most widely cited being Paul Kagan Associates.

Other references, where appropriate, are given throughout these Notes.

Journals

There is extensive coverage of television in newspapers, magazines, newsletters, and academic journals such as the *Journal of Communication*, the *Journal of Broadcasting & Electronic Media*, the *Journal of Advertising Research*, and the *European Journal of Communication*.

For professionals, important journals include the monthly *Channels* in the USA, which also publishes an annual 'Field Guide' to new media developments, the British-based monthly *Admap* (with an advertising focus) and *InterMedia* (with wide international coverage), and also *TBI* (*Television Business International*) launched in 1988. Weekly trade publications include *Variety* and *Advertising Age* in the USA, and *Broadcast* and *Media Week* in the Britain.

Audience Data

There are numerous reports on audiences by the regular ratings services in different countries. A US text is Beville (1985). A.C. Nielsen's annual report, *The Television Audience* (e.g. Nielsen 1987), gives audience data and trends for the USA. Arbitron (1981) describes the methodology of their one-week-diary surveys in the US, and BARB/AGB (1987) that of the panel-based measurement procedures in Britain. A brief summary of measurement procedures is given in Appendix B of this book. Procedures are currently changing somewhat because of the increasing number of channels and the increasing use of people-meters (see, for example, CAB 1983; ARF 1987; Twyman 1988; Cook 1988; Spaeth 1988; Soong 1988).

Assessments of the validity of measurement techniques include in the USA various reports by the Committee on National Television Audience Measurement (e.g. Mayer 1966; CONTAM 1969 and 1971) and more recent unpublished industry studies. In Britain there were reports by TAM (1961) and Ehrenberg and Twyman (1967), as well as frequent discussions more recently in the journals and the trade press.

Small-scale 'presence and attention' studies of the extent to which those measured as being in the room with the television set on are actually watching it have used observational techniques such as photographs or video (e.g. Allen 1965; Bechtel et al. 1972; Collett and Lamb 1986). Innovative *quantitative* research into this area was begun in Britain (e.g. Research Services 1962), with more recent work in the USA by Television Audience Assessment (TAA 1983a,b, 1984). The literature has been well reviewed by Twyman (1986a, b).

Chapter 2
Watching Television

In most industrialized countries television is in more than 95 percent of homes. Most households now have color television, and many have two sets or more – 50 percent in Britain for instance, and over 60 percent in the USA, making an average of almost one set per *person* there. Even in developing countries, where television is a luxury, ownership is rapidly growing: in 1984 Brazil already had a set for every six inhabitants, while the Ivory Coast in Africa had one set for every twenty.

People who have access to a television set generally use it a great deal. In most countries they are in a room with a television on for between 10 and 25 hours per week. In the USA, Japan, and Britain the average is higher still – 25 to 30 hours per week, or almost 1500 hours per person per year. The sets themselves are on for even longer, because different members of a household may watch at different times.

The so-called 'audience ratings' measure how many people in the population are in a room with a tuned-in television set at any given time. Some of this viewing is combined with activities such as housework, eating or talking, and can be at a very low level of concentration, as we have already stressed. Nonetheless, the audience ratings give a good indication of how much television people are exposed to.

In that broad sense people in many countries spend between a third and a half of their free time with television, more time than we spend on anything else except sleep and work. In the late 1960s, some people predicted that viewing might decrease: the novelty was wearing off, more women were going out to work, and people were acquiring wider leisure interests as they became better educated and more affluent. Television viewing has confounded these prophets: it has gone on growing. Even in the USA, viewing has increased by some 15 percent in the past ten years.

Although countries vary widely in their cultures, living standards, and political structures, viewing is widespread everywhere. Differences between countries' alternative entertainment and information media, or between their television systems, affect viewing levels less than one might expect. A city-dweller in the USA can typically choose from eight or ten channels in color (even more if on cable), which show the world's most expensively-made programming 24 hours per day. The schedules are fine-tuned to maximize patronage in a non-stop competitive quest for the viewer's attention. In contrast, a small Third World country may be served by a single, government-administered, monochrome channel. This may be on the air for only six hours per day showing a mixture of cheap, home-produced programs (including state-controlled news) and imported entertainment, dubbed or subtitled in local languages. Yet the medium's fascination transcends these inequalities.

The amount that we view varies seasonally. Other calls on our free time are more pressing in mid-summer, when viewing in the USA and Britain is a good 10 percent below the annual average. In the depths of winter, we view at least 10 percent more than average. In northern countries such as Finland the contrast is starker: on average people watch seven hours per week in June and 15 hours per week in February.

For most countries, however, these seasonal variations should not be exaggerated. Viewing less in the summer still means an average of more than 20 hours per week in the USA and Britain. Broadcasters possibly over-react. In most western countries the summer television schedules are full of cheaper or repeated programs, with new and high-budget material kept back until the autumn and winter. Would summer viewing drop off less if the most attractive programming were more evenly spread through the year?

Although households are becoming smaller, with at least one person in ten living alone in most developed countries, people usually watch tele-vision in company, often with close relations. Among those who do not live alone, about half of their day-time viewing is in the company of at least one other household member; in the evening after work, almost all viewing is in company.

In two-set homes it is fairly unusual for both sets to be on at the same time. When they are, for half of the time both are tuned to the same channel, even in the USA with its many channels. Thus the second set is used not only to extend the choice of programs at a given time but also to enable people to watch in different parts of the house, such as kitchen and the living room, and to keep in touch with a program if they are moving around.

DIFFERENT VIEWERS, DIFFERENT AMOUNTS

Individuals vary widely in the amounts of television that they watch. Figure 2.1 shows the distribution for New York housewives in a given week. The average number of hours viewed was 29 but the range was wide, with a quarter being in the room with the set on for less than 15 hours and a quarter for 40 hours or more. The top 10 percent viewed for more than 55 hours. This degree of variation is typical.

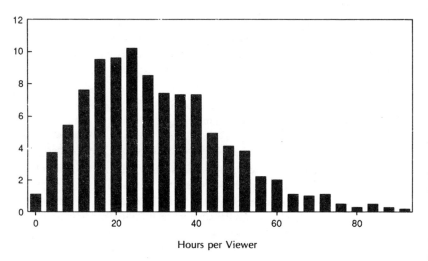

Hours per Viewer

Figure 2.1   *Television hours viewed in one week (New York City, November 1974)*

Part of the variation is systematic, differing consistently between different kinds of people because of the amount of free time that they have at home. The biggest single factor here is age. Older adults, particularly retired people and those who live alone, watch on average almost twice as much television as do young adults. Contrary to widespread belief, children in general watch rather less television than adults, mainly because they go to bed earlier. A striking change occurs in the mid-teens, the 'going out' years. While teenagers aged 12 to 14 are quite heavy viewers, older teenagers are on average the lightest.

The better-off and/or more educated groups watch a little less television than the rest, in Britain an average of 23 hours per week compared with 27 hours for all adults. Women watch more than men. People in large households watch less television *per person* than people in small households, but they still average about 20 hours per week.

Despite such systematic differences, how much television an individual views is not primarily determined by age, sex, income, or any other demographic classification. Within any subgroup there is still the kind of variation illustrated in Figure 2.1. Attempts have been made to match amounts of viewing to people's lifestyles or their 'psychographic profiles' (social characteristics, attitudes, opinions, interests, needs, personalities, etc.) but nobody has succeeded in strongly correlating such stereotypes with individuals' viewing patterns. This emphasizes that television is a true mass medium, too widespread to be closely identified with particular pockets or segments of a country's population. How much we watch is largely a matter of personal taste and habit, constrained by the competing appeals and demands of other activities and pastimes.

WHEN WE WATCH

During the peak viewing hours each evening, up to half of a country's population is doing the same thing: watching television. The numbers are vast, about 20 million will be watching in Britain and 100 million in the USA. Nonetheless, watching television is not universal. Even at peak time at least half of the population is doing something else.

The size of the television audience follows a recurring daily pattern. Figure 2.2 illustrates the percentage of US adults viewing at different times. The numbers build up fairly steadily during the day, reaching about 15 percent of the population by late afternoon and then climbing faster to a peak generally of almost 50 percent between about 9 and 10 pm. The percentage then starts to fall off quite rapidly, but is still between 10 and 20 percent at midnight.

The daily rhythm of these overall percentages changes little during the working week, even though different programs are screened. If 30 percent of a given population are watching television at 7 pm on an average night, the actual figures day by day will vary relatively little: perhaps 32 percent at 7 pm on Monday, 27 percent at 7 pm on Tuesday, 31 percent on Wednesday, and so on, but never 5 percent and virtually never 50.

The pattern at weekends differs marginally, since people have more free time then. There is somewhat more late-night viewing on Fridays and Saturdays, and more day-time viewing on Saturdays and Sundays, but most adult viewing is still in mid-evening.

The pattern of viewing by time of day also varies between subgroups of the population but mainly in their off-peak behavior. Women of all ages who do not go out to work and older retired men watch more television in total because they can watch more during the day and early evening. Among children and teenagers, the daily trend of viewing naturally differs

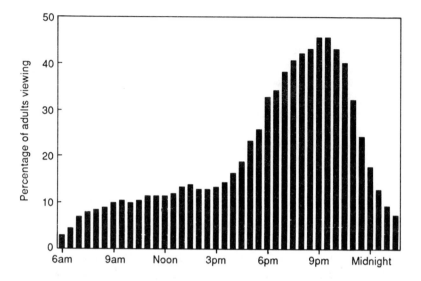

Figure 2.2   *The daily pattern of the television audience (New York City, November 1984)*

from the adult pattern, though perhaps less than one might think. In the pre-school group in the USA and Britain, some 10 to 20 percent tend to be watching at any one moment in the morning. On weekdays during school time, young people's viewing hours are roughly from 4 pm to 10 pm, compared with adults' 6 pm to midnight. Viewing is more prolonged during school vacations but not dramatically so. Like adults, children watch more television at weekends. Their viewing is notably high on Saturday mornings in countries where child-orientated programs such as cartoons are screened.

Audience levels can vary for cultural reasons too. At breakfast time, the peak adult audience levels in the USA and Britain are only about 10 percent. The figure for Japan is some 35 percent, partly because in many homes the television set is in the room where meals are taken.

Availability to View

A major influence on people's viewing is their availability to view at a given time. This has been defined as 'being at home but not asleep in bed'. During the working day in the USA and Britain, only half of the women and a quarter of the men are available to view. During the main part of the evening, the proportion rises to about 70 percent for both sexes.

But this is not the only factor governing whether we watch. Until early evening, less than half of those 'available' are watching television. During the peak hours this increases to as many as two-thirds of the much larger number of people 'available' by then, giving the peak total television audience of close to 50 percent of the total population (i.e. some two-thirds of 70 percent). While some of the other things that people do at home can be compatible with television viewing, some are not: vacuuming, mowing the lawn, talking with friends, studying, and so on. Some things, such as looking after a toddler or gardening, have to be done during day-time hours but others, such as most housework, could in principle be done at almost any time of day or night. However, it seems that, despite increases in leisure time, when people at home have the choice, most would rather finish their tasks during the day and relax with television in the evening, not the other way around.

Television did not dictate this order of work and play, although television channels do screen their most expensive and inherently popular programs in mid-evening. In the heyday of radio in the 1930s and 1940s, peak listening time was during the same hours as television's peak viewing today. Nor has the increase in day-time programming, or the adoption of VCRs, caused any reduction in evening viewing. The sequence 'chores first, relax later' seems to reflect fundamental human needs, not just the way that television schedules are designed.

HOW TELEVISION AUDIENCES OVERLAP

The rather steady number of people who watch television at a given time each day, say about 30 percent of a particular population watching at 7 pm each evening, can easily trap one into supposing that much the same people tune in each time. But in practice there is a fair amount of audience turnover beneath the steady total figures. Most of us know this from our own experience: we do not always watch television at the same time every day.

The detailed ratings data confirm this and also show some simple regularities. It turns out that during peak viewing hours only about 65 percent of those watching television at a particular time on one evening will also watch at the same time the next evening (or any other particular evening). Outside peak time the proportion is slightly lower, about 60 percent, so that some 40 percent of the audience are not the same individuals. The detailed figures differ from case to case but not by much.

The main reason for this substantial turnover in viewers is their availability to view: the fact that people are not always at home and free to watch rather than that they are free but are doing something else. In Britain, the data show that one person in four of those available to view at a given time on one day is not available at the same time the next day. Most of those who watch one day and *are* available also at that time on the following day therefore do watch again on the second day.

Television Audiences at Different Times of Day

The extent to which anyone watches television at two *different* times on two consecutive days is generally much lower. The majority of the television audience at 7 pm last Tuesday, say, did not watch television at 9 pm the previous day or at 10 pm the day afterwards. This is so whatever programs might be showing on the individual channels.

The size of this audience overlap is predictable. The broad rule-of-thumb is that it is slightly higher, by about a fifth, than the percentage of the whole population that are watching. Thus if 30 percent of the whole population were watching television last Tuesday at 7 pm, then the proportion watching at that time of those who had watched television at 9 pm on Monday would be roughly a fifth higher, i.e. some 36 percent or so. Almost two-thirds of the viewers on Monday at 9 pm would *not* also be watching television at 7 pm on the Tuesday.

As a rough approximation one can even ignore the 'one fifth more' factor and simply say that if 30 percent are watching television at some point, only about 30 percent of those who had been watching television at some other specific time will also be watching then. This means that most people, although they watch a great deal of television, are not all doing so at the same times but are exercising some choice, not necessarily a very considered choice, over when to watch. The degree to which this happens gives some background for the next chapter, where we describe the audience overlap for pairs of specific television programs.

There is one major exception to this rather low audience overlap, namely that between consecutive time-periods on the same day. People tend to watch television in sessions that span several programs. Hence as many as four out of five of those watching television at 7 pm, say, will typically still be watching at 8 pm that same evening. However, this high carry-over of the audience does not last very long. For times that are two or three hours apart in the evening the audience overlap is again quite low. It is then no higher than for two such times on two quite different days and follows the same rule-of-thumb as was noted above.

Given the extent of this in-and-out movement of viewers under the surface, why is the total size of the television audience at a given time of day so stable and predictable from one day to the next or even a week or more later? Why is it *always* rather like Figure 2.2? Presumably it is because people's alternatives to watching television vary irregularly from day to day and from one individual to another and, in large populations, the irregularities largely cancel each other out. There is also of course *some* variability between different days, perhaps ranging from 27 percent to 33 percent viewing at 7 pm instead of always exactly 30 percent.

The overall conclusion is that, although television audiences are huge and so many people watch so much, the audience is not monolithic and the habit is not all-dominant. It would seem that, except for a few favorite programs, we mainly watch television when we are free to do so and when nothing more important intervenes.

WHY WE WATCH

Television is so popular because it provides large amounts of distraction and relaxation at a trivial cost and with minimum effort to the viewer. Watching television can be almost as pleasurable as going to a movie, yet it is nearly as cheap and convenient as listening to the radio.

Research into the uses and gratifications of television tells us that people say they watch to be entertained, to relax, to 'kill time', or to 'escape from my worries'. But it also seems to be a force for social cohesion. Those who live alone may say they view 'to avoid being lonely'; those watching in company seem to get positive pleasure from sharing the experience. Television offers a convivial and reasonably neutral topic of conversation. It unites different groups within a society and even, to some extent, citizens from different countries. This common interest is reflected by the considerable space allotted to discussion of television programs and personalities in the press and on television itself.

Television also conveys information. In both a loose and a precise sense, it can be an educator. As described in various surveys, people may say that they watch partly 'to keep in touch with what is going on in the world', without referring solely to news programs. They may also say they 'learn' from television, again without speaking solely or primarily about any overtly educational strands in the schedule.

But television's informative and educative functions do not explain why people give it so much of their free time. Its main role in people's lives is to entertain, more often by soothing than by stimulating. Its functions as an instructor, conveyor of information, and intellectual stimulus are secondary to the audience. Indeed, few of us could handle mental and visual bombardment from demanding or deeply involving television programs for several hours every day, nor would many of us choose to do so or plan our free time in that way.

Some important social issues are raised by the vast role of television viewing in most people's lives: we consider these in Chapter 11. For the moment it is enough to appreciate that most television 'washes over' us. We feel little involvement in most of what we see each day, in line with the fact that we mainly watch to relax after the day's work is done. We return to this question of 'low involvement' in Chapter 10, where we discuss television as a medium in broader terms.

SUMMARY

Television is truly a pervasive mass medium. Virtually everyone in every developed country watches it. As individuals, many of us watch television for three hours per day, while some watch much more. People watch a little less in summer. The better-off or more educated watch slightly less. In Britain the figures build up to over 50 billion hours of television viewing per year, and in the USA to more than 200 billion hours.

If in such countries a typical viewer's total viewing during the year were laid end to end, it would fill two months, the whole of January and February say, for 24 hours each day! Although that may be hard to accept, it may be harder still to think of our imaginary television viewer having the set totally switched off throughout the other ten months of the year.

The daily pattern of television viewing is very steady over different days. Roughly the same percentage of the population watches at a given time day by day and week by week. But, except for the heaviest viewers, few individuals watch regularly at the same time every day or every week: typically only 60 to 65 percent watching on one day will be watching at the same time on another day.

Audience overlap at different times and on different days is usually even lower than this. A general rule is that it is slightly more (about a fifth) than the proportion of the whole population that is viewing at the particular time in question. Hence most of the people watching at one time are *not* also watching at another time, unless it is at the most popular viewing times in the evening (when almost 50 percent of the population are doing so).

Audiences are vast but not monolithic. Even during peak viewing hours, at least half of the population is doing something else rather than watching television and mostly it is a different half at different times. Viewers exercise choice, at least insofar as viewing seems to be what we mostly do when there are no other, more pressing calls on our time. These rival activities are very diverse and not as habitual as TV viewing. The audience totals across large populations can therefore be much steadier than individuals' behavior might suggest. To explore how far viewing is deliberate or selective rather than merely habitual, we need to consider the programs people choose to watch. We turn to this in Part Two.

NOTES

Viewing Patterns

The sources are the weekly or monthly tabulations of ratings data in the USA, Britain, and elsewhere. Figure 2.1 is for New York housewives from a tabulation of routine Arbitron data in January 1974, and Figure 2.2 from equivalent data in November ten years later (Arbitron 1984). The basic pattern changes little over the years.

Viewing Alone and in Company

The specific results quoted are from Aske Research (1981a), Ehrenberg and Goodhardt (1981), and unpublished work done for the Markle Foundation (Barwise and Ehrenberg 1982). Earlier studies of family viewing-choice, as summarised in Comstock et al. (1978), were by Wand (1968), Lyle (1972) and Chapter 7 of Bower (1973). See also CBC (1982). More recent studies are summarised by Gunter and Svennevig (1987).

Multi-set Viewing

The numerical results come from Nielsen (1976, 1981), Media World (1982), and Wightman (1982).

Breakfast Ratings in Japan

Possible reasons which have been put forward for the high level of breakfast-time viewing in Japan include (i) that 'Japanese salarymen' use the clock shown during the early morning news to make sure that they catch their trains in time; (ii) that Japanese wives stay tuned to watch the 15-minute NHK soap opera after their husbands have left; (iii) that (according to a Western bachelor in Tokyo) Japanese husbands and wives may have nothing to say to each other at breakfast time; (iv) that (according to a Japanese researcher who had never been to the USA), US breakfast-time ratings might be lower because many Westerners are Christians and hence breakfast-time is perhaps taken up by family prayers; (v) that the television set is often in the room where breakfast is taken (Webster 1980).

Availability to View

The analysis is based on a week's AGB data in Britain on 'being at home and not asleep in bed', reported ¼-hour by ¼-hour (Aske Research 1978a). More detailed surveys of how people spend their time generally cover only a single day per person (e.g. BBC 1980). People's daily availability to view through the day in the USA seems to be similar to that in Britain, according to an unpublished trade source citing data based on telephone coincidentals. See also Robinson (1969).

How Audiences Overlap

The regularity of watching television at the same time on different days is discussed in Barwise et al. (1978d) and Aske Research (1978a).

Duplication between total television audiences at two different times is generally higher than the product of the ratings because some people watch systematically more than others, as was reflected in Figure 2.1. Most studies of audience duplication focus on the overlap between the audiences of specific programs, as discussed in Chapter 3. Studies of total television duplication also include Aske Research (1977) and Webster (1985) in the context of 'lead-in': see Chapter 6.

Why We Watch

The classic on 'uses and gratification' remains Blumler and Katz (1974). A recent survey is Rosengren et al. (1985). Many of the books on television listed on page 10 also discuss people's reasons for watching television, especially CPB (1978) and Taylor and Mullan (1986). See also Tannenbaum (1980).

PART TWO
WATCHING PROGRAMS

When spending so much of our free time in front of a television set, we do not just 'watch television', we watch particular programs. Chapter 3 looks at how we do or do not differ from each other in the programs we watch. Chapter 4 describes how we are then less than regular in watching successive episodes of these programs. In Chapter 5 we discuss how much people seem to *like* what they watch.

Chapter 3
Choosing Different Programs

Someone who views television for 20 or 30 hours in the course of a week will typically watch at least 30 or 40 programs. Even though some programs are very popular and seen by many, the particular combination of programs that we choose differs from person to person. In the USA with three large and highly competitive networks and several other channels also available in most homes, few programs attract more than a third of those viewing at the time. Even in Britain, the most popular programs attract only about half of those watching television at that time; the other half is divided among the less popular programs on the other three channels. Except for major events such as American football Superbowl, a Royal Wedding or a World Cup soccer final, very few of the hundreds of programs broadcast each week are in fact watched by as many as 20 percent of the total population. Most get much smaller audiences, although usually still in millions or at least hundreds of thousands.

Thus, although television is very much a mass medium, the audience is not an undiscriminating crowd all watching the most popular fare. The average viewer watches only two or three of the top ten rating programs in the week. Nor are viewers divided into a mass audience, who always watch the popular programs, and separate smaller groups, who always watch minority programs. On the contrary, most viewers choose a mixed diet of programs of light entertainment, drama, films, sport, news, features. How much of their viewing time people devote to the different *program types* is remarkably similar for different groups of the population, as we will describe in more detail. But individuals differ greatly in their choice of *particular programs*, and different programs are mostly watched by different people.

To reflect these varied preferences, the television schedules in most countries consist of a mixture of different types of program. Which specific programs are shown depends on both economics (e.g. reliance on relatively cheap imports) and on the traditions and broadcasting system in the particular country. But overall in Europe, news and other factual programs take up about 40 percent of the broadcasts, with light entertainment, drama/films, sport, and children's programs taking up the other 60 percent. In the USA this broad split is more like 30:70 in favor of entertainment on the three networks, with the ratio being greater towards entertainment during peak viewing time and on most independent stations.

VIEWING DIFFERENT TYPES OF PROGRAM

If one classifies programs into about seven major categories, the way in which people allocate their time across categories varies surprisingly little between different subgroups of the population.

Table 3.1 illustrates this for some typical weeks in Britain in 1985. There are two main features to note. First, viewers spent something over 60 percent of their viewing time watching entertainment programs (game shows, light drama, sport, etc.), compared with some 30 percent on somewhat more demanding programs (information, features, news, etc.), with the other few percent going on a miscellaneous category which includes children's and educational programs. Second, this was almost equally so for those better off in socioeconomic terms and those less well off (described by British market researchers as ABC1s and C2DEs respectively, and making up about a third and two-thirds of the population). The less well off chose a slightly lower proportion of the more 'demanding' programs, 30 percent against 32 percent, but, since they typically watch rather more television (averaging almost 30 hours versus 23 hours per week), they in fact spent more hours on the demanding programs than their better-off compatriots.

Table 3.1 *Viewing of the main program types by socioeconomic background*

UK adults 1985	Average viewing hours per week	Percentage of time spent viewing						
		Entertainment				Demanding		
		Light e'ment	Light drama	Films	Sport	Drama, Arts, etc.	Infor- mation	News
Social class								
ABC1*	23	16	24	11	9	4	18	10
C2DE	30	15	26	12	9	3	17	9

* Better-off and longer-educated, professional, managerial, etc.

All of the many other population subgroups examined, men and women, old and young, heavy and light viewers, etc., show a very similar profile. On average, all tend to spend much the same proportions of their viewing time on the various types of program available.

There are some differences in these numbers but they are fairly small in relation to the total time people spend viewing. In particular, children and teenagers tend to watch fewer demanding programs and, of course, more children's programs. For adults, the main systematic differences are that sports programs tend to be somewhat less popular among women and that most soap operas are less popular among men. (Some other fairly minor differences occur due to some people not being at home during the day.) Thus, in the same UK analysis, men spent 11 percent of their viewing on sport, women 8 percent. But the difference is not that dramatic, especially in terms of actual hours of viewing sport, since women spend more time watching television generally (and more women than men tend to watch tennis, show-jumping, and wrestling). In any case, as a broad approximation, each sex spends about a tenth of its viewing on sport and nine-tenths on other programs.

These are all averages and individuals of course vary more in their viewing preferences, but mostly not by much. While British adults on average spend about 30 percent of their viewing time on the more demanding programs, only one in ten of them spends less than 20 percent.

The similarity in the spread among the different program types is not due to a shortage of choice in the supply of programs. For example, 30 hours or more of programming per week is broadcast in Britain for most of the seven categories, including many broadcast at convenient viewing times. People could therefore concentrate on only one or two types of program if they wanted to, by choosing such programs on particular channels at particular times. Instead they choose variety.

The same tendency to opt for such a range of different types of program shows up even for the people who have chosen to view a particular program. One might have imagined that viewers of a 'light drama' such as *Dallas* would differ markedly in their other program choices from those of a news or public affairs 'information' program such as the *McNeil-Lehrer Report* in the USA or *Panorama* in Britain. But again this hardly occurs. As Table 3.2 summarizes, they all tend to spend much the same proportions of their viewing time on light entertainment (about 15%), Sport (about 9%), News (9%), etc. These figures are typical of many more detailed results.

Table 3.2 *Viewing of the main program types by viewers of different programs*

UK adults 1985	Percentage of their other viewing time spent viewing						
	Entertainment				Demanding		
	Light e'ment	Light drama	Films	Sport	Drama, Arts, etc.	Infor-mation	News
Viewers of the average program of:							
Light entertainment	**15**	26	11	9	3	17	9
Light drama	15	**27**	12	9	3	18	9
Films	14	26	**13**	9	3	17	9
Sport	15	26	11	**10**	3	17	9
Drama, Arts, etc.	15	26	12	9	3	18	9
Information	15	26	11	9	3	**17**	9
News	15	26	11	9	3	17	**10**
Average	15	26	12	9	3	17	9

The most dramatic feature is the set of figures on the diagonal of the table. These show that the proportion of their television viewing time that viewers of one program spent watching other programs of the same type is almost identical to the other figures in the same column, i.e. to the proportions of time devoted to that category by viewers of *other* types of program. Viewers of *Dynasty* and viewers of *Panorama* both spent some 25 percent of the rest of their viewing time on light drama and about 17 percent on information programs.

Direct analyses in this format are not yet available in the USA or other countries but other types of audience analysis, such as by audience composition and audience overlap for different programs, imply that much the same flat 'unsegmented' patterns of program choice occur. Viewers choose from the range of programs available and different groups of viewers hardly differ in the overall proportions.

THE COMPOSITION OF THE AUDIENCE

Although audience sizes for different programs can vary greatly, the make-up of these audiences tends to be broadly similar, for example in terms of demographic characteristics. This is implied by the way that subgroups of the population in Tables 3.1 and 3.2 devoted similar amounts of their viewing time to the different categories. But it also shows up more directly. Thus there is generally little difference in the make-up of audiences for the different program types by (i) demographic differences such as age, sex, size of household, presence of children, or socioeconomic status; (ii) television-related factors such as being heavy, medium or light viewers, having one or more television sets in the household, having color or only black-and-white television, having a remote control, or having a VCR.

As shown in Tables 3.3a and b, the figures in each column for viewers of programs of the different types are generally very close to the average. About 8% or 9% of the adult audience of any type of program was aged 16 to 34, and about 35% had a remote control.

There can be exceptions for individual programs, although sometimes only for some specific week, and these are rarely large. The main systematic exception with these categories is Sport (65:35 in favor of men, as highlighted in the tables).

Table 3.3a   *Audience composition for different program types*

UK adults 1985	Age			Sex	
	16–34	35–54	55+	M	F
Viewers of the average program of:					
Light entertainment	%	9	46	45	41	59
Light drama	%	9	47	44	39	61
Films	%	10	50	40	44	56
Sport	%	9	43	49	**65**	**35**
Drama, Arts, etc.	%	8	51	41	42	58
Information	%	7	43	50	41	59
News	%	7	45	48	42	58
Average	%	8	46	46	45	55

In the USA, the same rather flat pattern applies as in Tables 3.3a and b, again with an exception for sport. This is illustrated in Table 3.4 for a selection of specific programs during the 8.00–8.30 time-slot on different days and channels. The small range of variation is typical. There are vast

amounts of such ratings data every week showing much the same kinds
of result.

Table 3.3b *Audience composition for different program types (continued)*

UK adults 1985		Hours of viewing per week			No. of sets		Remote controls	
		1–20	21–40	41+	1	2+	w	w/o
Viewers of the average program of:								
Light entertainment	%	14	41	45	62	38	38	62
Light drama	%	13	40	48	62	38	37	63
Films	%	13	36	50	60	40	37	63
Sport	%	14	35	51	62	38	35	65
Drama, Arts, etc.	%	19	43	38	61	39	37	63
Information	%	14	42	45	65	35	33	67
News	%	16	45	40	66	34	32	68
Average	%	14	41	45	63	37	35	65

Many commentators talk about the television audience as being much
more segmented than it really is, especially those people who use television as an advertising medium where even relatively small differences
can affect the costs of airtime. And there *are* differences: in Denver in
February 1979, fewer women and more young viewers watched *Dukes
of Hazzard* than *Quincy* (Table 3.4). However, in more than thirty years
there have been no reports, as far as we know, of any dramatic and
consistent examples of segmentation for different programs.

Television audiences are quite different in this respect from the
readerships of most print media, which are far more segmented. The composition of the readership of different kinds of newspaper and magazine
differs very markedly, as has been consistently established. For example,
the socioeconomic status of British television audiences hovers around the
30 percent ABC1 to 70 percent C2DE mark for all program categories.
This is slightly down-market of the split that occurs in the whole population and also not far from that of mass circulation newspapers in the UK
such as *The Sun* and *The Daily Mirror*, where the split is close to

Table 3.4 *Audience composition for individual programs*

Denver 1979	Audience size*	Percentage audience composition		
		Women 18+ years	Men 18+ years	Young viewers 2–17 years
Three's Company	26	39	30	31
Charlie's Angels	19	37	30	33
M*A*S*H	17	43	38	18
One Day at a Time	13	41	36	23
Quincy	12	49	36	14
Dukes of Hazzard	11	31	31	37
Hawaii Five-O	10	46	35	19
The Big Event	8	44	40	16
Average	15	41	35	24

* Viewers as percentage of total population aged 2+.

20% ABC1s and 80% C2DEs. But it is totally different from that for up-market papers in the UK such as *The Times, The Financial Times*, or *The Guardian*, where the split is 80:20 in the opposite direction, that is 80 percent or so of readers are ABC1s and only 20 percent C2DEs.

Television is much more of a universal or mass-appeal medium. Whether a program is seen by only 1 percent, 10 percent, or 30 percent of people, the audience generally reflects much the same broad cross-section of the population available at the time, with relatively small deviations. For advertising purposes, these deviations may remain worth exploiting, if they are predictable before the event, to increase the number of target viewers reached per dollar. But they do not make television a greatly segmented medium. The only real exception occurs where a program or channel is in a minority language. Obviously, only those who understand the language will generally watch.

AUDIENCE OVERLAP BETWEEN DIFFERENT PROGRAMS

Although the make-up of the audience for different programs tends to be similar, this is not because the programs are viewed by the same people. On the contrary, the audiences for any two programs are largely made up of different people.

The size of this audience overlap or duplication for two different programs can be predicted by using a rule-of-thumb similar to that noted in the last chapter for watching television as a whole. The rule is at its simplest where the two programs are shown on different channels and on different days. It then says that the percentage of the viewers of program B say, who also watch program A, is much the same as A's rating in the population as a whole. Thus if 10 percent of the whole population watch A, then roughly 10 percent of the viewers of B will also watch A, and so will about 10 percent of the viewers of programs C or D or E. The overlap on any specific occasion may be 9 percent or 12 percent but it will neither be 50 percent nor 1 percent.

Table 3.5 illustrates this pattern of audience overlap from some of the earliest evidence of this kind reported in the USA, for the New York stations WABC and WCBS. Few of the viewers of the afternoon and evening WABC programs on Wednesday watched the WCBS programs at various times the following Tuesday. Of the WABC Wednesday audience at 4 pm only about 1 in 6 (16 percent) also watched the WCBS station at 7.30 pm on Tuesday, and almost no-one (only 4 percent) did so at 11.30 pm. Most of the WABC 4 pm Wednesday audience, the other 90 percent or so, did *not* watch the WCBS channel on Tuesday at these times. So the audience overlap was low.

The overlap was also fairly low at all the other times shown in the table. The detailed numbers are predictable, being close to the WCBS ratings among the total population at each time: 14 percent at 7.30 pm, 26 percent at 8.00 pm, and 3 percent at 11.30 pm, which are shown in the bottom row of the table.

These similarities (especially between the row of average duplications and the Tuesday WCBS ratings) are typical of what has also been found in thousands of such cases in later studies. There are nonetheless also some variations in each column of the table. Some are due to sampling errors in the data but others will be real and may, for example, reflect some of the variations that do occur in the demographic composition of the audiences. But the variations are mostly small. Typically, the figures in each column of Table 3.5 are within an average of about two percentage points of the ratings for station WCBS. This will hardly affect one's overall view of how people choose to watch television programs (but can, as already noted, be more relevant when buying or selling airtime for advertisements).

The basic pattern shown here is known as the Duplication of Viewing Law. It is at its simplest for pairs of programs on different channels and

Table 3.5 *Audience overlap: the duplication law*

New York 1974	Percentage who also viewed WCBS on Tuesday pm at				
	7.30*	8.00	9.30	11.00	11.30
Viewers of WABC on Wednesday at:					
4.00 *	16	34	10	7	4
4.30	14	22	11	2	3
6.00	11	26	13	3	3
7.00	12	29	14	6	4
7.30	12	29	10	5	2
8.00	8	29	12	7	3
10.00	13	28	15	6	5
11.00	10	24	15	5	3
11.30	9	23	14	7	2
Average	12	27	12	5	3
Tuesday WCBS ratings	14	26	11	7	3

* ¼-hours starting

on different days, as just illustrated, when the percentage of the audience of one program who also watch the other is roughly equal to the latter's rating in the population as a whole.

A major feature of the Duplication of Viewing Law, highlighted by Table 3.5, is that the audience overlap between different programs can be successfully predicted as simply varying with the ratings without having to know the content or even the names of the programs shown. Perhaps surprisingly, the amount of audience overlap does not depend on what types of program they are but only on the size of their audiences. This reflects the fact that there is little or no tendency for viewers of one news program specially to watch other news or viewers of one soap opera specially to watch other soaps, as was illustrated earlier by Table 3.2.

Scheduling Exceptions

There are three systematic exceptions or subpatterns in this very simple picture of audience overlap between pairs of programs. They are due to the scheduling of the programs, i.e. at what times and on what channels they are shown, and do not relate to the content of the programs.

Two of the subpatterns apply to programs that are shown on the same channel. First, for two such programs which occur on different days, audience duplication is somewhat higher than if the two shows had been shown on different channels. However, the numbers still tend to be small: most viewers of one program do not see the other program even though it is on the same channel.

Second, for two programs on the same day and which are *consecutive or near-consecutive* on the same channel, audience overlap is much higher, often 50 percent or more. This is known as the 'audience inheritance' or 'lead-in' effect.

The third exception is day-time programs on weekdays. Although the audience overlap between different programs is then even lower than for evening programs, it can look relatively high when compared with the ratings of the two day-time programs. But it is these ratings which are unusual, in that they are depressed by the large proportion of the population who are regularly out at work.

The first two subpatterns are discussed further when we look at television channels in Chapter 6. All three must be allowed for when assessing the audience overlap between programs. Failure to do so has led some commentators to believe that the higher overlap observed in some cases is due to program content when in fact it is due to the time of day and channels of the broadcasts.

SUMMARY

Individual tastes in television programs vary widely. Viewers' program choices nonetheless follow a common pattern, mainly that each of us has a wide yet rather similar demand for a diet of programs of diverse types. There is remarkably little variation in the way that different subgroups of the population allocate their viewing across the different program categories. In line with this, the composition of the audience for most programs is also very similar, whether in demographic or television-usage terms. Systematic exceptions, such as for sport or soap operas, are few and not especially dramatic.

Although the audiences of different programs mostly have a similar composition, they consist of largely different individuals: the overlap between such audiences is generally low. The numerical size of this overlap is quite predictable, irrespective of program type. This does not mean that program content does not matter. Together with scheduling factors (channel, time of day, and competition), the content determines how many people watch the program but it has surprisingly little impact on what kinds of people do so.

NOTES

Audience Flow

Viewing data are routinely reported as cross-sectional ratings, i.e. the percentage of the population (or of a demographic subgroup) who watched each particular broadcast. In contrast, many of the results in Chapters 3 and 4 are based on analyses of 'audience flow', i.e. how many viewers of one broadcast also watch another (e.g. Goodhardt et al. 1987).

Viewing Different Types of Program

Tables 3.1 to 3.3 are based on analyses of AGB data in Britain in 1985 (Ehrenberg 1986, Ehrenberg and Goodhardt 1988). Corresponding tabulations of US data are planned. The lack of special addiction to particular program types has long been reflected in the close fit of the Duplication of Viewing Law (Goodhardt et al. 1987).

In Table 3.2 the classification of (a) viewers and (b) the amounts they viewed is based on two different weeks. This avoids double-counting the program used in defining a viewer of a program (Ehrenberg and Goodhardt 1988).

The classification of the seven main program types used in Tables 3.1 to 3.3 is adapted from that used in *AGB/BARB Audience Research Reports* in Britain (see Ehrenberg 1986:29 for more details).

Type	*Sub-types*
Light Entertainment	Variety & music. Quiz shows & panel games. Other light entertainment (mostly chat shows and other 'personality' programs).
Light drama	Series. Situation comedies. 'Light' plays/drama (including made-for-TV mini-series and one-offs).
Films	English language films made for cinema showing.
Sport	Actual sporting events. ('How to play . . .' are classified as 'general interest' programs.)
Drama, Arts, etc.	Limited serials (book adaptations, etc.). Foreign language films. 'Heavy' plays. Serious music & arts.
Information	News magazines. Current affairs programs. Documentaries and features. General interest programs (e.g. religion, motoring, gardening, cooking, consumer programs, etc.).
News	News Bulletins.
Miscellaneous	Children's programs. Miscellaneous (mostly formal School or University programs and Teletext broadcast as programs).

It seems that different definitions would not affect the general conclusions in Chapter 3. (See also CBC 1973; Williams 1974; Wakshlag 1985). Goodhardt et al. (1987) report an

analysis of 1980 data, using somewhat different program type definitions, showing the same
lack of variation as in Table 3.3 for 1985.

Audience Composition

Table 3.4 is based on Arbitron data for adults in Denver in February 1979. The other sources
are as above, together with regular ratings reports.

In Table 3.3 some 45% of viewers of one program watch television for more than 40
hours per week, which implies a very high level of viewing (well over the normal average
of 25 to 30 hours a week). This is a 'selection effect': viewers of any specific program tend
to be relatively heavy viewers, compared with the population at large. For example, they
exclude all non-viewers of television.

Little Segmentation

Segmentation refers to a program (or a certain type of program) being viewed mainly by
some identifiable population subgroup (e.g. younger people, owners of hi-fi equipment, etc.).
As and when segmentation occurs, it could be of particular value to certain advertisers, since
it would provide a possible target-group for their advertising, and of interest to program
makers and schedulers.

In practice, however, the audiences of different television programs are mostly very similar
in their make-up, i.e. largely unsegmented. Nonetheless, there appear to be sufficient variations
in the ratings data to lead to some savings in buying airtime for targeted advertising.

In television there is nothing like the striking segmentation which is regularly reported
for the readership of newspapers and magazines (e.g. AA 1987). Probably the largest
systematic segmentation study of television viewers was by Frank and Greenberg (1980).
In this, almost none of the differences in viewing of different program types could be accounted
for by classifying viewers into specific demographic and/or 'lifestyle' segments.

Audience Overlap between Different Programs

The Duplication of Viewing Law says that the percentage of the audience of program B
which also watches program A simply varies with the rating of program A, with only small
deviations. The audience overlap is usually low.

For pairs of programs on different days and different channels, the duplication of program
B with A generally equals the rating of A. For programs on the same channel, the duplication is generally higher (by about 50% in the USA or 70% in the UK), a channel-loyalty
effect, but the overlap is still low in absolute terms. For more or less consecutive programs
on the same channel, much higher 'lead-in' effects occur (see page 72).

A striking feature is the lack of any special tendency for viewers of one program to watch
others of the same type. There is extensive empirical evidence for this pattern as well as
theoretical back-up (see Goodhardt et al. 1987). The same kind of duplication pattern also
holds for people's choices of brands and of retail stores in the case of buying packaged
consumer goods (e.g. Ehrenberg 1972/1988a).

Analyses of audience flow in the USA are complicated by scheduling habits such as strip-
programming, i.e. the re-running of an old series on the five weekdays (Goodhardt et al.
1987; Barwise et al. 1978a). This leads to repeat-viewing levels at the same time on different

days tending to be higher than normal duplication levels if different programs are shown. Rust (1986) and some earlier writers have misinterpreted *scheduling* effects (channel, time, lead-in) as if they were *program type* effects, but they merely reported some overall 'statistical significance', without identifying any specific results. Once scheduling effects are allowed for, US viewing data fit the Duplication of Viewing Law within about the same limits as in Britain.

Late-evening Programs

Audience duplications appear high relative to the ratings for pairs of late-night programs because the same people tend to go to bed early and are not available to view.

Chapter 4
Watching Different Episodes

We have just seen that the audience composition of most television programs is much the same, although different individuals choose different programs. But how regularly do people watch the successive episodes of a particular program? To what extent is it the same viewers each week?

This question is relevant because most television programming in all parts of the world consists of series with episodes screened at regular intervals, e.g. weekly or daily. Even movies are often scheduled into series-like slots, such as *The NBC Monday Movie*, starting at fixed hours and edited to standard running times. Public affairs and sports coverage is similarly tailored for regularity and uniform lengths. This is especially true in countries such as the USA, where television channels are more directly competitive than elsewhere.

Several factors work to produce this kind of regular programming:

1 Once established, series are cheaper and less risky to produce than 'one-off' programs.
2 Narrative programs, which have a continuing storyline or cast of characters ('serials' or 'series'), benefit from developing plots and establishing characters over time and building audience appeal. In particular, the humor of situation comedies and the intrigue of soap operas are partly cumulative. Even for the news and game and chat shows, viewers find it relaxing to have familiar presenters and routines.
3 When we like a program, we appreciate knowing in advance when it will be on.
4 Channels which are supported by advertising revenue need reasonably predictable audience levels in order to sell their commercial airtime to advertisers in advance.

Most programs therefore appear as series of episodes. A series which makes the grade usually settles down to a particular audience size very soon after its debut. Some take longer to establish their audience, especially if they cut across familiar genres or styles. Examples in the last ten years include *Soap* and *Hill Street Blues* in the USA, and *Last of the Summer Wine* and *Minder* in Britain. But these are exceptional. Usually, over several months, if there are no big changes on the other channels, the audience-size ratings of a regular series tend to be pretty steady from day to day or week to week, especially relative to the ratings of other shows. Table 4.1 illustrates this for some contrasting shows aired in the early, middle, and late evening on four Wednesdays in New York.

Table 4.1 *The audiences of four successive episodes (household ratings)*

New York, November 1984		Week			
		1	2	3	4
ABC World News	(7.00 WABC)	9	8	8	6
Wheel of Fortune	(7.30 WCBS)	14	15	17	14
Highway to Heaven	(8.00 WNBC)	13	11	12	11
Dynasty	(9.00 WABC)	25	26	24	24
St Elsewhere	(10.00 WNBC)	11	10	8	12
Ch 2 News at 11	(11.00 WCBS)	8	6	13	7

THE LEVEL OF REPEAT-VIEWING

Given these mostly rather steady ratings, it might be thought that each program attracts its own more or less loyal following, that in Table 4.1 much the same 14 percent of the population watched *Wheel of Fortune* each week. But this is not what happens. In each case only about half or even fewer of those watching such a program in Week 1 would also watch it in Week 2. This applies to all kinds of program and is a very general finding, known since the late 1960s.

Recent evidence suggests that repeat-levels are even lower than they used to be, partly because there are more channels and thus lower ratings per program. In the USA, the average repeat-percentage for prime-time network programs is now down to about 40 percent or even less. With only four channels in Britain, the repeat-levels on the two main networks (ITV and BBC1) are a little higher but have recently moved down to between 40 and 50 percent, from an earlier average of about 55 percent.

Different types of program all attract low levels of repeat-viewing. Table 4.2 illustrates this with the repeat-rates for a range of US prime-time programs in 1985. Most series in this particular study averaged repeat-rates of less than 30 percent.

Table 4.2   *Repeat-viewing levels for different program types*

Boston adults	Percentage average repeat*
Games/Quizzes	32
News	26
Sitcoms	25
Drama	21
Action/Police	19
Average	25

* Viewers in Week 1 watching also in Week 2.

A partial exception occurs for some soap operas in the USA, including daily day-time soaps. These can have repeat-levels about 10 percentage points higher, e.g. averaging up to about 50 percent nowadays. To this limited extent, the results bear out the widespread belief in the television industry that, with stories and characters that can continue for decades, soaps command a somewhat more loyal and habitual audience than other kinds of series. This belief is also supported by the extrinsic signs of a cult, such as 'soap magazines' and telephone services that update viewers on story-lines. However, the very existence of such services demonstrates that even soaps are not viewed day after day without fail by their habitués. A relatively 'high' 50 or even 55 percent repeat-rate is not the 90 percent that one might have expected. On any given day, virtually half of even a top-rated soap's audience will not have seen the previous episode.

People's repeat viewing of weekly series has been studied more extensively in Britain (week-by-week data for this in the USA have in the past been available only sporadically). These studies confirm that repeat-viewing levels vary little by program type (apart from the marginally higher levels for some soaps). In particular, repeat-viewing does not differ systematically between: (i) most programs with continuing storylines ('serials'); (ii) programs where each episode has a separate plot but some of the main characters are the same ('series'); (iii) transmissions that are merely in the same general format (news, documentaries, etc). The low level of repeat-viewing does not therefore directly reflect program content but is a more general feature of people's viewing behavior.

Loyalty to Programs

Despite these remarkably low levels of repeat-viewing for regular series, viewers do show some loyalty to the programs that they choose to watch. This shows up in several ways.

1 The low repeat-viewing of, say, 40 or 50 percent for an established series does not mean that non-repeaters are lost to the series for good. Such low repeat-viewing occurs in combination with basically steady audience ratings and is not in itself a precursor of any decline in the popularity of the series.

2 The level of repeat-viewing is not appreciably lower for episodes that are more than a week (or day) apart. Lapsed viewers in one week will still watch episodes in later weeks.

3 Even with only a 40 or 50 percent chance of watching the following episode, viewers of a program in one week are much more likely to watch the next week's episode than is the average member of the public. For a series that has an average rating of 10, say, only one in ten of the public as a whole will see it the next week, whereas up to half of those watching the current week's episode will do so. Hence a marked degree of program loyalty exists, even if it never shows up as a 90 or 100 percent repeat-viewing rate.

4 We noted in Chapter 2 that no more than about 65 percent of those watching television at a given time watch again at the same time a day or a week later. However, with the repeat-levels just noted, some 40 or 50 out of these 65 percent will be watching the same program as before, so *most of those watching television again* at the same time do in fact watch the same program. This demonstrates considerable loyalty. The main single reason for not repeat-viewing is that one is not watching television at all at the time of the second episode.

NOBODY WATCHES EVERY EPISODE

For a regular series of, say, 10 or 20 episodes over a season, few people will see all or nearly all of them. Similarly, only a small proportion of viewers of a finite-length serial, such as a television adaptation of a book, watch each and every broadcast or anything like it. This reflects the 40 to 50 percent levels of repeat-viewing noted above. Conversely, however, the number of people who see at least one episode of the series over a period of time (called the 'reach' or 'cume' of the series) is much higher than the size of the audience for any given episode. If a series is seen by 15 percent of the population each week, typically as many as half the population will see it at least once over a 10-week period.

The combination of relatively low repeat-viewing with high reach does not come about because early viewers of the series drop out for good. Rather it occurs because the audience is made up of a mixture of frequent and less frequent viewers of the program. The less frequent viewers see perhaps only three or four episodes out of the ten or twenty, so they simply cannot be repeat-viewers of all successive episodes. They may see one episode this month, maybe a couple next month, and so on.

Table 4.3 shows how many viewers saw different numbers of episodes of three widely publicized programs in Britain. These were thought to be watched avidly by their fans but of the 60 percent of UK adults who saw at least one episode of *Brideshead Revisited*, over half saw only one, two or three episodes, and less than 10 percent saw all or all but one. The pattern in the table is typical of all programs. It is also theoretically predictable (see page 48).

Even for a finite serial, which may have had a great deal of publicity, very few viewers watch every episode. It seems that most of us do not care enough about most of the programs that we watch to make special efforts to see them each week or to sacrifice other activities or even to catch up by using our VCR. We might make a special effort to do so for our two or three favorite programs but, even then, the irregularity with which we watch television in general (noted in Chapter 2) means that we might have to go very much out of our way to be available to watch every single episode. Most often we only 'dip into' the series that we watch.

Often we perceive our own behavior as being rather different from this. At least for our favorite shows, we may think that we have seen every episode. Some people of course do so. As Table 4.3 shows, three percent of *Brideshead Revisited*'s viewers did see all 11 episodes. That means almost a million people (including one of the authors) but not the 10 million or so who saw it in any one week, let alone the 25 million who saw at least one episode. More generally, we will be aware of those episodes that we have seen but only barely of those we missed because we were out or doing something else. In our minds, 'I've seen every episode when I was there' can become 'I've seen every episode'. However, on being told of the general pattern, most people agree that it does also apply to

Table 4.3 *The number of episodes seen: some examples*

Program	(Number of episodes)	Reach* (millions)	Number of episodes seen by percentage viewers													
			1	2	3	4	5	6	7	8	9	10	11	12	13	14
Dynasty	(10)	20 = 100%	33	15	15	8	7	5	5	5	5	2	–	–	–	–
Brideshead Revisited	(11)	26 = 100%	28	18	13	7	5	5	5	3	7	4	3	–	–	–
Jewel in the Crown	(14)	23 = 100%	30	15	9	6	5	6	4	3	4	6	4	4	2	2

* Millions of UK adults who saw the program at least once.

themselves: one colleague, a keen football fan, told us, 'You're quite right. I watch *Match of the Day* religiously about every other week.'

LOWER RATINGS AND
LOWER REPEAT-VIEWING

Series that have few viewers ('low ratings') have even lower repeat-viewing levels than the roughly 40 or 50 percent levels mentioned so far. A low-rating series generally has only 20 to 30 percent, or even less, of one week's viewers also watching it the next week. The effect is roughly that the repeat level drops one or two percentage points for each one-point drop in the audience-size rating. Thus if Series X has a 10 point lower rating than Series Y, we can expect X's weekly repeat-level to be 10 or even 20 points lower than Y's.

This tendency is an example of a widespread phenomenon known as *Double Jeopardy*. It occurs when people have to choose between broadly similar items that differ in popularity. The less popular items are not only chosen by fewer people but are also liked somewhat less by those who choose them. This means that low-rating programs also attract lower repeat-viewing. This type of pattern occurs very generally. It was first noted by the Columbia University sociologist William McPhee in the early 1960s, when he was studying radio audiences. He regarded it as 'unfair' that the item chosen by fewer people should also be liked less by them and named the effect 'Double Jeopardy' accordingly.

The Double Jeopardy phenomenon also highlights the fact that the opposite pattern does not occur, namely low-rating 'minority' programs being seen by small numbers of viewers who particularly like them and thus choose to watch them exceptionally regularly. In practice, viewers virtually never respond in that way to television programs, though it is often thought that they do or might do in the future when there are still more channels and the audience becomes more fragmented.

Situations where repeat-viewing levels are particularly low are often explained just by low ratings and the Double Jeopardy effect, rather than by anything else which might be intrinsic to the situation. Thus programs on smaller television channels, such as most independent (non-network) stations and the Public Broadcasting Service in the USA, and BBC2 and Channel 4 in Britain, usually attract below-average repeat levels simply because of the low ratings of their programs. (This does include an element of chicken-and-egg.)

A second example is that young US viewers watch network programs even less regularly than do adults. Network audience ratings for children are lower and this accounts for the low repeat levels, not that children are exceptionally fickle.

A third example is light viewers, say people in the USA or Britain who watch less than 15 hours of television per week. They tend to have low repeat-levels for the programs that they do watch. In the USA, the evidence is that only 25 percent of such light viewers who watch one episode of a series also watch the next. This contrasts with an average repeat-rate of 40 percent, and with repeat levels as high as 60 percent for heavy viewers. Again, it is not a case of light viewers being especially discriminating; they do not concentrate their viewing on just a few programs which they like especially and watch devotedly. Instead, they watch less television in general and dip into programs even more irregularly than the average viewer.

REPEAT-SHOWINGS

One particular aspect of broadcast media is that any given broadcast, say an episode of a series, is essentially shown just once and then it is all over. Nobody can ever see it subsequently. This is quite unlike a play, film or book. A television program is even more ephemeral than an issue of a magazine or newspaper.

The single television showing will of course tend to attract a vast audience of millions or tens of millions. Nonetheless, that is not everybody. Other than for the very occasional blockbuster event, in multi-channel countries no more than about 20 or 30 percent of the population, and usually far fewer, will have seen such a broadcast. Most people will not have seen it and will have no chance of doing so. Even with a VCR to record the program off-air, people record very few of the many programs that they do not see and replay even fewer.

However, some programs are shown more than once. In Britain this occurs in three main ways.

1 A few weekly programs are shown twice each week, often on related channels, e.g. on Thursdays on BBC1, repeated on Sundays on BBC2.
2 A successful program may be shown again a year or two later.
3 Some isolated programs, particularly classic films such as *Casablanca*, may turn up every other year or so.

In the USA, repeat-showings are more systematically developed. The three networks (NBC, CBS, ABC) show virtually all suitable programs (other than news or sport) twice, the re-runs being in the summer off-season. Successful shows are later shown yet again, and sometimes repeatedly, 'syndicated' on the independent stations or cable, or on the network affiliates outside prime time (e.g. re-runs of *M*A*S*H*, the *Lucy Show*, or the *Flintstones*). They are then often 'stripped', i.e. shown at the same time each day on five days per week. In recent years, new movies have also been shown repeatedly, even within one month, on pay-cable channels such as Home Box Office. This will typically show thirty movies in a month, each perhaps eight or nine times.

The audience ratings of re-runs can be substantial, since most of the programs were initially popular. Nonetheless, the audience is usually smaller than for the initial screening, especially if the re-run is on a smaller channel.

The limited evidence so far is that people rarely use repeat-showings (or VCRs) consciously to catch up on those episodes of a series which they missed initially. This includes drama serials, where most viewers are used to missing episodes. If they see a later episode on the first run of the series, they will mentally fill in the gaps in the story-line, if it is continuous, and no longer feel any special need to see the episodes that they missed. This seems to be so for most people for most of the programs that they watch.

Partly because of this, perhaps, there is an impression that people object to re-runs, even just a second or third showing. Complaints are made, especially during the summer 'silly season', when re-runs tend to be bunched. In Britain, it may be partly because there are only four channels to choose from. More generally it may be because viewers object to a particular program being re-run if they had already decided not to watch it the first time. Perversely perhaps, people seem to object to re-runs at least as much on free or almost free television channels as on pay-channels such as HBO, where viewers know they can opt out by cancelling their subscriptions. Compared with the numbers viewing, however, such objections do not seem many. There might well be more objections if viewers never had the chance to see a program that they had earlier missed or to see an old one again.

SUMMARY

The proportion of the audience of a regular program in one week, who also watch it the following week, is generally only about 40 percent or even less in the USA, and 40 to 50 percent in Britain. We seem to find few programs sufficiently compelling to make us watch television instead of doing something else that interests or involves us. But if we do view television at the same time for two weeks running, we mostly choose the same program, which shows that there is some positive loyalty to most of the programs that we choose to watch.

Repeat-viewing levels are even lower for programs that have low audience ratings. This contradicts the notion that some low-rating programs cater mainly for devoted minorities of 'selective' viewers. In principle it could be so but television does not seem to work that way.

A consequence of these low repeat-levels is that, for serials or series, almost nobody sees all or nearly all of the episodes. The reverse side is that the 'reach' of such regular series is high: very large numbers will have seen at least one or two episodes over the season. Hence many people will have some direct familiarity with these programs.

Although a specific program may well be screened only once, in cases where programs are shown again (or remain available through VCRs), they can get quite substantial numbers of additional viewers. But people actually make little effort to 'catch up' with episodes they missed originally, even if they own a VCR.

NOTES

Steady Ratings

Table 4.1 is from routine Arbitron ratings in November 1984.

Repeat-Viewing

Goodhardt et al. (1987) cover repeat-viewing in Britain, and early results for the USA. More recent US or Canadian results are in Stewart (1981), Barwise et al. (1982b), TAA (1983a), Barwise (1986b), and Ehrenberg and Wakshlag (1987). The repeat-viewing patterns for television programs are also analogous to those for the repeat-buying of packaged consumer goods (Ehrenberg 1972/1988a). Table 4.2 is for the earliest US people-meter panel run by AGB; the overall rating levels in the market in question were lower than average, leading to exceptionally low repeat-levels.

Loyalty to Programs

There is a degree of real but weak program loyalty. The audience overlap for different episodes of a program is higher than can be accounted for by channel loyalty (see Chapter 6).

Watching a Series

Table 4.3 is based on AGB data in Britain. The programs in the table had ratings of 15 to 20 for each episode, and each program was seen by about 50% of the population for at least one episode. The pattern whereby few viewers see all or nearly all of the episodes of a series is closely predictable by the Beta-Binomial Distribution or BBD model (Goodhardt et al. 1975/1987; Greene 1982; Rust 1986).

Double Jeopardy

For the decrease in repeat-viewing with decreasing rating levels, see Goodhardt et al. (1987). The Double Jeopardy effect has also been found in many other contexts (McPhee 1963; Ehrenberg et al. 1988).

Repeat-showings

The available evidence shows no special tendencies to catch up on missed episodes either for repeat-showings over-air or in the use of VCRs (Aske Research 1981b, 1984; Ehrenberg and Goodhardt 1982; Nielsen 1974, 1976, 1978).

Chapter 5
How Much We Like
What We Watch

The main thrust of this book is to explore television in the light of people's actual viewing behavior: how much they watch, when they watch, the extent to which the same people watch different programs, audience overlap for different episodes of a series, and so on. However, we also need to consider how much people *like* the programs that they watch.

What viewers say about liking television programs is consistent with what and how they watch, as described in the preceding chapters. This is reassuring because, if the patterns of liking and viewing were wildly inconsistent, we would tend to disbelieve at least one of them. Thus the findings are that people greatly like television and are most unwilling to go without it. In interviews, most people's overall estimation of television is unambiguously favorable, both in absolute terms and in relation to other mass media. The public's expressed attitude towards television has, however, gradually become slightly less positive since the early 1960s. This may seem paradoxical, given the steady increase in viewing levels. But, as television has become ever more ubiquitous, it has also come to seem more ordinary. As one critic put it, 'When television was invented, it was such a revolution that you'd watch anything. We lived in Nebraska, and we would watch snow.'

The present, more blasé, attitude is reflected in the extent to which people like particular programs and episodes. Thus people's liking of most specific programs is less emphatic than for television as a whole, although each viewer may greatly like some particular shows. There is no evidence that minority-taste programs are especially well-liked by all their relatively few viewers: if anything, the opposite tends to be true.

These patterns of liking reinforce our belief that most television viewing is done at a low level of involvement. They also add to our understanding of people's program choices, especially those that demand somewhat more effort or involvement from the viewer.

AUDIENCE APPRECIATION OF
PARTICULAR BROADCASTS

In a few countries such as Britain and Canada, audience measurement routinely includes an index of how much each broadcast is liked by its viewers. The audience's expressed appreciation of programs has also been measured on a trial basis in the USA and elsewhere. The main methods involve individual self-completion diaries, in which viewers record what they watch and how much they like it. For instance, one catch-all question used is, 'How interesting and/or enjoyable did you find each program you watched?', with the possible responses 'extremely', 'very', 'fairly', 'not very', down to 'not at all'. The results of these measures are consistent across different countries and also for other somewhat different scales and forms of question-wording.

As one might expect, people who watch a particular episode of a program tend to say that they like it, some more so, some less. An episode's average liking score among its viewers is rarely less than neutral. Perhaps less obvious is that it is also unusual for a broadcast to be very well liked by all or almost all its viewers. There are few broadcasts whose average audience appreciation is near the top of the liking scale.

The net result is that, although audience appreciation for different programs does vary, it mostly falls into a fairly narrow range, about 60 to 80 on a 0-to-100 scale, with the average across all programs being close to 70. To put this in perspective, on the 'interesting and/or enjoyable' scale an average score of 70 would be well above 'fairly' (scored 50) but lower than 'very' (scored 75).

This 60-to-80 range for different programs has been found repeatedly in Britain, Canada, the USA, West Germany, and elsewhere. Studies of white South Africans found program appreciation scores averaging about 60 when there was only a single low-budget, bilingual, government-controlled channel (which is no longer the case). Conversely, a study of Welsh speakers in Wales found average appreciation scores of 80-plus for the (mostly English-language) programs watched over a week, although this may have reflected poor translation of the liking scale into Welsh! These studies in South Africa and Wales seem to represent the two extremes found to date.

For a regular program or series, audience appreciation varies little from episode to episode, with scores of say, 71, 75 and 72 in three successive weeks. But, within the overall 60-to-80 range, some programs fairly regularly score higher than others. For example, among US viewers a typical episode of *Dallas* might score 80 as against 70 for the *Muppet Show* and 65 for *Charlie's Angels*. Although these differences are still not dramatic on a 0-to-100 scale, they indicate some consistent variation in how much specific programs are liked by their viewers.

LIKING AND VIEWING

In Chapter 4 we discussed how the audience of a regular series consists of a mixture of frequent and infrequent viewers, with a few seeing many episodes and many others seeing only a few. This pattern of viewing also relates to how much people will like the program. Studies of audience appreciation show a strong relationship between how often people watch a given program (i.e. different episodes) and how much they say that they like it. People who see a program in two successive weeks will typically give it an average appreciation score of about 75 as against 65 given by those who watch it in only one out of the two weeks. (There is no difference in this between 'first-week-only' and 'second-week-only' viewers.)

The relationship between liking and frequency of viewing shows up more dramatically if we ask viewers how much they like the program in general instead of just a particular episode. For an established series, most people will have seen or dipped into an episode at some time in the past, or at least heard or read about the program. Typically, some 70 percent of the population are prepared to venture an opinion, including many who say they rarely or 'never' watch it but have seen it in the past. Among this 70 percent giving a definite response, their liking of the program varies strongly with their claimed frequency of viewing it. The results in Table 5.1 for the ABC sitcom, *Three's Company*, are typical.

Table 5.1   *Average liking score related to claimed frequency of viewing (of sitcom 'Three's Company')*

Frequency (out of 5)	'Never'	1/5	2/5	3/5	4/5	5/5
Average liking score	16	40	55	66	74	84

Those who said that they 'never' watched this program (but were nonetheless able to give a definite response) gave it an average liking score of only 16, somewhere between 'not at all' interesting and/or enjoyable (scored 0) and 'not very' (scored 25). People who said that they watched

'1 out of 5' to '5 out of 5' episodes gave average scores from 40 to 84, so those claiming to watch all given episodes, although only a small proportion of all viewers of the program, seem to have been quite involved with it.

The way in which most appreciation scores fall into the 60-to-80 range can be explained by a combination of: (a) the general tendency for liking to vary with viewing frequency; (b) people's general pattern of mostly irregular television viewing. Most programs are watched by a mixture of some frequent viewers, who say that they like the program a lot (average scores of about 75–85), and a larger number of occasional viewers who like it only marginally (scores of 40–60). The audience's appreciation for a given episode is a weighted average of these scores, typically about 70.

A 'Double Jeopardy' Pattern

We also saw in Chapter 4 that there was a small Double Jeopardy relationship between ratings and repeat-viewing levels. Programs with low ratings for the time of day when they were shown tend to get the worst of two worlds: fewer viewers and less loyal ones.

A similar pattern shows up in terms of audience appreciation for the broad run of entertainment programs, again as a general tendency with variations. Because scheduling factors, time and channel, can greatly affect audience size without necessarily affecting audience appreciation, one has to compare programs shown at much the same time of day on the same channel, or at least on channels of similar size and character. Table 5.2 illustrates the results for some prime-time entertainment programs on the three network-affiliated stations in Cincinnati in 1980.

Table 5.2   *Audience size and average audience appreciation*
         (of prime-time entertainment programs)

Audience size (percentage rating)	Audience appreciation
25+	74
20–24	70
15–19	69
10–14	67
1–9	65

The broadcasts seen by 25 percent or more of people had an average appreciation score of 74 among their viewers, while those seen by fewer than 10 percent had an average appreciation score of only 65 among these fewer viewers. The more popular programs have higher proportions of frequent viewers and this gives them somewhat higher audience appreciation scores as well as much higher ratings, other things being equal. Numerically the effect does not look very dramatic but it is sizeable within the relatively limited 60-to-80 range of most average liking scores. Such Double Jeopardy trends have also been found in Britain and Canada. There is, however, a good deal of variation for individual programs. Some with small audiences can get higher liking scores than others with larger audiences.

DEMANDING PROGRAMS

The simple pattern in Table 5.2 is typical for the general run of entertainment programs: the fewer the viewers, the less that they tend to like the program. These entertainment programs make little or no demand on the viewer and are watched mainly for relaxation.

The liking pattern is somewhat different for programs which are more demanding, such as most information programs (news, public affairs, documentaries) and some drama and cultural programs. A measure of 'demandingness' used in Canada and in some research in the USA is the number of viewers who say that a program 'made them think'. For the Cincinnati entertainment programs covered by Table 5.1, typically only 10 percent of their viewers said that such a show made them think, while 55 percent said that it helped them to relax.

In contrast, most information programs are regarded as much more demanding than this. When asked about local and network news bulletins, features and documentaries, news magazines such as CBS's *60 Minutes*, and some 1980 election specials, on average almost 60 percent of those who viewed them said that such programs made them think and only about 15 percent said that the programs helped them to relax. An almost identical program split was obtained just by separating information programs from entertainment programs according to their apparent content. The only exceptions were certain 'soft' information shows, such as some wildlife programs and the news magazine, *PM Magazine*. Viewers saw these as mostly relaxing, which would put them into the entertainment category.

There are many ways in which a program can make us think. Some game or quiz shows demand our concentration at the time but then leave no more trace than last week's crossword puzzle. Others may involve us more deeply, for instructive or emotional reasons. These deeper responses have been defined as reflecting a program's 'impact'. This can vary widely among programs but is also correlated with 'liking' or audience appreciation: high-impact programs tend also to be well liked by those who watch them but many (entertainment) programs can also be very well liked without making much impact. Less usual is a high-impact program that people watch but do not appreciate.

Because it takes more effort to watch a demanding program, we have to like it enough to justify this extra effort, otherwise we switch to a more relaxing one. Hence the audience of a demanding program tends to exclude those people who would find it only marginally interesting or enjoyable; in a competitive broadcasting system they can usually find something easier to watch on another channel. The overall evidence here is not yet very widely based but the effects seem to be three-fold:

1 The audience size for demanding programs generally tends to be lower than for relaxing programs, although it is often still substantial. (As noted in Chapter 3, in Britain people devote some 30 percent of their viewing time to demanding programs.)

2 For two programs with the same audience size (and allowing for scheduling factors such as time and channel), viewers of a demanding program tend to give it a 5 or 10 point higher appreciation score than viewers of a relaxing program give that, especially for low-rating programs of either kind.

3 There is no clear Double Jeopardy effect within the broad category of 'demanding' programs. The smaller-audience programs tend to be as well liked by their viewers as the larger-audience programs are liked by theirs, although there is again a good deal of variability for individual programs. This pattern probably occurs because different 'demanding' programs can vary in many ways; in particular, the lowest-rating programs tend to be more demanding than the higher-rating ones, so only viewers who are truly interested watch them. This cancels out the Double Jeopardy effect but still does not mean that demanding programs are passionately liked by most of their viewers.

Two further qualifications should also be noted. First, even the most demanding programs that have measurable audiences do not require great effort or attention on the part of the viewer (compared with, say, reading a college textbook). Any program that survives, especially in a ratings-dominated system such as commercial television in the USA, has to be easily watchable.

Second, some viewers might say that they like demanding programs merely because this seems to be the socially acceptable response. If so, one would then expect them also to exaggerate how often they watch such programs. However, the limited evidence available suggests that viewing claims are no more exaggerated for demanding than for relaxing programs. Viewers' stated appreciation of demanding programs therefore seems to reflect something deeper than mere snobbery.

HOW LIKING DEVELOPS: THE ROLE OF FAMILIARITY

As noted in Chapter 3, most of us watch a mixture of programs, some demanding and many relaxing ones. Our choices depend on how much we expect to like the programs, how much effort we think will be involved, and perhaps also how much effort we are prepared to make at the moment when the choice presents itself. This does not imply a deep or lengthy decision process but we will be more willing at some times than at others to make the effort of watching a program on, say, arms limitation talks or famine relief.

Program choice demands a similarly low degree of involvement as do many other routine choices, such as which brands of cereal to take from the supermarket shelf or whether to cross the road at this block or the next. People do not stop to think deeply before choosing.

What typically seems to happen in these situations is that when we first face a particular choice, we take one of the options because of some minor circumstance, such as a price offer or a gap in the traffic. If this works out, and we quite like the results, we may take the same option on future occasions, although we will also vary our choice either for the sake of variety or because of variable factors such as special offers, trying a different brand at a friend's house, traffic lights, and so on. Despite these variations, we are likely to keep coming back to the most familiar choices. Something similar seems to happen even for more occasional but still repetitive major items, such as choosing where to go on vacation.

This seems to be roughly how we first come to watch particular television programs. Importantly, we do not seem to have strong program-type preferences or loyalties: audience duplication is much the same between different program categories as within the same category, as noted in Chapter 3. This suggests that we rarely come to the television set with a predefined need which one program type would satisfy better than any others. (Tuning in for the news or a topical sports program would be exceptions.) Instead, over different viewing occasions we tend to try a good many of the new season's unfamiliar programs to see which ones we like. By the very act of trying them, and talking to each other about them, we then come to like some of the programs, especially as they become more familiar. These samplings will be influenced by some chance factors, such as whether we saw a trailer or magazine article about the program or heard about it from a friend or colleague. Our sample choices will also be based on our vast prior knowledge or impressions of program formats and styles, of actors, and so on. In this trying-out process we also form strong dislikes of programs, which we subsequently avoid (although sometimes we might have begun to like them had we given them more of a chance).

Our trial viewing, like our subsequent repeat-viewing, is mostly done in the company of other family members. Although each has somewhat different tastes, there is evidence that, within a household, people tend not only to watch the same programs but also to say that they like the same programs too. This reflects the way in which viewing leads to familiarity and liking, which in turn lead to further viewing.

By the same token, although family members (especially adults and their children) may argue about channel or program choice, and although control of the remote switch may be a sign of who has the power, there seems to be little 'strongly' forced viewing. Research shows that out of every eight people watching a program, about six will say that they are doing so because they 'really like to watch it' although not all of these will say that they themselves chose it. Only about one in eight will say, 'Someone in my family likes it', and another one in eight that 'There is nothing better on'. Even the latter two categories would not say that they actively dislike the program: they would on average rate it 'fairly' interesting and/or enjoyable (giving 50 on the 0-to-100 liking scale).

A further telling instance of the way in which we come to like programs is that audience appreciation among those viewing in company is at least as high as among those watching alone. This largely accounts for the fact that most viewing in multi-set homes is still done on the main family set.

Increased Choice

These insights also help to explain viewers' responses to the extra choices becoming available as the number of television channels increases. Where there are many channels, people switch between them frequently and with little apparent effort, as we discuss in Chapter 6. One result of this is that there is virtually no difference in the appreciation expressed by viewers who had to switch channels to see a program and those who merely stayed tuned to the same channel.

Conversely, where program choice is highly restricted, audience appreciation can be reduced. One example of this was the lower appreciation scores in South Africa mentioned earlier. Another example is the screening of the evening news in the USA, where in most markets similar bulletins are shown simultaneously on all three network stations, the main channels that people watch. There is some evidence that this restriction of program choice goes with lower audience appreciation among those viewing at these times (i.e. they did not all necessarily want to watch news then).

However, once viewers at a particular time have a choice of three or four different types of program, which are reasonably good of their kind, the addition of further choice does not seem to lead to further rises in appreciation. For example, initial indications are that US cable subscribers do not find the programs that they watch more appealing or stimulating than non-cable viewers find theirs. Against this background, we turn in Part Three to the role of television channels more generally.

SUMMARY

Viewers mostly say that they quite like what they watch and watch what they say that they quite like. Most programs are positively liked by nearly all of their viewers (otherwise why watch them when there is choice?) but are intensely liked by only a few.

These results about people's appreciation of programs fit in with how they watch them. As we saw in Chapter 3, the audience for a program includes a high proportion of viewers who see it only occasionally. Since these occasional viewers of the program like it only fairly marginally, the average level of appreciation among the audience as a whole is correspondingly reduced, falling usually into the 60-to-80 range on a 0-to-100 liking scale.

There is no evidence that within the general run of entertainment programs there are any which attract small but highly dedicated or enthralled audiences. Instead, there is a Double Jeopardy effect: low-rating entertainment programs tend to get somewhat lower liking scores than programs that have many viewers.

The more demanding types of program (e.g. information and heavier drama), which generally have smaller audiences, do not show a Double Jeopardy trend with audience size. The reason may be that watching such programs requires more intellectual or emotional effort. This deters some viewers at the margin but also makes these programs potentially more rewarding for those who do watch them.

However, demanding programs also rarely get very high liking scores. On average, viewers' appreciation of the demanding programs tends to be only about as high as for the entertainment programs, which attract larger audiences. As demanding programs also attract a mixture of frequent and infrequent viewers, their average liking scores are still within the 60-to-80 range.

NOTES

Liking Television

See for example Steiner (1963), Lo Scuito (1972), Bower (1973, 1985), Roper (1971 and periodic updates), Comstock (1980), Taylor and Mullan (1986). For Nebraskans 'watching snow', see Mink (1983).

Liking Specific Programs

The results for the UK are in Goodhardt et al. (1987), Barwise et al. (1979, 1980), and Ehrenberg and Goodhardt (1981).

The US results in Tables 5.1 and 5.2 are from a study in Cincinnati (Barwise and Ehrenberg 1982, 1987). For other US results see TAA (1983a, b, 1984) who also measured the 'impact' of programs. Barwise and Ehrenberg (1982) also discuss the exaggeration of respondents' viewing claims in simple questionnaire surveys and the greater reliability of diary data.

Earlier work in Canada was reported in CBC (1973, 1977) and Stewart (1981) and summarized in Aske Research (1981c). There have also been surveys of audience appreciation in other countries, e.g. Pretorius (1984) for South Africa, and Aske Research (1978b) for Wales. See also McCarney (1984).

Some isolated cases have been reported where a change in appreciation level has preceded a change in ratings (e.g. Meneer 1987). The correlation between changes in liking and viewing can, however, be negative in certain cases: a smaller audience, caused by a more popular competitive program, may exclude those who do not like the series particularly, so that the average liking score among viewers goes up (Barwise et al. 1979; Stewart 1981; Aske Research 1981c; Goodhardt et al. 1975/1987).

Demanding Programs

The pioneering work here was carried out at the Canadian Broadcasting Corporation (CBC 1973, 1977; Stewart 1981). For the relationship between the liking of demanding programs and their rating levels, see Meneer (1987) and earlier references there.

The low-involvement nature of most television viewing has been explored by Krugman (e.g. 1965, 1980), and the notion of 'viewing effort' by writers such as Cardozo (1965) and Kahneman (1973). Csikszentmihalyi and Kubey (1981) discuss how television viewing is generally less demanding than reading. One measure of audience involvement or 'impact' has been TAA's scale based on 'I learned something from it' and 'It touched my feelings'. The 'impact' of different programs was found to vary widely and was highly correlated with the programs' 'appeal', i.e. audience appreciation (TAA 1983a).

Familiarity

A seminal article on 'mere exposure' as a source of liking was Zajonc (1968). Follow-up experimental work is reviewed by Harrison (1977).

For findings on viewing alone or in company see references on p. 21. The results on 'Someone in my family likes it' come from Goodhardt et al. (1975/1987). The effort of switching channels was explored in a UK pilot study (Aske Research 1980a). The results on US evening news are from Barwise and Ehrenberg (1982).

PART THREE
HOW PROGRAMS REACH US

Traditionally, television has been broadcast on a small number of terrestrial over-air channels from fairly local transmitters. The organization and funding of such channels differ by country. Nonetheless, the way in which viewers choose programs from the channels is much the same.

As we show in Chapter 6, people tend to spread their viewing across several channels rather than being loyal to just one channel. For instance, there are virtually no 'CBS-only viewers' in the USA nor 'BBC1-only viewers' in Britain.

Technological developments are now leading to more ways of viewing television. Two of these, multi-channel cable and video cassette recorders (VCRs), have already achieved wide penetration in some countries. Direct broadcasting by satellite (DBS) may be about to do the same. However, as discussed in Chapter 7, the impact of the new channels on how and what people watch is gradual rather than revolutionary.

Chapter 6
Broadcast Channels

Countries differ in how they run their broadcasting. Television stations in the USA are nearly all privately owned, while in the Eastern bloc and in most developing countries they are run by governments. In these cases, the television is mostly or wholly funded by competing for a single source of money, either advertising revenue or taxes. Other countries increasingly have a mixture of public and private ownership and so a mixture of funding sources, such as license fees paid by viewers *and* commercial airtime fees paid by advertisers.

The number of channels in a country and their organization and incomes lead to somewhat different kinds of programming. Nonetheless, every major broadcast channel in the world transmits a wide range of different types of program. This leads to remarkably similar viewing patterns for most channels despite wide differences in their overall popularity or viewing-shares. In particular, where a country has several channels, each tends to be watched by many people for a part of their viewing time. Smaller channels not only have fewer viewers but also attract less of these viewers' viewing time than the larger channels. Almost no television channel caters successfully for a small exclusive minority.

TYPES OF CHANNEL

In this section we outline how the organization of traditional broadcast channels varies among the USA, the UK, and other countries.

The USA

Broadcast television in the USA is almost entirely funded by advertising. It is transmitted by local commercial stations in some 200 different areas or 'markets'. While people tend to think of US commercial television as a pure free market system, it has traditionally been highly regulated by a government agency, the Federal Communications Commission (FCC). Although regulation has been cut back during the 1980s, there are still elaborate rules on station ownership, for instance, to limit domination by a few interests.

Most of the programming is provided by the three networks, the American Broadcasting Corporation (Capital Cities–ABC), the Columbia Broadcasting System (CBS), and the National Broadcasting Company (NBC). These are allowed to own only a few local stations, so they mostly broadcast their programs and advertisements through separate, privately owned, local 'affiliates'. However, under the 'prime time access rule', the networks provide programming for only three out of four peak viewing hours, usually from 8 pm to 11 pm. The rule was designed to allow affiliates to show some of their own programs. In practice, they mostly use it to broadcast bought-in 'syndicated' entertainment programs, especially game shows and sitcoms, plus some of their own local news and sport coverage. Local news has grown in its scope and profitability, largely because of developments in technology for gathering news very quickly and perhaps the availability of local advertising revenues.

Most markets also have some 'independent' stations; many have one or two, and the larger cities may have four or five significant independents. They are so named because they are independent of the networks. Independents in different markets are often grouped under the same ownership and act as 'mini-networks', with transmission links and shared programs but without affiliates in yet other markets (except, very occasionally, on an ad-hoc basis). The independent stations show syndicated material that was originally screened on the networks. This they often 'strip' across five days per week, showing a series in the same time slot each weekday.

Although the three networks originate most of the programs shown on most broadcast stations, they are not permitted by the FCC to produce in-house, except for the network news, sport, and public affairs shows. Almost all of the rest they must buy in, in practice mostly from the large Hollywood production companies. However, these rules only last until 1990, when there may be big changes in business practice.

Since the early 1970s, the networks have also been prevented from broadcasting these bought-in programs more than twice. After that, ownership reverts to the production companies, who then syndicate the more popular shows to the independent stations and to the network affiliates (who broadcast them outside network time). The opportunity to broadcast re-runs of recent popular shows has brought bigger revenues to the independent stations. They have therefore become able to support the production of some first-run, non-network programs. However, these are still made for syndication to many stations (to share costs) and are in no sense designed to be 'different'. On the contrary, they usually aim to compete for advertising revenue by looking as much as possible like real first-run network programming.

The aim of regulation has been to limit the power of any one media owner. In itself, this hardly affects the viewer, who may not notice or care who owns the channel that screens the third re-run of *M*A*S*H*. There is little or no regulation of the kinds of program broadcast or of their content, partly because the First Amendment of the US Constitution guarantees free speech and partly for general ideological reasons. (The main exception is a rule on editorial comment by the stations, which must be specifically labelled as opinion. This 'fairness' doctrine is currently (1988) under review.)

Nearly all of US television is paid for by the sale of advertising time. The United States is unique among major countries in the extent to which its broadcast television is funded in this way, which leads to intense competition between channels for their income. Since a competitive commercial television channel's income in practice varies almost directly with the size of its audiences, this means that channels continuously compete for the maximum audience – what is often called the 'ratings war'. Virtually all of the time, therefore, they show the kinds of program that are most likely to win, with perhaps a very occasional prestige program for publicity or goodwill. The nature of television funding and its relationship with programming are discussed further in Part Four.

The Public Broadcasting Service in the USA is the exception to this funding rule, being paid for by donations from viewers and corporate sponsors, and by local, state, and federal grants. PBS has achieved some notable successes, for example with children's programming features, and drama (often imported and mostly British), but it has only been able to achieve an audience share of well under 5 percent. The initial design by the Carnegie Foundation, as well as government regulation, notably under President Nixon, has imposed a fragmented structure on public broadcasting, made worse by conflicting objectives within the system. Although PBS in its financially better days had a total television budget equal to that of the BBC, much of its revenue goes into running its local stations instead of being available for networked programming.

Britain

The organization of television in Britain differs markedly from that in the USA. Britain has just four channels, with a mixture of public and private ownership.

Two of the four channels (BBC1 and BBC2) are run by the British Broadcasting Corporation, a public body funded by a license fee levied on ownership of a television set. The amount of the fee is determined by the government.

Since 1955, a separate channel has been shared by 14 privately owned regional stations (Thames, Granada, Yorkshire, London Weekend, etc.), which are funded by advertising and which have franchises renewable every six to ten years. In 1983 a national breakfast-time franchise was added (TV-am). These stations are known as Independent Television (ITV) because they are independent of the license fee. They largely broadcast the same programs nationally, as a network. The government imposes a direct levy on them, over and above corporation tax, to cream off excess profits derived from their near-monopoly of television advertising.

In 1982 a further company was launched to operate a fourth national channel catering for minority tastes or interests. Channel 4 is publicly owned – by the Independent Broadcasting Authority, the public body which oversees ITV and (currently) Independent Local Radio – but is funded by advertising.

All four UK channels are regarded as part of 'public service' broadcasting, being subject to some broad programming guidelines and accountable to two 'arms-length' governing boards. The BBC and IBA board members are appointed by the government but are then expected to act as individuals in the public interest, as also with the FCC in the USA.

The guidelines for programming are non-quantified and more enabling than restrictive: a proportion of features and documentaries must be shown, with some aired during prime viewing times. When there is adequate advertising income (as there has been since 1975), this control system works roughly as intended. The real possibility of non-renewal of some of the ITV broadcasting franchises (as has happened repeatedly in the past) gives the system some teeth. The result is a wide range of programs of different types, sufficiently watchable to be viewed by all parts of the population. But sometimes, even with the arms-length system, there can be disputes. For example, in 1985 the British Government tried to interfere with the BBC's showing of *Real Lives*, a documentary about terrorists in Northern Ireland. The dispute attracted worldwide comment and the program was ultimately shown with just some minor additions 'for balance'.

One feature of the British system which is often regarded as special is that there is no financial competition between channels paid for explicitly by the viewers and those funded by advertising. Increased ratings would not directly boost the BBC's income nor would higher ITV ratings necessarily lead to advertisers spending more on television advertising (see Appendix A). Yet every channel has to obtain a 'viable' share of viewing.

Although in the UK there is no all-out ratings war to win at each point of time, there is still rivalry for viewing and audience appreciation. In particular, the BBC is far more aggressive in reaching and entertaining the audience than is PBS in the United States.

Again, Channel 4 has been deliberately shielded from a direct ratings war by having its advertising time sold by the ITV companies, in return for a fixed percentage of their total advertising revenues. Until recently, the ITV companies' payments for Channel 4 were not fully recouped in advertising revenue from it. This was seen as just another price that they had to pay for holding their otherwise near-monopolistic advertising franchises.

Although Channel 4 is not funded well enough to spend very heavily, it has been able to broadcast a wide range of programs which are not mass-orientated. It is mostly viewed by relatively small but still significant audiences of one or two million people from all parts of the population. While the BBC and the ITV companies make most of their own programs (other than imported ones), Channel 4 buys or commissions almost all of its material, with a substantial proportion coming from independent production companies. At the time of writing, the British Government is putting pressure on the other channels also to move in the same direction. The way in which Channel 4 has been shielded from direct free market competition for advertising revenue is also being questioned. Almost everyone agrees that it works in practice but some people seem concerned that it does not work in theory.

Other Countries

Broadcast television channels in other countries have traditionally been publicly owned, sometimes even as part of a government department. But moves towards privately owned television are now being made.

At present, many smaller and poorer countries have only one broadcast channel, while most other countries still have only two or three, with limited competition for audiences. This is changing however, as the number of channels grows and more channels are funded by advertising, for example in Canada, Australia, Japan, Latin America, Hong Kong, and Western Europe, especially Italy and France. Now Hungary, India, and on a small scale even the Soviet Union and China have television advertising, although Sweden rejected it again in 1985.

The less developed and Eastern-bloc countries have centralized national networks with strong state control, the senior management being appointed by the government of the day. French television has traditionally been organized in much the same way but in 1987 the largest national network (TF-1) was sold off and privately owned fifth and sixth channels were created. *Le Cinq* has run into some difficulties however.

Japan, with its booming economy and its large population of avid television viewers, already has six channels, combining many features of the US and UK systems. The government-owned NHK is organized and funded like the BBC, but with almost double the revenue because of the larger number of license payers. It runs two nationwide television channels and three radio channels. Most homes can also receive at least four commercial television stations linked to key stations in Tokyo (NTV, TBS, Fuji, and ANB). These compete ruthlessly, like the US networks. Virtually all of the programs are produced in Japan and include some distinctive genres and conventions.

The West German system is fairly complex, combining regional channels (ARD) and something like a national network (ZDF), with the controlling boards often based on proportional representation of the main political parties and social and civic groups. Funding is by license fees and limited advertising.

In Italy, the main political parties have also shared in the running of the rather centralized state service, RAI. In the early 1980s, however, television in Italy was completely deregulated. This led to a spectacular proliferation of privately owned local stations, funded by advertising. Most then quickly merged into three national commercial networks controlled by one man, Silvio Berlusconi.

In countries with central control, the lack of effective competition between channels, coupled with limited funding and sometimes rather lofty cultural or ideological aspirations, has led to programming which is often criticised as stodgy and boring. This is a common complaint about television in socialist countries but it has also been repeatedly made in Western countries, including the UK prior to 1955 when the BBC had the only channel.

A controlled degree of competition or rivalry for audiences has in many countries led to what is now regarded as more varied and watchable programming. However, when uncontrolled, competition can also lead to a narrowing in the range of programs shown, with minority or demanding programs tending to be squeezed out of the schedules, as discussed in Chapter 9.

CHANNEL REACH AND HOURS VIEWED

Television channels vary greatly in their audience size. In the USA, a large network affiliate attracts something like 25 percent of all viewing in its market and an independent station typically 5 percent or less. In Britain, ITV and BBC1 each have some 40 percent of viewing, while BBC2 and Channel 4 have roughly 10 percent each.

These channel shares tend to be stable. In the USA, the NBC network overtook CBS in 1986–7 but its lead was less than two percentage points. This is equivalent to many millions in advertising revenue but represents an insignificant difference in the average person's viewing choices. There are also differences between regions of a country: in Britain, ITV has long been slightly stronger than BBC1 in the North, but the difference is again small. The audience shares are stable mainly because a large channel has more income, which allows it to put on more costly programs. These tend to attract larger audiences, which in turn bring in or justify the larger income.

Channels do not win their differing shares by appealing to markedly different kinds of people. Indeed, viewers do not stick to one channel but choose programs from a variety. Even before the recent growth of cable, the typical viewer in the USA in the course of a week watched four or five channels out of the five to ten locally available and in the UK, an average of three and a half out of the four available.

Even a popular channel accounts for only a fraction of the 25 or 30 hours per week that its viewers watch television: most of them spend more hours watching the other channels than they spend watching that channel itself. In a competitive system, perhaps the best way for a channel to think of its audience may be simply as viewers of television in general (i.e. of the *other* channels), who occasionally watch that channel. As a result, the number of viewers that a channel has (its 'reach') is far larger than its share of total viewing time. A large US network station with a 25 percent share is not viewed by a quarter of the people for all of their viewing time but by most of the people for an average of something over a quarter of their time. NBC, CBS, and ABC are each watched by at least 80 percent of all US viewers for at least one program in the week. ITV and BBC1 are each watched by some 90 percent of British viewers.

Even small channels appeal to more than just a few viewers, in some cases reaching well over half the population. In Britain, Channel 4 has less than 10 percent of viewing but is watched by some 70 percent of people at least once in a week. PBS in the USA has a share of less than 5 percent but nonetheless is seen by over 40 percent of people in a week.

People 'dip into' a small channel for only a minor part of their viewing. Thus, a small channel attracts fewer viewers and they watch it for fewer hours than the more numerous viewers of a bigger channel watch that. Table 6.1 illustrates this Double Jeopardy effect.

Table 6.1   *Channel reach and hours viewed*

Denver adults 1979	Percentage share of viewing	Percentage weekly reach	Hours per viewer
Network affiliate	28	91	7.7
Independent	9	60	3.6
PBS	3	28	2.3

Similarly in Britain, the two smaller channels, BBC2 and Channel 4, are each watched for about two or three hours per week by the 70 percent of the population who view them, whereas BBC1 and ITV are watched on average for a good ten hours each by 90 percent of the population. How many people view a channel and how much they view it follows much the same numerical pattern in the two countries (see Figure 6.1). Such data show that the smaller channels do not provide exclusive programming for some specific minority but broaden the choice for most viewers.

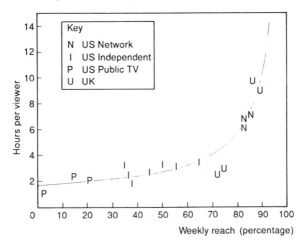

Figure 6.1   *Channel Reach and Hours Viewed*

Minority Channels

Two types of channel in the USA, namely Spanish-language and religious channels, are used very differently. They are treated more like the minority channel of popular imagination: just a few viewers watch them heavily. In both cases, there are special reasons for the exception. However, even these channels satisfy only a portion of their viewers' total viewing needs.

A Spanish-language station may be watched for an average of over ten hours per week by its relatively few viewers. This is longer than CBS or NBC are seen by theirs and, with a weekly reach of less than 10 percent of the local population, a dramatic exception to the main pattern in Figure 6.1. However, these Hispanic viewers still watch the standard English-language channels (mainly the networks) for a further 20 hours or more each week.

Similarly, a religious channel may be watched by only about 1 percent of the population in a week but for as many as six or seven hours on average. This is much more than the hour or two that a channel with a few viewers normally attracts. But here again, the bulk of these viewers' television time, over 30 hours a week, still goes to the main entertainment-type channels.

Such 'narrowcasting', a specialist channel addressing a small audience that is relatively interested in its narrow topic, could in principle occur more generally. (There are certainly other groups with fairly strong motivations, although perhaps few as strong as wishing to hear either their mother-tongue or evangelistic religion.) But full-blown narrowcast channels are rarely viable because of the high cost of producing programs with enough appeal to compete with well-made programs on other channels. The US minority stations have addressed these financial problems in two different ways. The Hispanic stations use low-cost programming (e.g. imports from Latin America, or dubbed cartoons) which can attract part, but by no means all, of the viewing of a group of people with a strong linguistic motivation. The bible stations receive special funding, such as donations and legacies from highly motivated viewers, as well as having low programming costs.

For specialist cable networks, the limited evidence to date is that they do not show the same distinctive viewing patterns as the Hispanic and religious stations. Some, such as those specializing in children's shows, music videos and financial news, may deviate somewhat from the main Double Jeopardy pattern in Figure 6.1. but this deviation seems to be limited, at least at the household level.

WATCHING DIFFERENT PROGRAMS
ON THE SAME CHANNEL

Although people tend to spread their viewing over many channels in a week, there is a limited degree of channel loyalty. Thus the audience overlap for two programs on the same channel is usually slightly higher than if the programs were on two different channels.

To illustrate, if an episode of *Dallas* on CBS were watched by 20 percent of the population, then about half as many again, say 30 percent, of those watching CBS at some other given time, such as 9 pm on the previous day, would also have watched that episode of *Dallas*. However, most of those watching at 9 on the previous day, the other 70 percent, would still not have watched *Dallas* and so audience overlap between programs on the same channel is still relatively low.

This pattern of only slightly higher audience overlap for programs on the same channel is another instance of the Duplication of Viewing Law of Chapter 3. It has been widely established in the USA and in Britain and largely holds true irrespective of the types of program involved, their time slots, number of days apart, and so on.

There are two major exceptions, both already noted in earlier chapters. The first is where the two broadcasts are different episodes of the same series. As described in Chapter 4, the audience overlap is then much higher. Up to half of the viewers of one episode also watch the other.

The second is for consecutive or near-consecutive programs on the same channel. With high-rating programs, more than half of the initial audience may stay tuned for the next program. This is the 'lead-in' or 'audience inheritance' effect introduced at the end of Chapter 3. Such higher audience overlap is not due simply to sheep-like inertia. If the program that we have been watching ends when the programs on the other channels have already started, or if there is nothing that we specifically want to switch over to anyway, it makes sense to sample the next program on the same channel – and perhaps get hooked. Lead-in also reflects our general tendency to watch television in sessions that span several programs, as noted in Chapter 2.

The lead-in effect rarely lasts for more than one or, to a lesser extent, two programs. If two programs are further apart, their audience overlap is not noticeably higher than if they had been shown on the same channel on two quite different days. In one study, of the viewers watching the *CBS Evening News*, the duplicated audience was three times the rating for the next CBS program that night (*Secrets of the Deep*) but the overlap with later programs (*Dirty Sally*, the *CBS Movie*, etc.) was only about the normal one-and-a-half times their ratings.

People therefore generally watch several different channels even on a single day. Typically, viewers in the USA watch about four channels on a given day and in Britain, about two and a half channels. This means watching the channels for significant periods of time, not just momentary 'flicking'. This multi-channel viewing was the norm long before remote-control switches.

SCHEDULING

The short term lead-in effect tends to be used by broadcasters in arranging their program schedules; for example, to help to boost the audience size of a weak or unpopular program or to profit from a strong one. However, although it used to be widely thought that a channel could dramatically enlarge its audience for a whole evening by catching viewers with a strong program early on, the short duration of the lead-in effect means that this is not so. Instead, when a network 'wins on Thursdays', say, and has a strong program early on, it is likely that some other inherently popular programs have been scheduled for later that same evening to build on the early success.

Both large and small channels tend to use mixed programming. Since most viewers watch a variety of programs, a channel which schedules varied programming could in theory hold the same viewers all evening. It might then aim to avoid too abrupt a change in mood or appeal. If one program is slanted towards older people, conventional wisdom suggests that the next program screened should have a similar demographic bias, so as not to disturb unduly the audience's continuity. But, since audience composition varies fairly little between most different types of program at a given time of day (Chapter 3), and because the lead-in effect is so short lived, there is more to successful scheduling than this.

At any given time, viewers have a better opportunity to choose a program that they feel like watching if the different channels are showing very different types of program. Such 'complementary programming' tends to be adopted when there is no ratings war and so no need for each channel to aim for the maximum audience size all the time. The channels' yardstick of success can instead be to achieve audiences that are large enough to be both economically viable and respectable for that kind of program in that time slot.

A related, more competitive approach is 'counter-programming', which means screening different kinds of popular entertainment programs against each other, such as a police series versus a soap opera. This is more common when channels compete directly for audiences in order to earn revenue. Counter-programming rarely means scheduling a demanding program against a popular entertainment program when the channels need to vie for maximum ratings at all times. However, if a program is known beforehand to be so strong that competing channels just cannot win in the ratings, the latter may counter it with a less successful, but at least cheaper, type of program in order to cut their losses and still pick up viewers who do not want the blockbuster.

A different policy occurs in the USA with the news, which tends to be shown in the early and late evening, so leaving prime-time free for entertainment shows on all channels. In most US markets this has led to similar, simultaneous news programs on all three network stations. This reduces the choice for the viewer, especially in a small market with few non-network stations. This type of problem is familiar to economists as a 'disbenefit' of straight competition and occurs in other situations, for example, when all morning planes to Kalamazoo leave at about the same time.

SUMMARY

The organization of broadcast channels varies widely between countries. At one extreme is the US system of private broadcasters and full-scale competition for advertising revenue; at the other is television run as a government department. In between are the more mixed systems which operate in most European and many other countries such as Japan and Canada. However the way in which viewers watch the resulting programs follows patterns that seem largely unaffected by differences in structure or in television managers' corporate objectives.

We saw in Chapter 3 how the audiences for different programs are largely made up of different people, even for two programs of the same general type. This also applies when two programs are on the same channel, unless they are consecutive or near-consecutive. It follows that, over a period such as a week, a channel has many different viewers who use it for only part of their total viewing time. Most small channels are viewed even less by their (relatively few) viewers.

Because the number of terrestrial over-air channels is technically limited and operating such a channel is a licensed or franchised privilege, broadcasting organizations have so far been regulated by economic or program-related controls. It is often thought that such regulation may come to be relaxed with the larger number of channels that are increasingly made possible by new technical developments. This we will discuss in Chapter 7.

NOTES

Types of Channel

Brown (1982) gives a brief description for most countries, as does the annual 'Field Guide' published by *Channels*. See also Blumler and Nossiter (1988) and Pragnall (1985). Detailed local descriptions are available from the broadcasting or regulatory authorities in each country. In most countries there is much day-to-day press comment on developments, especially in trade or professional journals (see page 11).

For the USA, see Chapter 6 in Vogel (1986) and the additional references given there. The numbers and types of channel receivable by US households are reported annually in some detail by Nielsen (e.g. 1987).

The big business changes coming in the US in 1990 partly concern the FCC's *syndication* ruling for the networks and more especially perhaps the *financial interest* ruling by which networks have been prohibited from investing upfront in new programs made by independent producers. This change may help somewhat to contain escalating programming costs.

Channel Reach and Hours Viewed

Following unpublished research by Dr Mallory Wober at the IBA, the main source is Barwise and Ehrenberg (1984); see also Aske Research (1976, 1980b) and Barwise et al. (1977, 1978c). Table 6.1 comes from our 1984 paper. The data in Figure 6.1 are for New York in 1976 and for the UK in 1987. (The reach of channels in Britain is now reported weekly by *Broadcast*.) For specialist cable networks, see Webster (1986).

Watching Different Programs on the Same Channel

The references on audience duplication on page 36 apply, especially Goodhardt et al. (1975/1987). The 'lead-in' effect is described further in Nielsen (1978), Aske Research (1980a), and CBC (1981). The latter also noted that lead-in was somewhat higher for breaks on the half-hour than for breaks on the hour, when there were more program changes on competing channels.

For an earlier contrary view on channel loyalty (e.g. that there *are* 'CBS viewers' etc.), see for example Hirsch (1977a). A still earlier discussion is Stewart (1970). See also Webster (1985) and Tiedge and Ksobiech (1986).

For discussion of 'middle-of-the-beach' consumer 'disbenefits' of highly competitive scheduling (e.g. of news across all the networks), see page 118.

Chapter 7
The New Channels

In the early 1980s it became fashionable to talk of the Third Age of Broadcasting – first Radio, then Television, and now perhaps many more ways of distributing video and electronic text services to viewers. A 'video revolution' was heralded: mass television audiences would fragment because each viewer could choose just what he or she wanted to watch. What has happened so far in practice?

There have been four main developments, each potentially adding to viewers' choice by removing different constraints. The first is that many households in many countries now have two or more television sets, including portables and even miniature 'watchmen'. This can free people from having to watch the programs chosen by other family members and from having to watch television in a particular room.

Second, video cassette recorders are owned by an increasing number of households. VCRs add a very flexible channel, allowing viewers to 'time-shift' broadcast programs – freeing them from the 'tyranny of the scheduler' – and also to rent or buy pre-recorded programs.

The third development is multi-channel cable, with the capacity for dozens of video channels to be wired up to individual dwellings. This can greatly extend the viewers' choices beyond the few channels which the over-air spectrum can accommodate.

Finally, direct broadcasting by satellite (DBS), which is potentially cheaper than cable, adds a few extra channels with a much wider geographical range. This can free viewers from reliance on regional or national broadcasting systems and from the need for cable, unless the demand is for more channels than the combined capacity of over-air and DBS technologies.

Other recent developments in using television screens include videotex (teletext and viewdata: see Glossary), home computers and video games, interactive or even read-write video disks, video cameras and camcorders for home video-movies, addressable, two-way or maybe even 'fully-switched' cable, and various so-called 'alphabet technologies', such as STV, LPTV, SMATV, and MVDS, which use different parts of the broadcasting spectrum to provide cable-type services in non-cable areas.

There are also numerous systems in advanced stages of development which will improve sound and especially picture quality, notably various competing technologies for high-definition television (HDTV). These are just beginning (in 1988) to reach some viewers through new forms of video cassette recorders (e.g. 'Super-VHS'), which are delivering a more detailed picture than are over-air broadcast channels. Some cable channels may also begin to deliver some kind of HDTV signal before the end of the 1980s. However, there are still major problems for any large-scale developments.

All of the new distribution channels for video (as opposed to text and data) are currently more expensive than traditional terrestrial broadcasting and are likely to remain so, except perhaps for DBS at some stage. But they allow a household to pay more (in a way which is now largely unregulated) for having extra choice about what, when, and where to watch.

Most of the new developments are still in their infancy. Even the three most popular – multi-set homes, multi-channel cable, and VCRs – still lack the almost universal penetration that terrestrial over-air television has achieved in developed countries. In assessing their impact on people's viewing, we must distinguish between their market penetration, i.e. how many homes have acquired a particular type of channel, and the degree of usage of that channel within those homes.

Usage, although significant, has been less dramatic than might have been supposed from the predictions and publicity. The main reason for this is that the new developments are essentially just channels of distribution. They have not led to people watching much more new and original programming because the production of high-quality new material has not matched the growth in channels. The new channels mostly give more convenient opportunities to watch existing network programming and, with pay-cable and VCRs, the option of paying to see new movies before they can be shown on mainstream television. Production and viewing of new specialist programming are still fairly slight. Why this is so and why it is unlikely to change fundamentally are discussed in Parts Four and Five.

MULTI-SET HOMES

The number of homes with more than one television set has grown markedly in developed countries. About half of the households in the USA and Britain now have more than one television.

What is remarkable is the way that the extra sets are used. To some extent they allow different people, especially those of different generations, to watch on their own and to choose different programs from each other. Media commentators, aware of some family tensions over what to watch, thought that this would lead to dramatic changes in the patterns of viewing in multi-set homes. This has not happened. As already noted in Chapter 3, second sets are hardly ever used to extend the choice of programs, either in the USA or Britain. For most of the time only one television set is on, possibly a different one at different times. It is convenient to have them round the house, say in the living room, kitchen, bedroom or children's 'den'.

When two sets *are* on, for about half of the time both are tuned to the same channel. On these occasions, the extra set is being used not to cater for a different program taste but to allow people to continue watching the same program if they have to move around the house. During the rest of the time when both sets are on, they are indeed being used to allow different family members to watch different programs but this accounts for under ten percent of the household's viewing.

THE VIDEO CASSETTE RECORDER (VCR)

The VCR has four distinct uses, each of which can in principle radically affect the way that we use television by giving us a more active role.

First, and so far uniquely, VCRs overcome the transient nature of television by allowing us to record 'off-air'. We can do so while watching the same or another program or, in our absence, by using a timer (if we can remember how to operate it successfully). We can then watch the recorded programs later or not at all. While most recordings are usually 'wiped' by being over-recorded with new material, some are kept, as viewers build up their own tape libraries.

Second, the VCR also gives viewers access to an almost infinite variety of programs, especially movies, in the form of *pre-recorded tapes* that are hired or, increasingly, bought. This process is more cumbersome than broadcasting and is more akin to publishers distributing books which we then buy or borrow. The cost of pre-recorded tapes is comparably high, about one hundred times more expensive than watching broadcast television. However, many of the tapes are already very widely available – there are now more video shops than bookshops, for instance – and the price is falling, especially for outright sale. Although pre-recorded tapes account for relatively little viewing time, they are a substantial and growing business, the fastest-growing part of the television market, and are already a formidable competitor to other types of pay-TV.

Third, combined with a video camera, a VCR allows one to make, record and play back *'home-movies'*. Hiring a camera is no longer very expensive but cutting and editing are cumbersome without access to costly equipment. Even with the right equipment, however, making videos that are watchable is a complex and skilled business and so the audience is likely to be limited to family and close or tolerant friends.

Finally, when playing a tape on the VCR, we have a new degree of *detailed control over how we watch*. The machine allows us to stop and 're-read' a passage, to zip fast-forward through parts that we do not want to see, to freeze-frame, to use slow-motion, and so on. But many VCR users touch no more than half of the buttons, perhaps because of the low-involvement nature of most television viewing. The feature used most is fast-forward, especially to avoid seeing commercials. Replay and slow-motion facilities are sometimes used for sport. Nonetheless, the VCR is not nearly as flexible as print media or even as interactive video disks, since the viewer cannot jump between different parts of the tape.

VCR ownership has grown dramatically in many countries. For example, there is now a VCR in roughly one out of every two homes in Britain, Australia, and Japan, and, after a slower start, in the USA and Canada. Viewing off the VCR averages about five hours per week per household, with 60 to 70 percent of the time being used for 'time-shifting' and the rest for playing pre-recorded tapes. The trend is towards the latter. Viewing of 'home videos' is negligible.

Up to 50 percent of households doing something for five hours per week amounts to a sizeable activity. But video-watching is still fairly marginal compared with the watching of broadcast television. Television sets are on for some 40 hours per week in the average US or British home and VCRs are mostly being bought by households where the set is on for even longer. VCRs are therefore used by most of their owners for perhaps a tenth of their total viewing time, to give extra freedom and choice, mostly by allowing them to watch selected over-air broadcasts at a more convenient time. There is also evidence of a small minority of VCR owners who watch very large numbers of rented movies, perhaps five or ten per week, equivalent to maybe half of their total television viewing. But, in general, watching television programs at the time when they are transmitted remains the norm for the vast majority, even in VCR homes.

MULTI-CHANNEL CABLE

Traditionally, cable television involved a household being connected to a transmitting point by a strand of separate wires, one for each television or radio channel. These were the local over-air broadcast stations. In areas of poor reception (e.g. mountainous terrain or some inner cities) cable gave a better picture. In these cases, the transmitting point was a large, well-sited, shared aerial or 'community antenna' (hence 'CATV').

In contrast, modern coaxial cable allows dozens of different channels, mostly non-local, to be transmitted. These non-local channels are usually distributed by medium-power satellite to a large dish aerial at the 'head-end' of the local cable system. Such satellite-distributed cable networks are now a major feature of television in the USA, as well as in countries such as Canada, Belgium, and Holland which have historically high CATV penetration.

Cable in the USA

The US cable industry is highly developed. Its annual revenue is almost half that of broadcast television. By 1987 three-quarters of US homes were passed by cable. Around two-thirds of these (i.e. almost 50 percent of all US homes) paid the 'basic cable' subscription of around $10 to $15 per month or $150 per year to be connected. In addition, homes can subscribe to what is called 'pay-cable'.

Basic cable typically gives viewers about fifteen or twenty channels: the local and near-local stations (networks, independents, and PBS), some more distant independent stations now distributed to cable operators across the USA ('superstations'), and a selection of national basic cable-only networks. These are funded by advertising plus a small charge per subscriber that is paid to the network by the local cable operator. One reason for people to subscribe to cable is still the poor picture reception of over-air transmission in many areas of the USA, but the main reason given by subscribers today is to have access to more channels.

In addition, more than half of basic cable homes (i.e. just over a quarter of all US homes) subscribe to at least one *pay-cable* channel by paying a further monthly subscription of around $8 to $10. Most often this has been a movie channel such as Home Box Office or Showtime.

Except for a brief 'honeymoon' effect, television viewing does not seem to have increased significantly in homes subscribing to multi-channel cable in either form. On average, cable homes, especially pay-cable homes, do watch somewhat more than non-cable homes but this is mostly because heavier-viewing households, which tend to be larger than average, are more likely to take cable.

At a price, cable gives the consumer a wider choice of programs: feature films (shown uncut, uninterrupted, and earlier than on broadcast television); more news, weather, sport and general entertainment (mostly re-runs of broadcast material); rock videos, children's shows, and other specialized types of programming such as business information, cultural, and nature shows.

In practice, people make fairly limited use of this apparently vast extra choice compared with their total viewing. The more channels that people have available, the smaller the proportion that they use regularly. In 30-channel homes, only about seven (including the three networks) tend to be used in a typical week, compared with four or five channels used out of the ten or so available in the average US home.

To illustrate, Lifetime, a basic cable channel devoted to women's health, fashion, and 'lifestyle' programming, is watched each week by some 30 percent of people in the homes able to receive that channel. But, instead of being light viewers of television and thus difficult for advertisers to reach on other channels, these people tend to be heavy users of television as a whole. Lifetime is therefore only a minor addition to their general viewing. There also seems to be a Double Jeopardy effect for cable channels: the fewer the number of people who use a channel at all, the less they use it. This is similar to the Double Jeopardy effect for over-air channels, discussed in Chapter 6.

Cable has led to some switching of viewing time away from the three broadcast networks but not to a radical redistribution. Much of the drop in the networks' viewing shares over the last ten years, from about 90 percent to 70 percent for the USA as a whole, has been due to increased viewing of independent *broadcast* stations, partly because of regulatory changes over re-runs of popular series. Broadcast channels altogether still command some 90 percent of overall viewing time. Even the quarter of US homes that subscribe to pay-cable allocate about 60 percent of their viewing to local stations which would have been available over the air.

Most cable television viewing is still of entertainment programs, e.g. sport, movies, and network re-runs. The extra choice brought by cable is clearly regarded as worthwhile but it has not been revolutionary. Moreover, there are signs that the slow erosion of the established channels may have stopped, at least for the time being.

By 1988, some dozen basic cable channels had become profitable, with others approaching break-even. The viewing level of each of these channels is still low and this raises problems of audience measurement. With low ratings and non-availability in some 50 percent of homes, basic cable attracts only about 5 percent of television advertising revenue in the USA, spread across more than 20 channels. The basic cable networks have thus been unable to afford original programming on a scale in any way comparable to the three broadcast networks and this in turn limits their appeal to viewers. The problem may get worse with deregulation, as local cable operators can start charging more for their basic cable packages and may lose some subscribers at the margin. (Cable operators have a local natural monopoly and can now price accordingly.)

It is widely accepted today that even specialist channels cannot offer advertisers a highly 'segmented' audience to compensate for the low ratings (as occurs with most magazines and some newspapers). As discussed in Chapter 3, television viewers are not strongly segmented by the program types that they watch. Some specialist channels, such as Lifetime and the music channel MTV, have therefore tried diluting their programming to broaden their appeal.

The pay-cable networks also have problems. The industry leader, Home Box Office, was highly profitable until recently but it now has some difficulty in maintaining revenue and in sustaining its investment in programming, especially first-run movies. Video cassette sales and rentals provide new and growing competition. Some households respond to price increases for the basic cable package by cancelling their pay-cable subscriptions. Even if the total number of subscriptions can be maintained, this steady total is made up of some subscribers dropping out as fast as others can be recruited, the problem of 'churn'. This leads to price cutting and cost escalation.

Nevertheless, US cable is a great success. Its annual revenue of over $10 billion makes it, alongside Japanese television, the second equal television industry in the world, easily outranking all others except the $25 billion per year US broadcast television industry. Half of the US population has chosen to pay an average of some $200 per year, double the whole license fee in many countries, for some extra or better television. But, because cable television uses an inherently expensive technology, almost three-quarters of this revenue goes into engineering, marketing, administration, and monopoly profits for the local operators, leaving relatively little for programming. In line with this, the impact of cable television on viewing has been fairly limited, a situation that seems unlikely to change much in the foreseeable future.

Cable in Other Countries

The penetration of cable television varies widely in other countries, for geographical and other reasons. In Canada, Belgium and Holland, cable transmits programs from neighboring countries and some 80 percent of television homes have it; in Australia, Italy, and Spain virtually none have it.

Governments in Japan, France, and West Germany have actively supported the development of high-technology cable systems as part of their wider industrial strategy. The long term aim is to encourage the supply of new interactive services and the products to support them. Cable penetration is about 10 percent in these countries and rising.

The British government was also enthusiastic about interactive cable in the early 1980s but chose to let market forces decide the speed of development, subject to limited control. To date, cable has hardly taken off and is in barely 1 percent of British homes. This reflects the varied choice of programs offered on the four broadcast networks, their good over-air reception, and high prior VCR ownership.

DIRECT BROADCASTING BY SATELLITE (DBS)

Satellites are giving a major boost to over-air broadcasting. A satellite in stable orbit some 23 000 miles above the equator takes a day to circle the earth and thus appears fixed ('geostationary'), relative to any point on earth. Hence it can receive from and transmit to fixed antennae without costly tracking. Being so high up, it can broadcast over a vastly wider area than a terrestrial transmitter.

Satellite transmission has had three applications so far.

1 The exchange between broadcasting organizations or agencies of worldwide 'instant news' for local over-air or cable re-transmission.
2 Providing feeder material for cable systems (instead of physically delivering master video tapes) and so facilitating multi-channel cable in a large country such as the USA. For pay-cable channels, the satellite signal is now 'scrambled' to reduce piracy.
3 Direct broadcasting by satellite (DBS) whereby individual homes or small groups of homes invest in a special 'dish' to receive the DBS signals direct from a high-powered satellite (again with scrambling in the case of pay-TV channels).

DBS gives viewers up to about a dozen extra channels. Although the size and cost of the required dish aerial has been decreasing quickly (already down to about $400 in 1988) take-up has so far been slow. Penetration has not yet reached a level to make separate DBS channels viable. With small audiences, the advertising and subscription revenues do not generate enough funds to cover the high fixed costs of satellites and top-quality programming. However, DBS already gives satellite-distributed cable networks some revenue from homes in non-cabled areas and is poised for a major assault on several European markets (including Britain) over the next two years e.g. with Sky Television.

In the longer term, DBS may largely replace terrestrial over-air trans-mitters if the cost of dishes keeps falling. It may then turn out to be a cost-effective way of giving viewers a wider range of say 10 or 15 channels, ample for most viewers' demands especially when combined with a VCR or its then equivalent.

The high penetration of cable in North America may inhibit the growth of DBS there, although by less than is sometimes supposed as some 20 million homes are not even passed by cable. Moreover, the replacement cycle for most physical cable plant is only about 15 years and some multi-channel systems already need replacement.

OTHER DISTRIBUTION TECHNOLOGIES

Other new distribution technologies have been developed in recent years but they have often failed in the market-place, sometimes spectacularly so.

Video disks are one example of failure. They have enormous technical advantages: they provide high-quality moving pictures by means of advanced electromechanical or (better but more expensive) laser-based forms of video recording; disks are potentially much cheaper to reproduce in large numbers than video tapes; they offer so-called 'random access', almost instant play-back of any chosen part of the recording. But the video disk of the early 1980s completely failed as a mass consumer product in competition with VCRs (RCA lost over $½ billion) because it could not be used to record new broadcasts off-air. Repeated viewing of pre-recorded material is not a high demand feature for most consumers.

Another hi-tech failure has been two-way interactive television, by which viewers can talk back through their television sets via a keypad. A brave experiment was Warner-Amex's Qube system, which included programs that allowed viewers in their living rooms to vote in debates, join in game shows, and so on. However, viewers' interest in actually doing so was minimal, even while the novelty lasted, and the experiment was stopped after six years of losses.

A third failure was the attempt to establish large scale on-line videotex (also called viewdata) in Britain in the 1970s. With this, viewers could access data on a central computer via the telephone network and display it on their television screens. Numerous attempts have been made to launch a similar information retrieval system in the USA, by using cable television wires rather than telephone lines, but demand has never materialized.

These three cases have important points in common which not only show the problems of launching new media but also give some clues about the real opportunities. For a new technology to succeed as a mass medium, it must obviously offer large numbers of consumers something that they will want at a competitive price and be simple to buy and use. With hindsight, video disk offered consumers no important benefit that they could not already obtain from VCRs, while Qube offered something that they did not really want anyway, namely interactive television programs.

Viewdata allows viewers to retrieve constantly updated information, which is at least of some real value to most people. But it can be provided more cheaply and simply via *broadcast* videotex ('teletext'), which transmits a more limited amount of data on the back of an ordinary television signal. This service, launched in Britain in 1973, allows viewers with a suitably equipped set (currently in 15 percent of UK homes) to look up the latest news, weather, sports results, and television schedules quickly and flexibly. Teletext, while less impressive to engineers than on-line videotex systems which use telephone lines or cable, serves consumers' practical needs, being more up-to-date (though much more limited), than newspapers, faster and more flexible than 24-hour news on cable or radio, and also free once the set is bought.

While teletext using a broadcast television channel is a cost-effective way of meeting a consumer need, it generates no revenue for the broadcaster. This may not be a great problem for a public service broadcaster, such as Britain's BBC or ITV, where it can be part of the overall service. But it is less attractive to a purely commercial channel such as a US network, for whom it might even reduce the audience during commercial breaks.

Although video disks, interactive television and videotex have failed so far as mass-market consumer media, each raises more limited opportunities as a 'niche' product and, indeed, on-line videotex may turn out to have more potential. All three technologies have specific applications in industry.

Video disks have specialized uses that exploit their flexibility and capacity (for video, sound, text, and data), especially in conjunction with

a microcomputer. Most applications to date are in training, the constraint
being the high cost of developing each teaching package.

A type of two-way television may be starting to be cost effective as
'video-conferencing', for instance between a multi-national company's
offices in different countries, at a cost of say $100 per hour. However,
effective usage is not straightforward; for example, it requires new
disciplines for running meetings, mutual familiarity of the participants,
and preferably a separate means of transmitting detailed visual inputs (such
as technical plans or data) which it is essential to see together.

Videotex via telephone lines is used as an inexpensive on-line computer
system, for example to give scattered branch offices and dealers instant
access to private information (such as the availability of spare parts) or
to allow travel agents to book holidays and flights.

Videotex may also blossom into several major consumer services. One
application has been for telephone directory enquiries in France. However,
the main emphasis now is on transactions such as home banking, home
shopping, and electronic mail, rather than just on one-way information
retrieval. Most of these transaction services can be provided by using
existing telephone lines. In most cases, the consumer has no need to see
moving pictures, so there is no requirement for high-capacity cable.

Although these various new applications all use the television screen,
none of them is of direct relevance to consumers as television viewers.

Payment Technologies

A different type of technical development has been in ways of charging
viewers for programming. Such 'Pay-TV' can be used with traditional
over-air, cable or DBS transmissions. Typically it 'scrambles' the video
and/or audio signal to restrict access only to those who pay a subscription
for a channel and have a device to unscramble the signals.

Subscription television (STV), based on scrambled broadcast transmissions, was briefly tried out in non-cabled cities in the USA in the early
1980s but did not then offer enough extra programming at a price that
was sufficiently attractive against the existing 'free' competition. The same
system was used in the mid-1980s for France's Canal Plus, which achieved
15 percent penetration in its first three years. Other European subscription options are being explored as possible additions or replacements to
all-in license fees.

Pay-per-View television is a special version which charges program by
program, either differentially for different programs or by the amount

viewed. Here the control is increasingly by 'addressable' cable, i.e. by technical interaction with the individual receiving home. Payments are made either well before viewing (by buying a 'smart card' to help to unscramble the signals) or by being billed in arrears. So far, Pay-per-View television has been tested several times but its financial viability on a large scale has not yet been established. We return to the role of payment systems in Chapter 9.

SUMMARY

The new electronic media have brought about significant trends in viewing but no revolutions. The new distribution channels, such as multi-channel cable, VCRs, and DBS, received much comment in the mid-1980s but, just because new technologies are developed, they are not bound to be a success in the market-place. There have already been resounding failures, such as video disks and two-way cable television.

More telling perhaps are the successful technologies, such as VCRs and cable in some countries. Their use by those who possess them is substantial although still small compared with the vast amount of mainstream television viewing.

All of the new video technologies cost more than traditional broadcast television. This extra cost is mostly used for distribution, rather than additional or costlier programming. Investment in extra production has so far remained very limited. Instead, the new channels provide more re-runs, slightly more sport and news, some more international interchange of programs, and so on. However, the FCC commissioner in the US who said that broadcasting is to cable what the garden hose is to Niagara Falls has not so far been proved right! This partly reflects the types of viewing pattern discussed in the first three parts of this book and partly the economic factors to which we now turn in Part Four.

NOTES

Description

For summary definitions of the new technologies mentioned, see the Glossary in this book. Because of the pace of change, books on the new media tend to become rapidly outdated. There is topical coverage of developments in articles, reports, newsletters, etc. (in particular the *Channels Field Guide*) but these contain more about business and technological aspects than about patterns of consumer response. The academic and monthly professional journals

listed on page 11 frequently include articles on new media developments, including some
measurement of audience behavior.

Multi-set Homes

The growth of multi-set ownership is monitored in each country as an aspect of audience
measurement (e.g. Nielsen 1987). On the use of the second set in a home, see Nielsen (1976,
1981) and Media World (1982).

The VCR

The *Channels Field Guide* (1987) gives VCR penetrations in different countries. The research
companies (e.g. A.C. Nielsen, AGB) have done ad-hoc studies of usage, including several
using diaries. These paint a fairly consistent picture. Routine measurement of play-back,
including identification of the programs, is in its experimental stage. Nielsen (1985) describes
a detailed US study. Reiss (1987) summarizes recent results in Britain.

Multi-channel Cable

See again the *Channels Field Guide* for an annual survey. A.C. Nielsen publishes periodic
cable-TV status reports for the USA. Vogel (1986) gives a good summary of the economics
of US cable. TAA (1983c) discusses the appeal of programs on cable.

Both cable and satellite have been the subject of government reports and comments,
especially in Europe (e.g. ITAP 1982; Hunt 1982; Ehrenberg and Barwise 1982a,b).

PART FOUR
PAYING FOR TELEVISION

How much does all the television that we watch cost and how is it paid for? While the making of a program can be very expensive, the cost to the viewer is always very low. We discuss this contrast in Chapters 8 and 9.

Producing watchable television costs at least half a million dollars per hour for a prime-time program on the US networks. The financial resources available for making or buying programs, however, vary greatly among different countries, mainly according to the number and affluence of their inhabitants. This economic factor, even more than culture and politics, determines the amount and quality of television in each country. There seems to be only limited scope for cutting production costs without also cutting quality.

So many people watch a successful program that the cost *per viewer* is generally very low, say up to about 5c per hour for broadcast television. Selective 'add-on' services, such as pay-cable or video cassette rental, cost some five or ten times as much for each hour's viewing.

A peculiarity of broadcast television is that the costs of a program do not increase with how many people tune in to watch it. A license-fee system of paying for television can therefore charge consumers a fixed sum for watching any amount of television. The amount is usually so low that letting people choose to pay selectively for individual programs or channels would cost them substantially more.

With television that is funded by advertising, viewers get their programs apparently free. However, there are two distinct markets, namely advertisers who pay the broadcasters and viewers who do not. The interests of these two markets overlap mainly for the most popular programs of the most popular types and much less otherwise.

Complexities also arise with the role of competition. Public service channels without competition can show a wide range of programs but these may be worthy rather than watchable. At the other extreme, channels which compete for advertising revenue have to show watchable programs but within a narrower range of program types. The challenge for policy makers is to obtain most of the benefits of competition without too many of the 'disbenefits'. Some countries aim to do this by adopting mixed funding systems.

Chapter 8
What It Costs

Making a television program which people will choose to watch when there are competitive offerings on the other channels is expensive. We first outline the cost factors for the broadcaster: (a) the high costs of making new programs; (b) ways of reducing such costs; (c) the much lower cost of re-using a program or acquiring it secondhand; (d) the relatively low cost of distributing programs to the viewer. The costs mentioned here generally do not vary with the number of people who tune into a particular broadcast.

We then describe how, despite technological developments, production costs will remain high because not only is there limited scope for productivity improvements when making television programs but also viewers prefer to have well-made programs rather than lower costs (especially as their television costs them relatively little or nothing anyway). We also note how broadcasters have to balance the high costs of production against the mixture of mass- and minority-audience programs that most viewers tend to watch, as we saw in Chapter 3.

THE HIGH COST OF PROGRAMS

Most television programs are complex enterprises, requiring inputs from many different highly skilled people. An hour of prime-time programming in the USA now typically costs between $500,000 and $1 million to make. Glossy drama such as *Dallas* costs even more.

To put these costs into perspective, producing a good book costs only a few thousand dollars, although the costs of distributing and selling books are higher. In complete contrast, a two-hour Hollywood feature film for cinema release would usually cost between $10 and $20 million to produce and almost as much again to promote and distribute. Indeed, the costs of movies are so high, and adequate returns so risky, that the big Hollywood studios now produce only about 400 hours per year between them. That is about four films per week. Instead they increasingly concentrate on producing television series and made-for-TV movies.

In most countries a single major television channel has to fill something like 100 hours of airtime each week or 5000 hours per year – over ten times as much as the Hollywood studios' total film production. What is more, each TV channel can transmit most of its programs only once or twice, yet must keep its programming costs within bounds. It can do so only by spending less on its own new programs and by sharing costs with other broadcasters.

Reducing the Cost of Making New Programs

There are three main ways of reducing the total cost of making new television programs: making them as a series, choosing cheaper types of program, and working with lower production values.

Series

As we noted in Chapter 4, most television programming consists of series rather than single programs. Series are cheaper to make per hour because the intangible costs of developing program ideas, devising a format, and putting a team together can be spread over the run, as can the cost of tangibles such as costumes, sets, and locations.

Similar economies of series production hold for factual shows such as newscasts, news magazines, and sports programs. All are able to gain some economic benefit from adopting a regular series format, although sometimes regular performers can become indispensible and can bid up their remuneration.

Cheaper Types of Program

A channel's collection of self-originated programs usually includes various cheaper form its and program types to keep down total costs. Some examples are studio-based situation comedies and day-time soap operas, simple children's programs, most education programs, and phone-ins. Other less expensive programs are game and talk shows which are recorded straight on to video tape in a single studio with little or no subsequent editing. Apart from the host, the participants cost the producer little or nothing. (When a young professor was asked after appearing on a talk show whether an $80 fee would be all right, he said, 'Sure, but where shall I send the check?')

Such cheaper types of program tend not to pull in very large audiences, although some game shows have proved exceptionally popular. In a competitive multi-channel television system such as the USA, the cheaper programs are mainly broadcast outside peak viewing hours and dominate the day-time and late night schedules.

Lower Production Values

Television producers can also cut costs by using fewer or cheaper production resources: fewer cameras, fewer locations, more work in the studio, fewer and lesser stars, less rehearsal, a lower allowance of film stock per minute of final output, less expert editing, and so on.

Throwing money at a program does not guarantee success. As Lord Grade said after his expensive flop, *Raise the Titanic*, 'It would have been cheaper to drain the Atlantic.' However, substantially reducing the production values almost inevitably tends to reduce the appeal of the program for the viewer. Other things being equal, most of us prefer to watch a program that has real locations, is well lit, has outstanding performers, and so on. This matters especially when channels are competing for audiences.

Neither small channels in large countries nor any channels in smaller or poorer countries can afford to make to make programs that cost as much as those of the US networks. They can achieve lower costs partly by paying lower wages but mostly by opting for drastically lower production values and cheaper program types (e.g. under-rehearsed drama, 'talking heads' in a studio, and lots of local light music). In round terms, the average cost of original programs in Britain, West Germany, or Japan might be half of the US figures. In Brazil, Egypt, and other major television production centers the cost might be half as much again or less: budgets can apparently be so low that actors are sent the script only the night before or are sometimes fed their words through earphones while performing. This is apparent when watching television outside the US, Japan, Britain, or a few other large and well-to-do countries.

Spreading the Costs of Production

Virtually all news shows and most sports broadcasts lose their appeal after one showing but the high production costs of some programs can be spread more because they can be shown more than once, either by the originating channel or by others. Thus successful drama series may be repeated, either in the same week (e.g. on a smaller channel in Britain) or a year or so later. Even for the US networks it is normal practice to show their main series twice. Indeed, in strict accounting terms, the networks tend to lose money when they first show their prime-time programs, although prime time is when their advertising rates are highest. As noted earlier, they re-run these programs over the summer season and so are able to charge much the same advertising rates but to pay only distribution costs and royalties (which can still be significant) for the repeat-showing.

A few programs, especially classic movies and sitcoms, can retain their value for decades and be played again and again. The main source of sitcom humor seems to be that nothing changes. Even the largest US network affiliates show old feature films and cartoons originally produced for the cinema. A pay-cable channel, such as Home Box Office, will typically schedule each of its recently released movies eight or nine times in a month, as already noted.

A channel can also reduce its programming costs by sharing them with channels in other markets, for example through networking, syndication, overseas sales, and co-productions.

Networking in a large country with local or regional television stations, such as the USA or even Italy, Britain or Australia, means that all of the affiliated stations show the same program (usually at the same time), thus spreading the cost across all regions of the country.

For such networking to be cost effective, there must be a central organization able to decide which programs will be made and when they will be shown. This organization may own the network station in each region (such as the BBC in Britain or RAI and the private networks owned by Berlusconi in Italy), or it may be given the power to make programming decisions at either main viewing times (such as the US broadcast networks or the main British regional ITV companies) or *all* times (as with US cable networks and Channel 4 in Britain). The main weakness of the Public Broadcasting Service in the USA is its lack of a central organization with this power.

Syndication is an arrangement whereby one producer sells the same program to many stations. This is another way of spreading costs within a country such as the USA where there are many independent television stations and a sizeable number of independent producers. Since the three US networks are allowed to show their bought-in programs only twice, further re-runs have to be syndicated to other stations, usually independents, either for cash or under a 'barter' arrangement in which the station gives the producer advertising time to sell.

With an increasing number of channels, and only a limited amount of good program material available, the prices for re-run programs have been bid up and the syndication and barter markets have become very lucrative. For example, re-runs of the *Cosby Show*, the top-rated US network program of the mid-1980s, were said to have been sold for over $250,000 per hour for reshowing in the New York area alone. Although this is an extreme case, the general growth of re-run syndication has enabled the networks to restrain rises in the price that they pay for the first two runs of a program, with the production companies now having to make their profits from later syndication and from overseas program sales.

Overseas sales of television programs also bring in extra revenue but tend to be made mostly from the USA to other countries, for three reasons. First is the high production values of much US programming, which are initially justified by the networks' vast revenue per hour at home. Second is the familiarity of US programming styles to other audiences, a legacy of Hollywood films. Third is the international usage of the English language.

Broadcasters and viewers in many countries benefit from this trade. It gives them the most expensive television in the world at a tiny fraction of its original cost. Since little extra expense is involved for the producer, most of the revenue earned is profit.

Overseas selling is a buyers' market, particularly for a small country with a single channel having limited hours to fill and no competitors bidding for the same program. A top-quality program may then be priced at under $1,000 per hour. By comparison, very simple, studio-based local programming may cost $5,000 per hour and will usually have far less appeal than *Dallas*, made for over $1 million per hour. Even for a country such as Britain, buying an hour of *Dallas* at $50,000 is not expensive when original, high-budget drama costs at least six times as much. Thus it is not surprising that television schedules in smaller and in developing countries include so much US programming. The basic reason is economics.

Co-production is yet another way to reduce the burden of financing new programs. Producers in two or more countries agree to share costs. This is done especially with expensive new drama and documentary series. One limiting factor here is who has 'editorial control'. Different countries have different traditions, styles, and languages. Editorial control vested in an international committee may be less likely to produce watchable television.

DISTRIBUTION COSTS

In addition to the costs of program production, broadcasters face the costs
of distributing and marketing the programs. Distribution to the viewers
is of course electronic, mostly over-air from local or regional 'terrestrial'
transmitters, and also nowadays by cable and/or satellite. Once the equipment is installed, distribution costs are usually totally unaffected by the
number of viewers tuning in. In contrast, pre-recorded video cassettes
and disks have to be shipped like other tangible products, with extra
production and distribution costs for each separate customer. Such
program material, however, represents only a tiny fraction of what people
watch.

The main cost of electronic channels to the broadcaster is the capital
cost of the transmitting equipment. Running costs are low. For a television
channel that is used for 10 to 20 hours every day of the year, the cost
of distribution is far less than that of the programs transmitted.

Physical distribution, marketing, and administrative costs have propor-
tionately more impact where television is fragmented. Large countries
usually have some regional programming to try to reflect local flavors
and interests but the degree to which this can be achieved is limited,
compared for instance with local radio and local press, by the high cost
of making watchable television programs. The main scope is for some
regional news programs.

How far the cost of separate local broadcasting companies may be
justified is debatable. An extreme case is the USA, which has over 1000
separate stations in more than 200 markets. The result is that only some
50 percent of net television revenue goes into making programs, compared with over 65 percent for Britain's less regionalized ITV and about
80 percent for the BBC's license fee.

With the costs of satellite channels and reception dishes decreasing over
the years, DBS may in due course become the most cost-effective way
of distributing television, especially in a large and scattered country such
as India, which does not yet have a fully-fledged terrestrial transmission
network.

THE LIMITED SCOPE FOR LOWERING COSTS

It is tempting to think that there must be scope for reducing the high costs
of making quality television programs by using new technology or greater
efficiency.

Manufacturing industry has seen continuous increases in productivity over the last two hundred years, often with a large number of skilled craftsmen being replaced by fewer semi-skilled workers using the latest techniques and equipment. Consumer services such as retailing and banking are also being increasingly 'industrialized', especially by means of information technology. A similar process has occurred for newspapers, which are a combination of a physical product and an information service: production can now be done by a small number of workers in a plant physically separate from the journalists.

Television is different. Here writers, producers, designers, performers, and key craftsmen such as lighting cameramen, sound recordists, and video tape editors, may need to interact closely for days, weeks or even months to make one single program. They are seldom replaceable by fewer or less skilled workers without a noticeable loss in quality, even with the latest technology.

The main impact of new technology on television has therefore been to increase quality rather than to reduce costs. For instance, video cameras allow instant electronic news gathering, showing us events as they happen anywhere on the globe. We now take this for granted, along with instant slow-motion replays in sport and the latest intricate computer graphics. With video tape, while immediate playback is possible (without film processing costs) and the tape is reusable (again unlike celluloid film), the output can cost more to edit and a video camera can cost more to maintain. There are also many cases where film is still preferred over video tape by producers and often, it seems, by viewers. Typically, video tape has revolutionized and expanded what viewers can be shown but it has not led to a general or major reduction in costs.

The idea that new, low-cost technology can provide a large influx of diverse, pluralistic, and cheap programs which people will actually watch is a romantic fable. It is true that for a thousand dollars anyone can have the use of a video camera and a simple editing system and that the results could in principle be shown inexpensively on the new channels, but on the screen the effects of amateurism are enormously magnified. No-one outside one's immediate friends and family would voluntarily watch these films in competition with network programming, especially not week in and week out.

The new technology has, however, reduced the cost of *distribution*, even for broadcast channels. This has made it financially feasible to give viewers more channels and hence more choice between different programs at a given time. Viewers seem to want that but it does not in itself provide extra money for programming nor does it lead to lower production costs. If anything the reverse is true: the more channels there are, the more they have to spend competitively on each program to attract the same number of viewers.

Once we viewers have the choice, we tend to choose the more expensive programs with the higher production values for the great bulk of our viewing. This holds true across the whole programming range and is shown at one extreme by movies. These are popular because more effort, skill, time and hence money are spent on making them. As viewers we respond to that especially perhaps when the movie is otherwise mediocre ('At least the helicopter chase was good!') While television programs are creative products for which money certainly does not guarantee success, the combination of time, talent, and technical resources explains why inexpensively made programs are seldom popular, whatever the program type.

Efficiency

The television industry is often criticized for being inefficient and greedy. Restrictive practices, overmanning, high pay, padded expenses and first class travel for the undeserving are common charges in many countries. The worst excesses tend to be gleefully publicised by the press (in some cases with the fervor of the reformed harlot). There is no doubt that excesses do occur and have done for many years but there is no simple textbook solution. Abuses and inefficiency have been as endemic in the most commercially competitive parts of the industry, such as in the USA, as in the more protected systems in Europe. (The union leader who originally negotiated the rather generous 'television residuals' deal for the US Screen Actors' Guild was its then-president, Ronald Reagan.)

One major factor is that a channel's output is needed every day and so it can cope less well with strikes than, say, the coal industry. This applies particularly to channels funded by advertising, which immediately lose revenue if they are unable to broadcast, unlike license-fee or tax-funded broadcasters, who actually save some money if there is a strike. Hence in almost every country, people working for commercial channels are earning more than their non-commercial counterparts. In any case, budgets are often easier to adjust by cutting or by delaying the making of some of the more expensive programs than by facing up to the unions.

A second factor is that competition induces pressure to buy expensive talent (such as anchor people for US network news shows at up to $2.5 million per year), to cancel expensive series on which much has been spent because their large audiences are not quite big enough in the ratings war, and to buy peace in order to avoid operating problems or lost revenue.

In-house production involves costly overheads but the economic case for external or 'independent' production is not clear cut. Cost comparisons are not straightforward. Not only has one to allow for bankruptcies and perhaps lower levels of maintenance, training, research and development, and so on, among the independent producers, but to compare like with like in terms of quality is very difficult when the aim in making television programs is always to make ones that are *different*. Television producers never really tender to the same specification, at least not in terms of the end result.

Independent production is dominant in the USA (partly for regulatory reasons) and in West Germany. In the USA the large independent production companies have enormous costs in selling to the networks. A pilot episode may cost far more than anything actually seen by the viewer subsequently. The independents are also dominated by their clients, becoming slaves of their own success and ever more averse to taking risks (the '*Rocky IV*' syndrome). West German programming on the whole is not exceptionally outstanding or cost effective.

A major effort to cut staff and expenditure has recently been imposed on the US networks by new owners or managers who are concentrating on bottom-line profitablity. While there *is* room for cuts in the television industry, it is doubtful whether it is any greater than in, say, accountancy firms, business schools or, indeed, government, especially if one allows for product innovation, quality, and value for money rather than mere conventional accounting figures.

Some of the criticism of television seems to be misguided or, in the case of some vested interests, disingenuous. Broadcasting is unique in the extent to which it is in the public eye. The output is seen by millions and there is intense public interest in it. Much of the criticism of, for instance, camera crews 'standing around doing nothing' comes from politicians who are themselves rightly accompanied by assistants and policemen who mostly stand around but who may be needed occasionally. Such comparisons are tricky but so is the question of cost effectiveness. For example, it is not uncommon to find that broadcasters are criticized for lack of cost controls and simultaneously for 'bureaucracy' (having accountants and managers whose job it is to control costs).

Although cutting waste and inefficiency can have quite a marked impact at the margin (e.g. to the surplus or profits of an enterprise), it would be overoptimistic to expect that such savings can very noticeably bring down the total cost of making watchable television programs (e.g. by much more than 10 percent in all). Cutting costs is therefore unlikely to make substantially more resources available for more or better programming or to reduce greatly the price that either viewers or advertisers have to pay. (As discussed in Chapter 9, this is little or nothing in the case of viewers, while the amount paid by advertisers for commercial airtime is not directly related to program production costs.)

ACCOUNTABILITY TO THE MARKET

Being allowed to broadcast on one of the few available wavelengths has in the past been rather a monopolistic privilege. There is a feeling that it is 'they' – whether some gray bureaucracy, commercial tycoons, politically-controlled broadcasters, a cultural élite, or trendy television producers with personal axes to grind – who determine what can be watched rather than the market that decides. Without a pay-per-view system, are 'they' not too sheltered from a direct market response?

As with all products and services, it is certainly the producers and management who produce and decide. However, we as the market can respond by whether we watch a program, watch all of it, watch it again next week, say we like it, discuss it with friends and family, or write letters if we feel strongly. Audiences in developed countries are very extensively measured for every minute of transmission time each week, as noted in Chapter 1 and Appendix B. These aspects are also very much taken into account by broadcasters, e.g. in looking at the ratings.

Even without having to chase maximum audiences at all times, few broadcasters continue to show programs that almost nobody watches. The broadcasters' problem is where and how to draw the line between sheer audience size and providing the wide range of varied programming which the ratings data show that viewers watch in substantial enough numbers if given the chance. There is also the question of motivating the broadcasters themselves, which involves their producing varied programs and being allowed or prepared to take risks but *not* their showing programs that viewers do not watch. Every producer wants a sufficiently large audience, large at least for the particular type of program and the competitive scheduling conditions.

Television differs from most other industries in the sheer number of new 'products' (i.e. programs) that have to be developed. This is inherently risky and the appropriate predictive market research is difficult. In marketing the saying is that 'nine out of ten new products fail'. However, while new television programs are costly, they are less expensive and risky to develop and try out than are new products in many other industries. For example, developing a new car model can cost in the order of $100 million; developing and launching a new brand of detergent nationally in the USA has been estimated at $250 million. The stakes in television are not so high.

There is little problem in assessing the market response to the most popular programs once they have been made. A lot of viewers like them enough to watch them. On channels funded by advertising, the advertisers like the programs too because they bring in big audiences. Unless a high-rating program is exceptionally expensive to make, its costs can be met whatever the revenue system.

The problem lies with the provision of lower-rating programs, which only a few percent of the population watch. A program with an audience rating of only 1 is viewed by some two million people in the USA (or half a million in Britain). This may be a huge number but in television terms it is 'hardly anybody'. How many (if any) of these programs should be made, what kinds should they be, and how much should be spent on them? The cost *per viewer* of such a program is typically above average but is still only a matter of a few cents: unlike say opera, no vast cross-subsidies of $10 or $20 per person are required either from the budgets of the top-rating programs or from outside the system.

One approach is public service programming, which in its most extreme form could be defined as 'showing programs that nobody watches (but wouldn't it be good if they did?)'. The other extreme is to aim continually at high ratings and let the lower-rating programming be squeezed out of the schedule.

However, as noted in Part Two, people spend most of their viewing on middle- or lower-rating programs, for which there is therefore a vast demand. This holds true for all segments of the population, so any cross-subsidies between people tend to cancel each other out. It is *not* a case of the many subsidizing the few.

Also, as noted in Chapter 4, far more people choose to watch occasional episodes of lower-rating series than the series' weekly rating would suggest: audience demand is spread more widely than it might appear from the ratings alone. Whilst no simplistic rule emerges on how to operate a cut-off point for lower-rating programs, the issue is less fraught in practice than in principle.

SUMMARY

Making watchable television is very expensive. Although there are ways of spreading the costs somewhat, such as making series, networking, overseas sales, and co-production, the nature of television program-making is such that no dramatic gains in productivity or efficiency appear feasible.

Automation and high technology will not reduce costs but will, if anything, lead to more ambitious and costly programming. This is determined by market demand. As viewers we mostly watch the programs that have higher production values – bigger budgets, better performers, more rehearsal, better scripts and locations – especially when we have otherwise comparable choices on other channels. This will lead to increased spending on program quality as more channels become available and have to compete more for viewers' attention.

NOTES

Program Costs

Program costs vary widely by program type, level of production values, and country. An entertainment show might typically cost two or three times as much per hour as a public affairs program but be cheaper *per viewer* because of its larger audience. Costs of individual programs and even of episodes can also differ markedly. Worldwide, production costs are increasing in real terms, partly because wages and salary costs are rising faster than general price inflation and partly because of improving standards that viewers take for granted.

Accounting conventions also vary and hence cost comparisons are not straightforward. See, for example, Greenfield (1987) on assessing the costs of television news programming in the USA. Much is known by broadcasters about the costs of producing their programs and of the major factors involved but, as in other industries, program-makers seldom reveal their detailed costs, especially for in-house productions. Even for bought-in programs, the price for a single showing may not reflect at all closely its production costs.

Distribution Costs

The low cost of physical distribution by terrestial transmission can be gleaned from the published accounts of most public service broadcasters. Distribution costs for the newer channels are always very much higher and vary widely and they also tend to change rapidly over time. Vogel (1986) again gives a good summary and references, and there are numerous trade sources.

Productivity and Efficiency

There are frequent public enquiries into the efficiency of broadcasting organisations, especially those not operating on a profit-distribution basis (e.g. Peacock (1986) and PMM (1985) in Britain recently). Such enquiries may be seen as one equivalent to commercial market forces. However few if any allegations of either large or very specific inefficiencies have been published nor have major recommendations. In the late 1980s the BBC set itself the target of improving its efficiency by 1% each year, which is in line with an earlier Peat Marwick Mitchell recommendation (PMM 1985). There tends to be much press comment on overmanning etc., and increasing public recognition of these criticisms by broadcasters, but there is little quantification of whether possible savings would add up to, say, 5% or 20% of turnover. (The press itself has had similar but worse problems of overmanning etc.; these could be reduced earlier in the USA than in Britain because the US newspaper industry is more dispersed and competition between titles less intense – see e.g. Willman 1986.)

Broadcasting organizations funded by advertising revenue have in some countries had a quasi-monopoly. For ITV in Britain, excess profits have been reduced by imposing government levies. These matters are discussed in the trade press, parliamentary debates, etc. (e.g. Colllins et al. 1987; Blumler and Nossiter 1988).

Accountability

In countries such as Britain, there is nowadays frequent media and political debate about the extent to which broadcasters are or are not accountable (e.g. Peacock 1986; Ehrenberg and Barwise 1983a; Graham 1985–6; Ehrenberg 1986; Home Office 1987). The argument hinges largely on the extent to which consumer demand is reflected by the measurement of the audience's viewing choices and on whether monetary payments are needed as well.

Chapter 9
How We Pay

There are three basic ways in which television is funded: (i) directly by the viewer by means of license fees or subscriptions; (ii) out of general taxes; (iii) from the sale of advertising airtime. Some countries use just one of these methods but many now use a combination. The dominant factor is that the cost per viewer is always very low.

A FEW PENNIES

The cost of watching an hour's television works out at only a few cents per viewer because of the vast size of most television audiences. This is regardless of how the programs are funded and yet the method of payment can influence the range and quality of the programs that are provided.

A major factor is the size of a country's population. If, in a large European country with some 50 million inhabitants (Britain, France, Germany or Italy), 10 percent of the population see a $100,000 program, that is 5 million viewers and the cost per viewer is only 2 cents. In the USA, with almost 250 million people, it would be less than half a cent. For a much smaller population of one million people, a $100,000 program watched by 10 percent would cost $1 per viewer. This is closer to the price of a movie ticket and few people would pay a dollar per person per hour for 25 hours of viewing every week. Hence there is virtually no expensive original television programming aimed at small populations. Small countries have either very little or very cheap television or else rely mainly on imports. Conversely the USA, with its large population and high income per head, imports little and produces more television and with higher production values than any other country. Next in line to the USA is Japan. Neither a small but affluent country, such as Switzerland, nor any large but poor one can in any way compete with such big spenders.

In the USA the total television advertising revenue in 1987 was some $25 billion, which amounts to roughly $100 per head per year, or less than 8 cents per viewer per hour. In Britain the total expenditure on BBC television and ITV was some £40 per head per year, or about 3p (say 5c) per viewing hour. Television is not only most people's largest leisure activity but is also among the cheapest, compared with, say, reading, knitting, drinking coffee or beer, or almost anything else other than doing nothing.

Although the ultimate cost to the individual viewer is always low, how we pay and how much we pay for television can be a politically sensitive topic. (A partial exception is the USA, where funding by competitive advertising has long been taken for granted.) There are several reasons. One is that payment covers a mixture of information and culture on the one hand and sheer entertainment on the other. Another is that until very recently there were only a few channels available and hence very limited freedom of entry for anyone wanting to broadcast. A third is that viewers of any of the main systems do not pay directly for each program or viewing session nor yet for each separate channel by means of a daily, weekly or monthly subscription. If this were technically and financially feasible, many of the problems and arguments over television funding would disappear. Rightly or wrongly, nobody seems to worry or argue much about how newspapers and magazines are funded. In this chapter we describe the various payment methods and their apparent strengths and weaknesses.

VIEWERS PAYING BY LICENSE FEE

In many countries, for example in Western Europe and Japan, viewers pay some or all of the cost of television programs by means of an annual license fee. Usually the fee also funds the country's national radio services.

Although the license fee may appear to be a tax, because its level is set by the government, the proceeds go to the country's broadcasting organization and do not become part of the government's own revenue and expenditure accounts. In this sense the fee is more like a state-controlled price, an annual contribution that households pay if they want to watch television (which nearly everyone chooses to do). To make the system legally enforceable, it is usual for a 'license' to have to be bought for having one or more television sets in the home.

A color-television license costs around $100 per year in most countries, roughly the same as the annual cost of the television set itself. A license for a black-and-white television set is usually a good deal cheaper, as is the cost of the set itself, but few households nowadays choose to make these savings.

There are several problems as well as advantages with the license system. A major problem is that a household has to pay the fee as an all-or-nothing subscription for television as a whole. This is a consequence of the low level of the license fee. If the fee were much higher, say $500 or $750 per year (still only 25c per viewing hour), it might be cost effective to split it up into so much per channel or per program (and also to pay for a reasonably effective enforcement system). At around $100, however, any such form of pay-TV would be much more expensive to run, even if it were done electronically. Almost all viewers would then have to pay more than with a general all-in-one payment (or, less likely, they would correspondingly have to watch much less than now or have fewer channels from which to choose).

A related problem is that the fixed cost of the license fee falls equally on both rich and poor. But the old and the needy tend also to be the heaviest viewers. They would certainly not benefit if the payment level were based on usage instead. In their case the low level of the fixed fee is a distinct advantage. Some countries nonetheless make allowances for the needy. In Britain for example, the government has in the past assumed at least notional responsibility for the license fee as part of its 'Supplementary Benefits' payments, while in Austria 13 percent of the population are fully exempted from paying.

A lesser problem is that some evasion occurs, as with income tax, paying for the telephone, for cable TV, or whatever. About 7% do not pay for the license in Britain for example. The problem of collection would be worse if payments were selective, e.g. for separate channels.

Another drawback with the license system is that the government is involved in deciding how much the fee is to be but has little control or responsibility over how it is spent. This raises questions of accountability, as discussed in Chapter 8. Broadcasters are sometimes accused of giving viewers what they think is good for them rather than what viewers might themselves want. However the more channels there are to choose from, including VCRs, the less weight such an accusation carries. As noted, there have also been criticisms concerning inefficiency and bureaucracy but these faults occur also with television funded by advertising and seem to be linked more to management styles and objectives and also union pressures than to the funding method. The license fee system can also seem rather 'cosy' for the broadcasters. On the other hand, no matter how well the broadcasters do their job, their revenue is arbitrarily held down to the level of the fixed license fee.

One major worry is that governments in most countries seem to begrudge the approval of an adequate, let alone an adventurous, level of license fee, regarding it as if it were government expenditure and as if a higher fee were just giving money to the broadcasters instead of determining the quality and range of programs that viewers would have. Thus television funded by license fee tends to be short of money, especially compared with that funded by advertising. Quite often the shortage of funds means that broadcasters are forced to broadcast, and viewers to view, third-rate or fifth-rate material in order to keep down costs.

Consumer research, however, suggests that merely keeping down (let alone actually reducing) the cost is not what viewers really want from a service that they use so much. Despite a half-felt belief that television programs should perhaps somehow be free and that broadcasters ought to provide better programs, the cost of the license fee does not appear to be a significant consumer concern. But the range and quality of programs is.

Pressure on the all-in license fee as a way of paying for television programs may increase over time because of the emergence of more channels that are paid for separately by advertising or subscription. Why should we pay a license fee if we could watch these other channels for free or if we have to pay extra for them anyway? Pooling license-fee and advertising revenues across different channels might help, as is already done in a number of countries such as Canada, Finland, West Germany, and Italy. But it might also further encourage the tendency of governments to hold down the level of the license fee. We return to this issue in a more general evaluation of future possibilities in Chapter 12.

On the positive side, and despite these various problems, the license fee system is thought to have quite a number of advantages.

1   It is the only major funding system whereby viewers pay directly for their television (which in a market-orientated sense might seem right), even if the payment is so highly 'bundled' into an annual all-or-nothing commitment.
2   The amount is small for most viewers and, at a few cents per viewing hour, it is regarded by them as good value for money.
3   Fee-collection costs are usually lower or even much lower than any alternative way of raising money directly from viewers. This was confirmed by a report published by the British Government in 1987.
4   Even when there is a mixed payment system, with some channels paid for wholly by advertising or by subscription, virtually all viewers make use of the channels that are funded by the license fee unless these are

so underfunded as not to achieve a sizeable audience share. In practice few if any households pay the fee without using what they pay for. This ties in with the way that each channel's weekly reach is much higher than its share of viewing, as discussed in Chapter 6.

5   The system can provide a wide range of quality programming.
6   The audience measurement systems that are used in most countries give market feedback for every program without a more specific and costly pay-TV system.

The fixed charge aspect of the license fee system faces up to the peculiarity of broadcasting that the costs of production and distribution are not affected by the number of viewers. An extra viewer or an extra million viewers costs the broadcaster no more. (Broadcasting is what economists call a 'public good'.) Since the extra viewers cost nothing, it is not clear how much, if anything, they ought to pay. The license fee system turns this into a benefit by avoiding complex metering and payment costs and by doing it as cheaply as possible. However, for this system to work, the programming must be sufficiently popular and well liked by all sectors of the population.

TAXPAYERS PAYING

In most socialist and developing countries and in some others, television and radio are funded by the government out of general taxes. The money is even cheaper and simpler to collect in this way than by means of a license fee. Being only roughly 1 percent of government expenditure, it also seems a fairly painless way of keeping people amused and informed for so much of their free time. It also places less of a burden on people who are less well off and who therefore tend to pay less tax, even though they still have to pay in full for their television sets.

However, with payment coming out of taxes, the government needs to ensure that its money is well spent, which may involve it in the management of broadcasting. The government will in any case want to influence the content of broadcasting and not only because it pays for it. Whether or not one regards this as an advantage depends on one's view of the role of the state. Most people in western countries believe that media such as television should be well separated from direct government influence, let alone control.

There is also a financial drawback to paying out of general taxes, namely that the level of funding is then determined by television having to battle directly against the competing claims of other much bigger government services such as education, health or defense. In contrast, when there are public or parliamentary debates about the size of license fee that viewers should pay or about what controls there should be on channels funded by advertising, the discussions are separate from those about the government's own expenditures.

On both grounds many feel that it is better to have maximum independence from the government, for example with viewers paying more directly for their entertainment and information by a license fee or similar, especially as the cost is so low that it is hardly a real factor.

ADVERTISERS PAYING

In most market economies, some or most television funding is a by-product of advertisers being willing to pay the broadcaster very high fees for the airtime used to show their commercials. The USA is unique in that almost all of its television has been funded like this from the outset. In other countries, television funded by advertising has come about increasingly as a way of adding to the license fee or tax funding.

Television advertisements generally appear as short commercials. They are so short because the amount of airtime devoted to commercials has to be kept within bounds in order to maintain audience levels. The price paid by advertisers for this limited airtime is high. For example, it costs about $100,000 for a 30-second spot to be shown nationally in the USA at peak viewing hours. The price can be a lot higher for spots during top-rated shows.

Several advertisements are usually shown together in a 'commercial break'. In some countries these breaks occur only between programs; in West Germany advertising is limited to 20 minutes in one or two big blocks during the early evening. In Britain commercials are restricted to an average of six or seven minutes per hour on two of its four channels (ITV and Channel 4), which is equivalent to just over 5 percent of people's total viewing time. In the USA, commercials and promotions take up to 12 minutes per hour on virtually all channels, amounting to some 15 to 20 percent of total viewing time (a condition somewhat exaggeratedly described by some foreigners as 'commercials interrupted by programs'). One of the claimed attractions of VCRs and pay-cable in the USA is that they are ways of avoiding interruption by commercials.

Over the years, despite economic recessions, the price paid for advertising airtime (and hence television advertising income) has usually increased.

In both the USA and Britain, it has been growing at some 6 percent per year above general inflation since the mid-1970s. The reason is competitive demand from advertisers who, as in an auction, bid up what they are willing to pay for the limited airtime available. This has long been happening not only in the USA, where there is intense competition between different commercial channels, but also in the more monopolistic selling of airtime by the network of regional ITV companies in Britain. The cost of airtime is determined largely by demand not by supply.

Television advertising can therefore generate a large income: over $25 billion per year in the USA, as already noted, and in Britain over $2.5 billion (as opposed to about $1.5 billion from the television/radio license fee). This means that advertising can pay for much or all of television programming as if it were free, i.e. without any money directly changing hands between the viewers and the broadcasters. However, since broadcasters' programming and distribution costs are not directly linked to their advertising revenues, any drop in revenue has a disproportionate effect on their profits. A slight 'softening' of the advertising market or just a temporary slowing down of its rate of increase can therefore seem like a disaster to the broadcasters (although it is of no direct concern to viewers).

Given the well known difficulties of proving the precise quantitative value of advertising, it is conceivable that the market might one day devalue television as an advertising medium. This could also reflect (a) more cost-effective advertising in print media using new production technology; (b) concerns about viewers 'zapping' away from television commercials to other channels by using their remote controls; (c) viewers 'zipping' through the commercials during playback on their VCRs. However, it is also likely that there will be a continually increasing demand for reaching the finite television audience, despite the ever-increasing price.

Some people criticize television commercials either in principle (e.g. for selling people things that they supposedly do not want) or more often merely as a source of distraction when watching programs. But most viewers enjoy at least some of the advertisements, which are much more expensively made per 30 seconds than any other television program, often by a factor of 50 or 100. They also regard them as perhaps fulfilling a useful function and as being a 'fair price to pay for free television'. There certainly does not seem to be any strong popular groundswell against television advertising, at least not when the amount is reasonably limited.

Television advertising is something of a gift horse for the viewer. It subsidizes the cost of television in the amount of roughly $250 per year per US household for virtually all of their viewing and roughly $120 per year per British household for about half of their viewing. This is attractive, although the amounts are fairly small for most people, especially in relation to the amount of viewing that they do for it (e.g. a total of over 3500 hours per year per household in the USA). Hence the 'gift' is not all that large. Further questions are whether it is really free and whether there are hidden costs or side-effects, such as over the kind of programs that the system provides.

On the first point, advertisers have to pass on at least some of their advertising costs to the customer, which in total can be as much as 5 or 10 percent of the retail price of some advertised goods or services. Commercial television would be really free only if the advertising paid for itself by leading to sufficiently higher sales volumes for all products or to sufficiently large economies of scale of other kinds. But there is no evidence that this is what happens, as is discussed in Appendix A. We believe instead that television supported by advertising is paid for at least in part by consumers paying extra for the advertised brands. They have no choice about this: they have to pay the extra even if they do not watch television. (The only way to escape might be to watch all the commercials to try to see which brands *not* to buy!)

Even if such television is not really free, two advantages for the consumer are that the payments are both invisible and made in dribs and drabs. Advertising can therefore be a painless way of channelling consumers' money into the television system, like a small hidden sales tax. A third attraction is that the system, being market-based, is often thought to give viewers what they want, automatically. This, we believe, is something of a fallacy.

Two Markets: Viewers and Advertisers

In a television system funded by advertising there are two distinct markets for the broadcaster: viewers and advertisers. Their interests often overlap, otherwise the system would hardly work, but basically their requirements are not identical. Insofar as this affects the range and mix of programs that are actually shown, it is a price that viewers have to pay for having their television 'free', i.e. paid for by the advertisers rather than directly by themselves.

In brief, an advertiser places commercials in a few time-slots each week and generally wants the largest possible audiences for each of these. This is because the composition of the audiences, by factors such as income, age, or usage of the product in question, is, to a first approximation, much the same (i.e. television audiences are largely unsegmented). For programs in prime time in the evening, say, the viewers of one program would be little more valuable for an advertiser to reach than would the viewers of another. Hence the sheer number of viewers (the ratings) has to be the advertiser's main criterion. The advertiser need hardly be concerned with the content of the programs in which the commercials appear and certainly not with the range of other programs shown over the whole week.

If broadcasters funded by advertising want to maximize their income or, more especially, if they see any real or perceived *short-fall* in their income, their only sensible policy is to broadcast programs that have potentially high ratings and so will bring in more money. Such broadcasters must therefore concern themselves chiefly with audience size (the ratings) rather than with the specific content of their programs, let alone the range or variety of their offerings over the weeks.

What viewers want from television programs differs markedly from this. An individual viewer judges a program not by how many other people also happened to watch it but by how much s/he and the rest of the family liked the program. Viewers' more general concerns are: (a) whether there are sufficient programs each week that they and their family quite like; (b) whether there are at least a few of these that they like very much; (c) whether there is a sufficient variety of different kinds of programs from which to choose over the weeks. None of this has anything directly to do with the ratings, i.e. how many other people in the country watch each program.

People will necessarily choose to watch programs that a good many other people also watch, otherwise the programs would not be broadcast nor would there be many other people with whom one could talk about them afterwards ('Did you see...?'). Here viewers' and advertisers' goals overlap. But viewers do not restrict themselves at all times to the most popular programs, i.e. the ones that get the maximum possible ratings. As we already noted in Chapter 3, the average viewer watches only two or three of the top ten programs in the week. And at least half of those watching television at any given moment do not tune in to the most popular program then showing but choose to watch one of the less popular programs instead. Thus broadcasters who have to chase the ratings cannot in practice always 'give viewers what they want'.

Some of the programs that people watch either cater for their special interests or are of the more demanding types which inherently never achieve top ratings. With funding by advertising, broadcasters have to squeeze such programs out of their schedules, even though their audiences would still be counted in the millions and the programs would be economically viable on a cost-per-viewer basis. In the case of such programs the requirements of the two markets, viewers and advertisers, markedly diverge and there is a narrowing of choice for the viewer.

The striving for top-rating television programs becomes more intense, and is likely to turn into an all-out 'ratings war', when there are several channels competing directly for the same limited advertising revenue. If most such channels always aim at the highest ratings, then a channel which does not do so will see its ratings fall and hence face a real financial disadvantage.

Competitive channels funded by advertising must therefore concentrate on a relatively narrow range of potential winners, especially in prime viewing times, all with high or extremely high production standards, i.e. each channel is trying for a better *Kojak* or a better *Dallas*. Developing an unusual program is not ruled out but, if the program is successful, it is soon imitated and there is again a tendency for more of the same to be made. Thus an innovation which does not quickly attract a very large audience tends to be abandoned fast. (New network series have often to be scrapped after just a few episodes because they fell fractionally short of their expected audience levels.) In general, risk has to be avoided under such competitive conditions.

To summarize, television funded by advertising is often described as 'commercial' or 'market-based' but the commerce is between advertisers and broadcasters, not viewers and broadcasters. Broadcasters funded by advertising have rightly to be concerned with selling audiences to advertisers, not programs to viewers.

MIXED FUNDING

Most western countries now have mixed funding, with advertising used to supplement the license fee or the tax contribution to broadcasting. In some countries, a single channel is funded in both ways. In others, some channels are totally license-based while the others are totally advertising-based (e.g. in Britain, Japan, and Australia).

It seems that this mixed approach can provide at least a partial solution to the narrowing of program range. The main potential benefit seems to occur when different channels do not have to compete directly for the same source of funds. This can reduce the ratings-war type of competition and the adverse effects on the range of programs shown. It also enables channels to practice complementary programming in order to give viewers a wider choice at a particular time. However, since even license fee or tax-based channels feel that they have to attract a large enough share of total viewing to justify charging the public, mixed systems can still result in a healthy rivalry for audiences. They usually lead to less stodgy programming than a system relying wholly on license fees or taxes.

In some countries the dual funding structure has been further supported by some broad 'public service' guidelines or targets for the range of programs to be broadcast, as discussed in Chapter 6. These guidelines try to ensure that certain proportions of more demanding and lower-rating program types are shown. The regulations are enabling rather than negative for the broadcaster: 'thou shalt' rather than 'thou shalt not'. The 1986 Peacock report on the funding of the BBC in Britain was explicitly based on the belief of liberal free-market economists that only by paying for each program could full consumer sovereignty be established. Yet the report also stressed that, even without such pay-per-view television, the joint license fee and regulated commercial system already 'mimicked the effects of a true consumer market'. This was meant as a compliment.

Nonetheless, given that most governments prefer to reduce the license fee element in the funding equation (irrespective, it seems, of real consumer demand), the non-commercial channels in mixed systems tend to be kept increasingly short of money for programming (e.g. in Australia, New Zealand, Italy, Canada, and recently also the BBC in Britain).

VIEWERS PAYING SELECTIVELY

Modern technology has begun to make it much more feasible to move towards payment systems whereby viewers pay selectively for what they watch (pay-TV), in such a way that the payments can be enforced. Transmissions (either the picture or the sound, or both) are 'scrambled' and can be viewed unscrambled only by those who pay. This can occur in one of two main ways.

1 *Pay-per-view* means that viewers pay for specific programs or by amount viewed, as with films in a hotel bedroom or with hired or bought pre-recorded video tapes for the VCR.
2 *Subscription television* (also known as 'pay-per-channel') means paying for a channel, usually monthly, as for pay-cable in the USA.

To date, all such pay-television systems are used for 'add-on' services, i.e. those that are additional to the universally available 'mainstream television' which people still watch for most of the time. They cost very much more, up to $1 or $2 per viewing hour rather than a few cents, a factor of 30 or 50, with pay-per-view usually costing more per hour than subscription television. Such pay-TV services are therefore bought only by a proportion of viewers and used for fairly small proportions of their viewing time, but are nevertheless clearly judged to be worth the money in order to provide some extra choice at the margin.

In theory, pay-TV would overcome the main drawback of the all-in-one license fee for mainstream television by letting people pay only for the programs or channels that they choose. In practice this would raise several problems, of which the most obvious is purely financial. The marketing, administrative, and collection costs involved in any pay-TV system are higher than for a license fee. With an add-on service, charged out at about $1 per hour, this matters little (as pay-TV is then providing a service which would not otherwise be available and at a cost which is high but still reasonable for occasional use). However, if people were charged more for the mainstream television, which now costs only a few cents per hour or is even 'free' and which is viewed for a total of some 60 hours per week by the different individuals in the average household, the extra costs would quickly mount up. This has inhibited any such development for mainstream television.

Another problem is the degree to which the freedom to pay selectively would in fact be used. In a country with, say, three or four main channels, few families would want to reduce their choice of programs by opting out of one or two of these channels in order to save a few dollars per month. This is especially true if, at the same time, they actually had to pay more than at present for the remainder because of the inherently higher costs of a subscription system. Nor does there seem to be much advantage to the consumer in not opting out of any of the channels and yet paying more for them than with an all-in license fee!

The main factor is practical not theoretical, that mainstream television is too cheap to make selective payments a worthwhile option for the viewer. As noted before, if television licenses were to cost, say, $500 per year, selective channel subscriptions would be a much more viable proposition.

It has also been pointed out that paying a lump sum for a 'bundled' service is in any case not uncommon, as in paying a single all-in tax to the government (to cover education, social security, defense, etc.) or as in buying a newspaper, many parts of which one may never read. In the latter case people do of course have the choice of buying different papers and they can usually change their mind from day to day. Few people seem to argue that the all-in license fee form of payment is altogether ideal, but only that it can work well and no more cost-effective alternative has yet emerged.

For newspapers the equivalent would be for one to have the choice of any paper or papers that one wanted each day and yet to pay less than the current price of a single paper. The costs of printing and distributing the required extra copies make such a miracle impossible for the press. However as extra viewers of mainstream television cost nothing, that is precisely what the all-in payment can offer. The license fee system turns television's 'public good' feature into a consumer benefit.

Selective pay-TV payments would in principle allow consumers to express the monetary value or utility that they put on their program preferences but the market already gives detailed feedback of consumer demand for each program via the various ratings measures, without viewers having to make direct monetary payments. Direct pay-per-view television would in practice introduce little extra market discipline, for four main reasons.

1 The payments would usually be made not by the individual viewer but by the head of the household.
2 They would have to be made as *charge*-per-view not pay-per-view. Thus the householder would either have to pay well in advance of the viewing occasion (e.g. by buying a 'smart card') or be billed well in arrears.
3 The specific charges would remain so small as to provide little test of demand, even if they were levelled directly from each viewer on each viewing occasion (e.g. 3 cents for *Dallas*, 4 cents for *Miami Vice*, and 6 cents for the *News*).
4 Because the proper costing of a program is complex (taking into account not only overhead allocations but also the subsequent benefits of re-runs, syndication, overseas sales, etc.), the prices charged to the viewer would be rather arbitrary.

It seems, therefore, that selective systems of paying for mainstream television would not reflect individual viewers' preferences particularly well. While such systems are not yet being operated, pay-TV systems are already well established as the chief source of extra revenue for relatively expensive *add-on* services and are likely to be used even more. The VCR is the prime example worldwide.

One possible benefit of pursuing the principle of pay-TV is that it would show up graphically that television currently tends to be underpriced and under-funded.

SUMMARY

Although television programs are costly to make, the cost per viewer is very low, a few cents per viewing hour. The reasons are that successful programs have vast audiences, in the millions, and that extra viewers cost nothing. A consequence of the low cost is that cost-effective payment systems have also to be cheap and therefore simple.

Most television is funded by viewers paying an overall annual license fee or by taxes or by the revenues that television channels earn by airing advertisements. Many countries now have mixed funding. There is political pressure on broadcasting systems around the world to reduce the payments by viewers or taxpayers and to increase the advertising element.

Add-on services such as cable tend to be paid for by more direct pay-TV channel subscriptions, but at a much higher cost per viewing hour. Another example is pre-recorded video tapes. However, such selective but more expensive forms of payment have not become economical for mainstream television.

When television is funded by advertising, advertisers basically pay for the size of the audience that is reached by each of their commercials. Broadcasters who are funded in this way therefore have to try to maximize their ratings if they are not to lose income, especially when different television channels compete for the same advertising revenue. Programs of types that inherently have relatively low ratings, even if they still reach substantial audiences, tend to get squeezed out of the schedules. The problem is that the broadcasters are then operating in two different markets, which are made up of *viewers*, who are concerned with the content, quality and the mix of programs over time, and *advertisers*, who are rightly concerned with how many viewers that they attract at the specific times that they are advertising, irrespective of program content. This partial conflict of interest is more marked for television than for other media (press or radio), because the TV audience is largely unsegmented.

The ratings-war problem has been reduced in some countries by having different channels funded by different revenue sources (e.g. a license fee for some, advertising for others) and also by setting broad targets for the variety of programs of different types that are to be broadcast. These targets can fairly closely reflect the preferences and habits of the viewing public: in Britain for example, even the minority-taste programs that are broadcast attract sizeable, if not maximum, audiences. The aim of such systems, it is said, is to 'make good programs which are watchable, and watchable programs which are good'.

Perhaps the over-riding factor in how and what we pay is that people greatly value being able to watch television. Most would pay a good many hundreds of dollars per year for this (as they do for running a car) rather than totally give it up. In that sense, it seems that television may well be underpriced in terms of what the market would bear.

NOTES

Payment Systems

For brief descriptions of payment systems in different countries, see Brown (1982) and the other references cited in the notes for Chapter 6, such as Blumler and Nossiter (1988). The low cost of television per viewing hour was emphasised in the early 1980s (Ehrenberg and Barwise 1983b).

License Fees

As the license fee is a monopolistic payment, governments sometimes keep back a part of the receipts, e.g. during the biggest spurt of conversions to color television in the UK between 1977 and 1983. Insofar as the fee is regarded as a tax, this would be like a tax upon a tax.

Recent discussions of the license fee system in Britain include Peacock (1986) and Ehrenberg (1986). There appears to be no more cost-effective alternative (see Home Office 1987; Ehrenberg and Barwise 1987b). The efficiency of the system has been illustrated by the notion that something like 25 cents per person per week would give the USA the equivalent of the BBC.

An earlier Japanese study of viewers' willingness to pay found that: (a) as many as 88 percent of viewers said that they had never thought about the price of the programs that they watched; (b) if viewers had had to, they would have paid far more than the cost of the license fee or advertising, by a factor of at least ten (Onoe and Sakamoto 1979). This is qualitatively in line with the priorities and perceptions of US and UK viewers.

Advertisers Paying

See Poltrack (1983), Kleppner (1986), and Broadbent and Jacobs (1984) for the technicalities in the USA and Britain. Concern among advertisers at the high and sharply rising cost of airtime is frequently expressed in both countries (e.g. ISBA 1985; Barnard 1985; Barwise 1985; Barnard and Barwise 1986; Auld 1987; Jacobs 1987; Spaeth 1988). UK advertisers commissioned a study of advertising economics in 1988 from Booz-Allen & Hamilton.

For the 'two markets' argument, see Ehrenberg and Barwise (1983b) and Ehrenberg (1986). The 'sheltered' funding of Britain's Channel 4 by advertising has begun to be questioned for ideological reasons of freedom and competition (e.g. Peacock 1986; Barwise and Ehrenberg 1979, 1987; Budd 1987).

A classic textbook illustration (Hotelling 1929) of how market forces do not necessarily maximize benefits for either sellers or buyers arises from the positioning of two identical ice-cream vendors on a uniform two-mile beach. To minimize customers' average walking distances, the vendors should station themselves half a mile from each end so that no-one has to walk more than half a mile. However if one vendor were to station himself closer to the middle of the beach then the other would lose custom and therefore have to move closer to the middle as well. In the end they would finish up next to each other in the middle of the beach. Hence average walking distances would be doubled and total sales could be less, although they would still split competitively 50:50. It is this kind of mechanism that, in the case of unregulated competition in television, can lead to stereotyped ('middle-of-the-beach') sameness of program offerings rather than to variety.

Regulation in this case, requiring the vendors to position themselves half a mile from the ends, would seem to be to everyone's advantage. It would be especially so if consumers remained free to choose which vendor to use, so that the one who provided a better or cheaper service would get some extra sales.

This type of hypothetical analysis of why 'rivalrous competitors market products of striking similarity, even though consumer desires would seem to dictate a more diverse product mix' illustrates a 'disbenefit' of direct competition. It occurs widely in practice and has been extensively discussed by economists (see Owen et al. 1974 for references).

Some antagonists of television funded by advertising have argued that as a result all American television is mindless rubbish, even if well (or 'slickly') made. This is certainly not wholly true (e.g. Dunkley 1985, Ch. 10), but is the US system's output as varied or as good as one might expect, given that it generally has had a total revenue of as much as eight times that of British television, say?

Mixed Funding

The notion that the more extreme ratings wars can be avoided by means of different broadcasters not having to compete for the same pot of gold was developed in the Annan Report in Britain (Annan 1977).

Subscription Television

Subscription methods are now standard for add-on services such as cable and have been widely discussed in the literature of the industry (e.g. *Channels* magazine in the USA). See also Vogel (1986). For mainstream television, subscription TV is in principle straightforward. Instead of an all-in license fee, so much per channel is charged to those who want to use it (payable, say, per month or per year). This would overcome the main criticism of the license fee as being a kind of universal 'poll-tax' which anyone who wants to watch television is forced to pay. The problem lies with costs and enforcement.

In Britain, the practicalities (essentially using scrambling of the signals as an enforcement system) and the theoretical justification for pay-TV have been extensively debated (ITAP 1982; Hunt 1982; Barwise and Ehrenberg 1982; Peacock 1986; Home Office 1987; Ehrenberg and Barwise 1987b). Further developments are likely.

PART FIVE
TELEVISION TODAY
AND TOMORROW

In this last part of the book we try to bring into focus the overall picture of television that emerges.

The various patterns in people's television viewing which we have discussed lead towards a model of viewing behavior that is mostly of 'low involvement', as Chapter 10 now explores. It also notes the similarities and more especially the important differences between television, radio, and print as media.

Television has a far greater social than economic impact on the public: for better or worse, it keeps people occupied for many hours at a very low cost. Partly for this reason, many aspects of television, such as violence in programs, raise concern. Chapter 11 looks at some of these concerns in the light of the evidence available. Our view is that so many people watch so much television that it would be surprising if any single program that they watch could have an obvious effect on their day-to-day attitudes or behavior. But are there important exceptions? Does television have an insidious longer term influence on people? On the whole we believe not, but the evidence on this is not clear.

Chapter 12 looks to the future, for which today's patterns serve to give clear indications. How we watch television and how we pay for it will no doubt evolve, and the type and number of channels used for distributing programs will certainly change. But, given the nature of the television audience and the costs of program production, what people actually choose to watch may change less dramatically than some think. In particular, we doubt whether the new channels will turn television into a medium with highly segmented audiences of highly involved viewers. Thirty years from now, we believe, television will still be a mass medium with largely unsegmented audiences watching varied programs for many hours and mostly at a low level of involvement.

Chapter 10
Television as a Medium

In this chapter we ask what television is like as a medium of communication. In particular what do the various patterns of people's viewing behavior tell us about it? If most viewing is done with rather low involvement, is there then a contradiction with the vast amount of time that people spend watching each week? We also try to understand better the characteristics of the medium by seeing how they compare with those of radio, the print media, and also manufactured products. Finally we ask to what degree television gives us the programs that we want.

A LOW INVOLVEMENT MODEL

People mainly use television to relax with and be entertained. We do not want to spend 25 hours per week worrying all the time about what we are seeing; quite the reverse. There may be two or three programs where we are rather concerned about what is happening on the screen or are highly involved with the characters, but we watch the news mainly because we do not like to be out of touch rather than because we necessarily care all that much about the stories themselves. There is usually *some* involvement in what we watch but mostly it does not go very deep: *Low* involvement but not *no* involvement.

Television is relaxing because it takes our minds off other things without giving us too much else to think about. We may chat about a program the day after, describing what it was like and what we thought of it, but we seldom go on caring about what we have seen or talk about it a week or more later. Choosing a television program to watch is not a major decision like acquiring a car, a house, or a spouse, where we then live with the consequences day after day.

Watching television is a passive activity in two senses.

1 It involves little physical, emotional, intellectual or financial effort or investment.
2 Most of the time it seems to be something that we do as a 'filler', when we have nothing better or more important to do.

There is abundant evidence from audience research that people rarely go to much trouble to watch particular programs. The fact that we are little involved in most of what we watch explains, for example, the low use of VCRs relative to the total amount of television viewing, the steady day to day size of the total television audience regardless of what is being shown, the low repeat-viewing of all program series, the often fairly moderate levels of audience attention and appreciation, and the tendency for people to avoid watching demanding programs.

Availability to view seems to be the main determinant of whether we watch television at a particular time. This is not to say that our viewing is then haphazard or unplanned. We do make a real effort to see certain programs. We may also routinely glance at program schedules on the day or earlier in the week to tell us what is on and may even plan our other activities accordingly, at least when we are at home. We do not all want the same thing. As noted in Chapter 3, although some 40 million Americans (an awesome number) are all tuned to the same highly popular prime-time program, another 60 million or so have chosen to watch one of the less popular programs while the other half of the population, 100 million or more, are not watching television at all then.

If we did not plan beforehand, we do not merely sit and watch the first program that comes on but we search through the channels until we find something that we like. What we then choose depends on the range and quality of programs available at that time, on our mood, and on our need for variety in the programs that we watch.

There are indeed times when we feel too relaxed or lazy to switch off the television and do something else instead, even though we do not much like what we are watching. But we do not stay glued to the same channel all evening out of inertia. Admittedly we are more likely to stay tuned to it if the alternative channels are not changing programs at the same time. However, even before the advent of remote-control switches, this 'lead-in' effect was neither all-powerful nor long-lived, lasting only for one program or two. Today, switching channels is even more frequent. To this extent, our choice of programs is active rather than passive but, as we often choose a program that we are used to seeing, our viewing is also influenced by habit. Although this habit may be fairly weak and irregular, we do find it easier to watch that which is already familiar and we seldom worry greatly before selecting a program. As Jean-Paul Sartre said: 'Obviously I do not mean that whenever I choose between a *mille feuille* and a chocolate éclair, I choose in anguish.' It is *rational* not to think too much about what programs to watch: elaborate 'information-processing' models seem inappropriate to this kind of low-involvement choice. Although viewers may sometimes complain that two programs, both of which they would like to see, are screened at the same time, it is remarkable how seldom this occurs, given how much we watch. This may again be explained by the fact that most of our viewing is at a fairly low level of involvement.

Although we usually choose a program that is enjoyable, relaxing, and fairly familiar, at times we choose one that is more demanding if it is also more rewarding in some way. This was discussed in Chapter 5. Some minor factor may also cause us to try a new program or series. If we continue to watch it, it becomes more familiar and familiarity can then breed liking. Choosing a new program to watch does not, we think, depend upon some neatly formed prior needs, attitudes or preferences regarding what we want to watch. While people may over time develop quite complex attitudes about a program, we think that these attitudes are formed in parallel with or after continued viewing of that program and so are not the prior cause of the initial decision to watch it.

Occasionally we watch unfamiliar programs or one-off 'specials', but none of us chooses to watch such programs for 25 hours per week. Films are an odd example of this. Although films tend to be very popular and are mostly very entertaining, even the heaviest television viewers do not watch two or three every day. It takes some effort to 'tune into' the locations, characters and plot of a film and doing so two or three times on most days would be too demanding. Consequently, most of the extra hours that the heaviest television viewers watch are spent on more familiar and relaxing, if less gripping, entertainment.

The majority of most people's television time occurs in the context of *family viewing*. The evidence here is that there is not very much 'strongly' forced viewing: people very rarely watch a program that they actually dislike just because someone else is watching it. If they really dislike it, they may leave the room or try to ignore it. People who have watched in company usually say that there was no program on another channel that they would have preferred to watch. They also tend to like the program at least as much as those who watch it alone and who must therefore have chosen it for themselves. This again suggests that people who watch programs together come to know and enjoy the same programs. People may also derive some extra satisfaction from viewing in company (e.g. laughing together) and from the social benefit of having the same program as a shared topic for conversation afterwards.

Glued to the Box?

Most viewing can be described as having a low level of concern or involvement but watching television often seems to be almost physically compelling. We think that this apparent paradox occurs because the act of watching television is to some extent compelling, irrespective of the program. If we are in a room with a television set on, our eyes are almost continually drawn to the screen. We are so made that we are attracted by a moving picture with sound. The degree of attention required for television viewing is at a comfortable level: less than for reading or speaking, and far less than for writing, but enough to distract us. We can watch television rather as we drive a car for hours on end, hardly aware of doing so yet able to react instantly when needed. (There appears to be some evidence to suggest that most television viewing, like routine driving, is done by the right brain, while reading is mainly a left-brain activity.)

Should we leave the room in the middle of a program and shut the door, our interest typically turns off with a snap. We seldom ask afterwards what happened. With serials we are content to wait until the next episode but on at least half of the occasions we are not even there to see it when it is screened.

One reason why much of our television viewing can be so relaxed is that the regularity of the programming makes us familiar with the characters, settings, plots, presenters, and general formats. Although we watch most programs irregularly, seeing only a few episodes of a regular series will be enough for us to recognise some of the people and to be able to pick up the threads of the story well enough and with little mental effort.

Television is far from unique in being a low-involvement activity. Many other things that we do, including most routine day-to-day activities such as travelling to work, chatting to colleagues, shopping, and using other media, also entail little involvement. For example, we may read a newspaper report of a murder or some foreign news development from beginning to end on one day but not the follow-up on the next day – and we hardly notice this omission. Newspaper illustrations are an extreme case of using the familiar to make for easy reading. When, say, the President of the USA meets the Prime Minister of Ruritania, the papers may well print a photograph of the President (which looks pretty much like the photograph of him on the day before) and not that of his so far unfamiliar visitor, who is the trigger for reporting the story. We like to keep up to date with the fact that they are meeting but are unlikely to be very concerned about what they have discussed.

Despite watching so much television, people tend to decry what is on it as 'cheap entertainment', 'absurd soaps', 'mindless game shows'. However, what we watch may not be as mindless as what we gossip about, what we read, or what we do if we are not watching television. When Turkish villagers living in the hills beyond ancient Xanthos were asked forty years ago, 'What do you do in the winter?' they replied, 'We sit'.

Virtually all of us spend most of our leisure time unwinding and passing the time rather than, say, reading Tolstoy or going to see an Ibsen play. It follows that we must not expect too much from our television viewing either. However, as is often noted, more people have seen Shakespearean drama in 40 years of television than in 400 years of the theater.

COMPARISONS WITH OTHER MEDIA

For sheer entertainment, television may come second best to actually going to the cinema, theater or a live sports event (although sometimes we do see more of an event on television), but television always has the major advantages of great convenience, minimal cost, and low risk if we do not like what we have chosen to see. As we discussed in Chapter 9, a television program is a product in which the economies of scale are enormous: the unit cost falls almost directly with the number of viewers. While this is also true for broadcast radio, it is far less so for cassettes, newspapers, books, groceries or motor cars, where each extra item costs a good deal to manufacture and distribute.

Although a program recorded on film or tape is tangible, television is more of a service than a product. Every program has to be individually created by people using equipment rather than being mass-produced by equipment serviced by people. With a branded product such as Heinz baked beans, the aim is to ensure that every can is the same. With television, every program and episode must be different and in that sense television is a cultural service. As noted in Chapter 8, new technology can help to raise quality and productivity but the scope for 'industrialised' production of television programs is fairly limited. If the service is run too much like a production line, both quality and range suffer. Thus, when it comes to making different episodes and programs, there are only limited economies of scale. The economics greatly favor mass consumption but not mass production.

This accounts for the co-existence of both large and small production companies in one television industry. Each can provide an environment where creativity can flourish. The large companies can or should provide security for costly experimentation; the small ones can sometimes provide the non-bureaucratic freedom to pursue particular enthusiasms.

Television programs also reflect the wider culture of their audience and to some extent contribute to it. The appeal of a program, more than for most products, is greatest within the society in which it was produced, which mostly means society at a *national* level as the program has to cut across most regional and demographic differences within a nation because of production costs. For some programs, such as news and sport, the appeal can be more local. The situation will also be more complex in, say, a bilingual country. But in general, and discounting language problems, Egyptian programs appeal more to the Egyptians and American programs more to the Americans than to anyone else.

The national nature of this cultural factor, combined with the size and prosperity of the total US market, enables American producers to make programs with very high production values, which they can then export at much lower prices. However, even without import quotas, cultural factors elsewhere put a natural limit on the extent of such 'cultural imperialism'. Acceptance of foreign programs varies widely. For example, the television audience in Hong Kong loves US programs, the audience in Taiwan does not; *The Cosby Show* was a huge success in the USA and in most other countries but something of a flop in Britain. One way in which to combat an undue proportion of imports may simply be to have more lively and adequately funded local production.

Television scores over radio and print in its 'viewability', vividness, and immediate impact. The other media cannot compete with moving pictures and sound in bringing the 'world' into our living rooms at little effort or cost to us. We actually *see* a flood, an earthquake, a moon landing. We feel familiar with President Reagan and the other celebrities of the moment, almost as if we had met them. Although appealing the effect is nevertheless often superficial. We do not actually know these people. We are able to see what the fighting is like in Lebanon, say, but our viewing experience does not make us feel as if we actually lived there and we would not choose to watch if it did.

The Speed of Information

One limitation of television as a medium of information is that it is slower than just hearing the spoken word, which in turn is slower than reading, especially in the case of fairly technical information. The comparison is fair, even although a television script (e.g. for the news) can be more succinct, using fewer adjectives and adverbs because the pictures convey much of the detail. In general, television has to illustrate things with pictures, preferably moving pictures, and this takes time. Merely saying 'Professor Einstein said...' takes less time than simultaneously talking and showing a still photo, let alone showing him turning the pages in a book or scratching his head. The impact of the latter is greater but the point takes longer to communicate.

Also, the name caption for a face appearing on the screen has to be left there for several seconds to allow viewers to absorb the information. In contrast, we can be aware of a newspaper photograph out of the corner of our eye before looking at it directly and each of us can decide how much time, if any, to spend looking at it and whether to read who or what it is. Television and radio are less flexible in the pace at which they can present verbal information and especially in its sequence. Print allows the reader to have much more control: skipping, pausing, re-reading, and so on. This shows up particularly when conveying extended technical information.

Largely as a result of television's slow information flow, it seems that experts watch televised information programs in their own subjects far less than might be imagined. The evidence is that they may watch such programs more often than the average viewer but usually not very much more. While a gardening program, for instance, can show us very graphically how to do a graft, it will take a long time over it. Expert gardeners may no longer need to see this. Should they want more details, they would instead quickly look at a specialist magazine or book or they would talk to another expert. On the other hand, if a television program itself showed such highly specialized information, it would find few viewers; even experts are not interested in *all* of the specializations in their subject area. Television does not lend itself to specialized communication to specific target groups ('narrowcasting').

This vicious circle is aggravated by the high production costs of watchable television. As already noted, a good-quality book can be made relatively cheaply, costing about $10,000 for a few thousand copies; this can be a viable proposition, offering several hours of reading per user. Making one hour's good television programming costs at least five times as much and often ten or fifty times; anything less and it would not attract even a few thousand viewers, if it were screened at all. To cover its cost, the program therefore has to appeal to a large audience: half a million viewers is a ratings failure in the USA, whereas a tenth of that number of book purchasers makes the book almost a best seller. Hence there are few 'advanced' information programs; to get the number of viewers that they need, information programs must be introductory, watchable, and fairly superficial.

Thus a gardening program, to cover its cost (or to justify its budget as opposed to alternative program ideas), must typically appeal to a wide rather than a 'narrowcast' audience. These will be people who occasionally quite like to watch programs about gardens or gardening rather than just people who garden seriously. The need to make television watchable and to attract large audiences is pervasive and can, for instance, also influence news values (what is covered and how) as well as entertainment.

More generally, television predominantly creates rather than deepens awareness. No other medium could have had the world-wide impact, in terms of either the vast numbers reached or the effect on individual viewers, of the 1984 BBC program about the Ethiopian famine or of Bob Geldof's subsequent Live Aid Concert. Yet even here, television created awareness, 'mere exposure' in the words of the psychologist Robert Zajonc, rather than deep involvement. Enormous numbers of people gave $5 or $50 to save a life but not $500 or $5,000, which would have been a perceptible sacrifice (e.g. no summer vacation). Nonetheless, many millions of us felt affected. Print or radio could not have done that.

Radio

Radio is more like television than are other media but there are also marked differences. Radio, like poetry, can picture events in the mind's eye or concentrate on meaning and sound; it can similarly defy space, time, and nature. This freedom can on occasion make radio listening a memorably powerful experience. However, it requires exceptional writing and performance, and considerable effort from the listener. Even during the heyday of radio, this happy combination was rare: Ed Murrow's wartime broadcasts from London, Dylan Thomas' sound-play *Under Milk Wood*, the surrealist humor of *The Goons*. More recently the original radio version of *The Hitchhiker's Guide to the Galaxy* has been notable. Alongside these rare examples of high-involvement radio there have also been a few broadcasters able to exploit its intimacy as a medium for clear, personal writing. These include Alistair Cooke's long-running *Letter from America* for the BBC, and recently Garrison Keillor's *Lake Wobegon Days* in the USA.

However, these and other radio masterpieces account for an infinitesimal proportion of listening. Apart from the news, radio is mostly background music or chat, e.g. studio discussions and phone-ins. Because it is usually a secondary activity, most radio listening is done with even lower involvement than television viewing. Hence audience measurement is much more difficult than for television: the practical definition of 'listening', or 'hearing', is so ambiguous. This is not to decry such background radio: it makes housework, driving, and many other work experiences more agreeable for most people for many hours each week.

In line with the background role of radio, there is less switching among stations than there is for television, a possible exception being in-car listening with push-button radios. Since the advent of television, radio in the USA has evolved from mixed-programming networks (like television) to a multiplicity of mostly single-format stations, each with a different style, especially of music: top-40, 'easy listening', country, classical, etc. As listeners, we find one or two stations to our taste and almost invariably stay tuned to these: we devote about 75 percent of our listening to our single favorite station. (One reason for resenting other people's radios being played is that we do not share their tastes in music.) This makes the radio audience much more segmented than television's, especially by musical taste, which correlates strongly with age and race and, to a lesser extent, class and sex.

Radio can thus be a more targeted advertising medium than television. Its other great virtue is cheapness: the cost of producing an hour's programming is minimal compared with television. This allows large numbers of small stations, including specialist music, local, and ethnic stations, to be viable. It also makes radio cost-effective not only for small advertisers but also for large ones as a supplement to their television and press campaigns. In all of these ways, radio differs markedly from television.

The Print Media

The contrast between television and the print media is even greater. This is important because much recent comment about television – its programs, audience, funding, control, etc. – has been based on analogies with print, which can be misleading. For example, Table 10.1 compares television programs with books and shows that there are many ways in which the two differ radically.

Table 10.1 compares books with television *programs*. The appropriate comparison for newspapers or magazines is with television *channels*: each provides a bundle of items (news, entertainment, sport, features, advertisements, etc.) and each tends to be looked at or dipped into repetitively for different issues. But there are again many production and consumption

Table 10.1 *Television programs versus books: major differences*

	Television	Books
Production factors		
Fixed production costs	Very high	Fairly low
Distribution costs (per user)	Low	High
The cost of extra users	Nil	Almost pro rata
Re-runs or reprints	Limited	Common
Payments (actors or authors)	Largely at the time	By results
Continuity of production	Regular (mostly)	One off
Creative input	Team work	The author
Consumption factors		
The number of consumers	Millions	Thousands
Consumption mode	Mostly shared	Solitary
Consumer segmentation	Low	High
Cost per hour's consumption	Very low	So-so
Information flow	Slow or very slow	Fast
Impact/actuality	Very high	Mostly low
Availability	Mostly once only	Any time
Replaying/re-reading	Impossible or rare	Easy and convenient
Attention & effort	Low to medium	Low to high

differences between the two types of media, e.g. in numbers of readers/
viewers and in costs. For instance, there is far more audience segmentation for the press than for television. Gardening magazines are bought
or read almost solely by people with a real interest in gardening. Quality
newspapers such as the *New York Times* or *The Guardian* in Britain are
read mostly by the better-off and more educated minority (who may also
read the popular press). Even the readership of the middle-of-the-road
press, such as *USA Today*, *The Daily Mail* in Britain, or Japan's *Asahi
Shimbun*, is more upmarket than the television audience. The composition of the latter largely mirrors that of the population as a whole but with
a slight 'downscale' skew, almost equally so for news or public affairs
programs as for entertainment, as we saw in Chapter 3.

QUALITY AND RANGE

Does television give people what they want? They do seem to want what
it gives them: most people watch it a lot; they mostly like doing so; it

is very convenient; in developed countries people can choose between several or many channels; it is very cheap – apparently free if funded by advertising, otherwise just a few cents per viewing hour. Paradoxically, however, people often complain that 'there's nothing on', that better programs should surely be provided.

The polarized value judgements of 'It's all trash' for light entertainment and 'It's too stodgy' for information and culture ignore the fact that most people choose to watch some programs of each kind (but usually not the ones that they deprecate). As discussed in Part Two, three requirements for television which most of us as viewers have in common are:

Range: the number of different *types* of program,
Good of its kind: the quality of programs of each type,
Choice: the variety of different programs within each type.

There is much agreement on what the different program types are, namely that a reported crime is news, *Kojak* a police drama, and *Macbeth* art. Despite some fuzziness at the edges, little subjective judgement is required. Even program quality expressed in terms of 'good of its kind' need involve no big cultural value judgements: the question is not whether Shakespeare is better than Soap Opera but whether *Hamlet* is better Shakespeare than *Titus Andronicus* or *Dallas* is better soap than *Knot's Landing*. This is so by almost any criterion – critical acclaim, peer group judgements, audience appreciation and, indeed, audience size. *Hamlet* has always been far better box office than *Titus*, although both were presumably given much the same exposure and publicity during their first runs.

Given how much we view and how our tastes differ, we need more than the ten 'best sellers'. It is commonly thought that producing the most popular, highest-rating programs gives viewers all that they want but the facts show that this is not so. As already stressed more than once, the average American, for instance, watches only three of the top ten programs each week, which is a couple of hours of viewing. The rest of the average viewer's 25 hours or so per week is directed at less universally popular programs.

Programs which attract audiences of half a million or a million (rather than 20 or 40 million) are needed to give viewers the varied diet or program range and choice that they actually use when they have the chance. Such programs can be financially viable without all giving identical value for money. It requires only the degree of cross-subsidy that we take for granted when we buy a newspaper with its mixture of items, or order meat and potatoes in a restaurant.

SUMMARY

Although we watch so much television, our viewing remains largely ephemeral. We use television mostly to relax and are seldom deeply involved. Even information programs have to be 'good viewing' if they are to keep our attention. Television is a very effective medium for making us aware and for giving us the feel of things but for detailed information we have to turn to other media. The basic reason is that moving pictures, although their immediate impact can be great, are slow and inflexible at conveying specific information compared with speech or print.

In judging television as a medium, we need to take into account what viewers do with it. The evidence is that viewers differ greatly in their tastes and preferences; that these are real and traceable even if our viewing from week to week is rather irregular; that watching merely the most popular programs would not satisfy us because most of us watch varied diets of entertainment programs and also some of the more demanding fare. Giving viewers what they want therefore depends on three factors: the range of programs of different types that are provided, whether a program is good of its kind, and the choice of different programs within each broad type.

NOTES

Low Involvement

This has been explored over the years by Krugman (1965, 1971, 1980), mostly in the context of television advertising. Krugman notes that learning can take place despite low involvement, while Gerbner (1987) suggests that low involvement viewing may make viewers *more* open to the effects of persuasion. Krugman (1980) has also suggested the possible relevance of left and right brain functions. Related issues, such as the 'passive' role of television viewing and how it mostly leaves 'no trace', are often raised. The notion that television viewing provides a comfortable level of distraction, without being too demanding or stimulating, has been explored in some detail by Watt and Krull (1974), Krull and Watt (1975), and Krull et al. (1977). The approach has also been applied to children's viewing (Krull and Husson 1979).

The notion that viewers often watch the 'least objectionable' program was articulated by Paul Klein (1971). The pregnant 'We sit' of pre-television villagers in the winter was elicited by the archaeologist George Bean (Darke 1986).

For references discussing the role of family viewing, see page 21.

TV and Other Media

We are not aware of any detailed public discussion or data on television being a 'slow' medium for passing on technical information. Here we report our personal interpretation. See Ehrenberg (1988b) for a related comparison of graphs, tables and text for communicating numerical information.

Early papers on 'mere exposure' already noted are Zajonc (1968) and Harrison (1977). Sluckin et al. (1982) summarize some unusual British studies using real-life data to show how familiarity, but not overfamiliarity, can lead to liking. Gorn (1982) explores the effects of mere exposure versus classical conditioning in advertising.

The view that television will become like the printed media was developed in particular by Jay (1981) and is widely referred to (e.g. Peacock 1986). For 'narrowcasting' see e.g. Crook (1984), Zenaty (1984), Wilson and Gutierrez (1985).

Quality and Range

See Ehrenberg and Barwise (1983b), Ehrenberg (1986), and Taylor and Mullan (1986). For the opposite view, that 'in the fully deregulated market place, the highest bidder would make the best and highest use of the resource', see Fowler (then chairman of the FCC in the USA). However, the view that high ratings give viewers what they want is rarely as explicit as this: it is more often seen as a self-evident assumption.

Chapter 11
Concerns About Television

Because of its vast audiences, television inevitably raises concerns in the minds of the public and social commentators. A number of specific issues, such as the effects of television sex, violence, and profanity, generate a great deal of comment and controversy. Less seems to be written about two more general concerns, namely the programs offered and the large amount of time spent viewing. We turn first to these more general concerns.

BETTER PROGRAMS?

People's primary concern about television seems to be the choice of programs available.

In social researchers' group discussions and consumer surveys, and also, we think, in ordinary conversation, people say that they mainly want more good programs and less repeats. Although this concern about programs may seem obvious, it is not reflected in the academic research literature, which is mostly about specific issues such as violence or political coverage. Nor is it adequately reflected in most public debates about broadcasting policy, which also tend to be about the more specific issues, and what the Government should or should not do about them, or about costs. Even the recent policy trend towards deregulation has involved little analysis or understanding of consumers' actual preferences. The restricted aim of encouraging competition is assumed to be able automatically to give consumers what they want, principally by making program supply more 'efficient' financially.

As we saw in Chapter 9, however, even in countries where viewers have to pay directly for their television its cost is at most only a few cents per hour. That is why, without prompting, the efficiency or cost of television does not appear as a significant consumer concern, in contrast with the cost of food, transport, housing, health care, taxes, and so on.

To illustrate, in Britain the cost of the television license fee was increased by a quarter in March 1985. Six months later only 30 percent of UK adults were aware of the increase and only 10 percent knew that it had happened in March. The BBC received a total of some 1500 critical letters before and 200 after the rise in fee occurred, compared with about 500 000 letters per year commenting on *programs*.

Perhaps one reason for the lack of formal public debate on program range and quality is that economists in particular have virtually no useful theory to apply to these issues and prefer to concentrate on costs, prices, and efficiency – issues of relative non-concern to the consumer. We ourselves believe that it would be much more helpful to focus on consumers' real concerns, especially since the range and quality of programs are far more affected by big economic factors, such as the funding system used and the degree of regulation, than by marginal if welcome increases in efficiency. After all, much is known about viewers' preferences, as revealed in their patterns of program and channel choice and in their liking responses. We return to this subject in Chapter 12.

THE TIME SPENT VIEWING

The other general concern about television is the sheer amount of time that we spend watching it. Most of us harbor some guilt feelings about spending, or 'wasting', so much time in front of 'the box' with so little to show for it. Whereas the other specific social concerns about television worry about the effects that it can have on viewers, this concern is the opposite, namely that so many hours of viewing pass without leaving a trace.

Feelings of guilt about television are very widespread but are not especially strong. In group discussions, although viewers of different backgrounds usually confess to some such feelings, many then counter this by saying that television viewing *does* at times leave a trace. They may say, for instance, that they have learned quite a lot from watching television and that it gives them topics to think about and to discuss with family and friends. They could have picked up this information in half an hour's reading or skimming of books, newspapers or magazines, rather than by watching several hours of television. But it would not have had the same immediacy nor have been quite so relaxing or entertaining, nor yet have been so open to discussion with others who had seen, or knowingly missed, the same programs.

Like the general concern about programming, people's nagging disquiet about the time spent viewing is mostly centered on themselves and perhaps their children: should they be doing other, more constructive things instead?

(People tend to forget that much reading is also done merely to 'pass the time'.) With the exception perhaps of a few teachers and moralists who may regard television with a kind of blanket disapproval, few members of the public express concern that everyone else is wasting time watching television. Conversely, people's more specific concerns about television relate more to its possible effects on others than on themselves.

SPECIFIC CONCERNS ABOUT TELEVISION

People's specific concerns about television are limitless and seem to include virtually all of human life. Television is assumed to have contributed towards, or even caused, almost every fault in modern society. Concern focuses on social problems such as violence, inadequate child development, sexism, promiscuity, and racial prejudice. It also touches on political issues (bias and television's effects on elections) and on even broader cultural factors such as materialism ('the consumer society') and 'media imperialism'. Among these many areas of concern, there are several recurrent features.

1 The concerns are largely negative. Of those people advocating change, far more lay stress on combating the assumed anti-social influences of television than on using it as a positive, pro-social force. It is fairly unusual (although not unheard of) for someone to say that anything good has been caused or reinforced by television. This tendency to ascribe all the ills of the world to a particular mass medium predates television: blame was first laid on books of any kind and then later on popular fiction, the movies, and radio. The concerns include an element of suspicion, fear or snobbery about popular mass culture. One factor in the case of television is its sheer scale. If it were like VCRs, with say only 40% of people using it for just a few hours per week, it would not create the same anxieties. People fear television's potential influence because it is hard to believe that so much viewing can have no effect.

2 Most of the concerns relate to specific types of program content, such as the behavior shown within entertainment programs and to a lesser extent within advertisements. Information programs raise a largely different set of concerns, such as political control and editorial bias.

3 The criticisms involve an implicit presumption that program content affects the audience's subsequent attitudes or behavior. If there were no such effects, there would presumably be little or no logical objection to any program content.

4 People's concerns are mostly about the effects on other viewers. People rarely say that *they themselves* have been made, for instance, more violent, oversexed, materialistic, or racially intolerant by watching television programs.

As noted above, it is usually considered obvious that, because of the sheer scale of television viewing, it must affect audience behavior. Although there have been a good many studies of the effects of television, the conclusions are seldom clear cut or startling in their size (e.g. that *many* viewers have been affected). Instead they appear always to be complex and difficult to quote. Nonetheless it could be argued that some issues are so important that significant effects on the audience should perhaps be presumed, even if they have not been proven.

Against this is the argument that what matters is the very *lack* of evidence that television viewing has large or dramatic effects on the vast majority of viewers most of the time, apart from occasionally creating sheer awareness (e.g. programs on child abuse or the African famine). It is not simply that big effects have never been proved but that they have never even been seriously claimed. For instance, criminologists do not claim that television has caused a doubling of the crime rate. Attila the Hun, Genghis Khan, Stalin, and Hitler managed to do what they did without growing up watching television and this is not a trivial point. It is therefore argued by some that the benefit of the doubt should go towards freedom of information: both the broadcasters' freedom to transmit and the viewers' freedom to watch whatever they choose.

One of the most heavily researched questions in broadcasting is the possible effects of television violence and aggression, especially on children and adolescents. We explore this now, as the issues raised illustrate the wider problems of television's alleged effects, and then look at some other specific concerns.

Violence and Aggression

Two problems in assessing the effects of television violence are deciding what constitutes violent material and how to quantify the amount of violence. For instance, viewers very rarely see a real person killed on television (e.g. on the news or in the boxing ring). But one such real occurrence seen in close-up may be more disturbing than any amount of stylized fictional violence. In late 1986 the Treasurer of Pennsylvania blew out his brains at a televised press conference. There was much discussion of whether the footage should be shown on the television news and, to some extent, of whether the press should show photographs. No-one queried whether the incident should be discussed in either medium. Nor was there much concern that someone had killed himself. This illustrates the difference between the media. Pictures, especially television pictures, have a much more vivid impact than cold print or discussion. But how does one assess or measure their long-term effect on attitudes or behavior?

The surrealist violence of traditional cartoons such as *Popeye* or *Tom and Jerry* is rarely regarded as likely to disturb people. In practice, concern and research have mostly focused on fictional violence portrayed by real-life actors, especially in 'action-adventure' series. These series vary widely. Elements of their appeal can include sitcom-type humor, the triumph of good over evil, human interest, a 'whodunnit' plot, beautiful props, locations, music, clothes, and people. Presumably, however, they derive much of their appeal from the excitement of watching the 'action', which may be, say, physical violence between people or car chases or buildings being blown up.

Viewers also derive excitement from suspense, the pleasurable fear that we experience in waiting for something violent or disastrous possibly to happen. Perhaps this is why we also watch motor racing and other dangerous sports; an uncomfortable thought, but there is a difference between enjoying the suspense and enjoying the disaster itself if it does happen (and anyway the Romans were much worse). The human dilemma is that, whereas almost no violence in real life (i.e. actually hurting somebody badly) is ever justifiable, most of us sometimes like watching it on the screen or reading about it. We may even peer at it in real life following road accidents.

Children, like adults, watch action programs because they like the excitement, as long as it does not become too exciting. This certainly does not mean that they would want to be involved with real-life violence. The data suggest that children do not like realistic, disturbing violence on television, although they may very occasionally chance upon it, but choose to watch a great deal of television's ritualized, not too graphic violence. For example, many children love watching the extremely violent *A-Team* and do not seem to find it at all disturbing because they know that no-one will get hurt. The characters and the predictably happy ending are all reassuring, like the happy ending of a frightening fairy tale. (In contrast, one of the authors was recently woken up by his eight-year old daughter who just had a nightmare about rattlesnakes after having earlier watched a low-key nature program in the presence of a parent.)

Under controlled laboratory conditions, several studies have found that children exposed to more violent programs can show somewhat more aggressive attitudes and behavior in the short term, e.g. in their subsequent play. The data seem to support a possible, if limited and short-term, excitement or 'arousal' effect in the laboratory. To our knowledge there is no evidence showing that children learn more permanent attitudes or behaviors from the portrayal of aggression (or of kindness) on television.

In real-life field studies (as opposed to laboratory experiments), the results show either no correlation at all or correlations that are statistically significant but very small. The causality is even harder to establish.

Typically, researchers first look for some correlation between aggressive behavior among a sample of teenage boys, say, and a measure of their previous television viewing, especially of violent programs. Practical difficulties include sampling, the measurement of aggression, estimating previous viewing over a period of years, and the fact that some of the children may guess what the study is about. In addition, any apparent correlation may prove nothing about causality or its direction. For example, some children may be predisposed towards violent behavior by heredity and/or environment and may even be working off aggressive feelings by watching violence on the screen. Insofar as any small statistical correlation has not been accounted for by other known factors, the question therefore still remains whether it means that the viewing of violent programs has actually caused the aggressive behavior. An alternative explanation of any correlation is that a few people simply like violence, both watching it on television and in real life.

The very occasional specific acts of apparent imitation by criminals or suicides reported in the press (with varying degrees of imagination) leave open the question of whether some other form of violence would not have been used regardless of the television. Similarly, all of the many other crimes and suicides which occur, are left unexplained. It should also be noted that if people spend 25 hours per week watching television then at least they are not spending that time out on the streets attacking other people.

To try to pin down the causality better, researchers have sometimes monitored the same individuals over a period of several years, which raises its own technical problems. The two main panel studies to date, by NBC in the United States and by SABC and academic researchers in South Africa, both found little or no correlation and hence no evidence pointing towards a possible causal relationship between television violence and violent behavior in real life, let alone proving it.

Despite the fact that this is a heavily researched area, at this stage we must still conclude that although sustained television viewing involves seeing a great deal of mostly fictional violence over time, no *dramatic* long-term effects have ever been claimed by serious researchers. The verdict is undecided as to whether there are some vestigial effects at the margin. In particular, there could be a small long-term 'drip' effect: television might for instance seem to be suggesting that it is fairly normal for people to settle their arguments with physical violence. However, for nearly all viewers that is not the norm in their everyday lives.

Some evidence has been reported that elderly US viewers, especially those who watch the most television, tend to believe that the world is more violent than it is in reality. Other researchers have questioned both the evidence and its interpretation. Nevertheless it is often argued that showing no violence would be unnatural in a violent world. Thus broadcasting authorities try to distinguish between showing 'gratuitous' violence and violence that has 'artistic justification', such as the Duke of Cornwall's sadistic blinding of Gloucester in Shakespeare's *King Lear*. In this particular instance the enormous difference between the media shows up again: the contrast between reading 'Out, vile jelly! Where is thy lustre now?' in the text, seeing the act performed on the stage, and watching it in close-up on television.

Another controversial aspect of the question of violence is war coverage. There are some who seriously doubt whether a democracy could conduct even a 'just' war, if the public were receiving full color television coverage, because war is so bloody and causes such obvious and immediate suffering. The alternative – surrender – would in contrast be relatively invisible and its effects would be delayed. Most people would argue that television news should be free to report to the public on the war and to debate the questions it raises. However, while the war is being fought, some censorship and delay in transmitting pictures (as was much discussed during Britain's Falklands war with Argentina) might seem to be justified, and not only for reasons of military security. For television news to bring real violence on that scale into the home could be too disturbing for most people to accept.

Bad Language

An issue which generates numerous letters to the broadcasters is 'bad language', especially profanity. Many viewers find this personally offensive as well as being concerned about other viewers. The main concern is simply that people find such language objectionable, not that it has any deep, long-term effect on society (though it can also be regarded as setting a bad example to children). The question for the broadcasters is how much they should sanitize the language in television drama in order to avoid giving offense; there is probably already less 'bad language' on television than in the world at large. Thus it is hard to imagine a fictional US President on television using the kind of language that was recorded in the Watergate tapes. Nevertheless the offense caused by bad language on television is very widespread indeed.

Sex

Sex on television produces almost as much criticism as profanity. There is actually very little explicit sex on television but much of televised drama involves people having sexual relationships, often with a couple obviously limbering up to have sex immediately after the end of a scene. These relationships are almost always heterosexual, and extra- or pre-marital. They are quite often casual, and there has been virtually no reference in television drama over the years to contraception or the risk of sexually-transmitted disease. (The recent AIDS publicity is quite separate and is also more about death than about sex.)

Many people feel that television should be more tightly controlled than other media because it is 'there in the home' and watched by all members of the family. It may be that a portrayal of sex, which each family member might find quite bland if seen alone ('there is more sex in real life than ever occurs on the television screen'), becomes upsetting or embarrassing when viewed together by the family, especially if it includes much younger or much older viewers. Critics can be roughly split into two groups: those who think that sex is a bad or at least a private thing and that television should pretend it does not exist, and those who think that sex is a good thing on the whole (quite unlike violence) but that television provides bad role models.

Media Portrayals

Television drama – soap operas, sitcoms, action series, movies, and general drama – tends to portray people of higher status living in a more glamorous world than most viewers live in. This, together with the common presumption that broadcasters share a fairly narrow set of values, leads to accusations that television reinforces existing differences in the power and status of different groups within society. In the words of a US Government report: 'There are more men than women on entertainment television and the men on average are older. The men are mostly strong and manly, the women usually passive and feminine. . . . Television characters usually have higher status jobs than average people in real life. . . the elderly are under-represented.' Some groups (e.g. homosexuals and, in the past, blacks) argue that not only are they under-represented on television, but also that they appear as a negative stereotype when they *are* represented.

In recent years some of these limitations have been redressed but the results can look sadly self-conscious and artificial. For instance, it seems to be a cliché of current British sitcoms that women are more competent than men, and of US police shows that black policemen are more competent than white.

Why might all this matter? Up to a point, it matters because some people say that it matters to them. Usually, however, these people claim to represent a particular group. They argue, for instance, that television portrayals of the handicapped influence those people's own self-esteem and the attitudes of other people towards them. There may be no evidence proving that it is so but some would argue that this merely reflects the limitations of social science research, or indeed would argue that the portrayals would still be objectionable even if they were known to have no social effects.

Against this, it has been argued that the world portrayed in entertainment television is determined by what viewers select to watch of their own free will, and that people want to spend their evenings relaxing, not being socially engineered. In fact, as we saw in Chapter 3, subgroups of the population (by gender, social class, etc.) do not differ radically in their broad viewing preferences. More specifically, programs 'for the black community' achieve minimal ratings among blacks, little more than among whites.

In some cases there are strongly felt values which prevent change. An example is the typical portrayal of homosexuals as comic stereotypes. There *are* signs that majority opinion is shifting against such portrayals but a more sympathetic portrayal in the spoof soap opera *Soap* drew strong criticism from the self-styled 'Moral Majority'. Even today, few heterosexuals regard homosexual marriage as a valid lifestyle and few want it presented as such on television, especially in front of their children.

Children

Many concerns about television apply particularly to children's viewing. It is felt that children are more likely than adults to be affected by program content, including commercials, and that if children spend too much time watching television, this will slow down their development.

Children and young teenagers spend a great deal of time watching television, although somewhat less on average than adults since they tend to go to bed earlier. Just as we saw in the case of violence and aggression, it is far from clear what effect, if any, all of this viewing has on them. Researchers have studied the patterns of attention and comprehension among infants of different ages, and what children do and do not seem to learn from television. In itself, television generally seems to supply little material for imaginative play. It may in some cases take up so much of a child's time that it slows down the development of reading ability, encourages passivity, and allows less time for other activities.

Good informative programs, however, can introduce children to a wide range of people, places, and ideas. This is a special case of television's phenomenal ability to introduce subjects superficially, rather than greatly deepening the viewer's existing knowledge of them. Thus television can broaden children's horizons and perhaps lead to further understanding if programs are watched with an adult who helps to discuss and interpret what is going on. The balance of opinion among researchers is that children learn little from unlimited, unselective, unsupervised viewing, but can have their lives enriched by limited, selective, partly supervised viewing.

The longer-term effects of television on socialization (the kinds of people that we become as we grow up) are debatable. But, in the short term, some viewing of popular programs helps children to keep in touch with their peers who watch the same programs. There is also evidence that television helps children to understand the two-dimensional representation of three-dimensional space, as well as visual movement and change. However, these skills can be learned with far less television viewing than most children actually do.

News and Public Affairs

A common concern with news and public affairs programs is allegations of bias, e.g. that television news is pro- or anti-Government, or biased to the left or right. However, media bias is very much in the eye of the beholder. Surveys in the USA and Britain show that most viewers regard their country's television news as balanced. Those who do not (including politicians) disagree on the direction of the bias. In 1986, when the Chairman of the (governing) Conservative Party in Britain publicly accused the BBC of an anti-government bias, a routine sample survey at the time showed that the great majority of viewers thought that the BBC was balanced and that most of the few who did not, felt that it was *pro-government*.

In Britain and many other countries, few newspapers expect to be regarded as balanced. (Newspapers in the USA are often different about this.) However, television has the inherent problems that its audience is enormous and represents all political opinions and that its visual impact is thought to be so powerful. Thus it is under greater pressure to be objective and so tends to avoid controversial political positions, partly through fear of alienating large groups of viewers and partly because 'editorializing' may not in fact be permitted.

Contrary to widespread belief, this striving for fairness extends to the way in which most interviews are edited. Usually the producer uses the interviewee's clearest, most lively statements, those which come across best on television. This can lead to distortions at times but it is less machiavellian, and more trivial, than is often assumed. More generally, television news-values favor what makes watchable television, which tends to mean action pictures and personalities. Television has thus been accused of trivializing politics, which in turn has led to concerns about television influencing reality.

One example is the idea that the way in which a politician happens to come across on television is a major factor affecting his popularity and election. Another is the increasing tendency for television news to be dominated by incidents which look real but are in fact performed largely for the cameras (e.g. certain aspects of riots and demonstrations, party conventions, sport, and even religion). Terrorism also sometimes plays to the television cameras to increase its effects. However, anyone monitoring even just the small proportion of cases reported in the media will find that most are unfortunately just for real.

More generally, our view is that some people and events do come across more vividly on television than others, and that this can influence their popularity or at least our awareness of them. For instance, American football may have become the most ardently followed sport in the US because it televises better than baseball. But such influence should not be overstated. In Britain, Mrs Thatcher's television image was a major handicap initially. Similarly, President Nixon has never been regarded as a TV natural, yet he won well in 1972. If John Kennedy won the US presidential election in 1960 because he knew how to use television, it was only by a hair's breadth; in fact, if not in mythology, the polls showed no marked swing towards Kennedy when he 'won' his famous televised pre-election debates with Richard Nixon. At the time of writing we also wonder which new president will have been 'made by television' in 1988.

One of the biggest effects of television may be its ability to popularize new people or issues instantaneously by exposing them to a vast audience. Beyond a certain point, however, over-exposure can lead to reduced popularity. At the same time, because television's moving pictures and sound are inherently much more pleasant and easier to watch than newsprint, television news can select a somewhat less trivial range of topics than the popular press without losing its audience.

Societal Values

It is sometimes suggested that much of television, especially commercials, game shows with big prizes, and many glossy drama series, encourages greed and materialism. This is part of a wider concern with the overall set of values implied by much television programming.

Again, proof is lacking. Causality is likely to flow the other way: we like to watch certain programs because we are rather greedy and like our creature comforts, such as preferring a washing machine to beating clothes on flat stones in the river. In researchers' group discussions and in general conversation and letters, there is no suggestion that people personally envy the glamor of *Dallas*; in the case of game shows, viewers are glad when someone like themselves wins the prize. All of this reveals a less selfish and much less naive response than some critics seem to assume.

Outside the United States, a related concern is 'Media imperialism', the domination of one country's national culture by another's – especially by that of the USA ('Coca Cola colonialism'). Because television is a cultural product, most programs inevitably portray and reflect the culture in and for which they are made. Other things being equal, they also tend to appeal most to people within that culture. However, other things are rarely equal. As discussed in Chapter 9, the economics of television production strongly favor the large countries against the small, and the USA against all others. Thus an American program, made to the highest production standards in the world, can be bought by broadcasters in a smaller country for vastly less than it would cost them to produce something comparable themselves. We believe that a local soap opera, made to production standards even just approaching those of *Dallas* and *Dynasty*, would do even better in the local ratings in most countries.

The degree to which US programs are acceptable to a foreign audience is itself a question of national culture. The country that has felt itself most vulnerable to US 'media imperialism' is probably Canada but the Canadians themselves argue about what they mean by 'Canadian culture'. American programs have proved popular throughout the world (except in parts of the Far East including Japan since the late 1960s) and especially in English-speaking countries. It is debatable in what ways it matters that people in a small country spend so much time watching Americans on television. For instance, it may not always inculcate a pro-US stance. Conversely, the fact that Americans see virtually no programs made by and for foreigners has reduced their opportunities to understand other cultures. Neither aspect of the USA's one-way trade in television programs seems of much concern to most Americans.

All of the social concerns about television's effects which we have touched on here pose similar problems of evidence. Many studies have been done but as yet very little is actually known about the real effects.

Nonetheless, broadcasters have made some attempts to deal with the concerns, especially those regarding violence, sex, and language. For example, Channel 4 in Britain has experimented with a small warning symbol in the corner of the screen when a program contains material likely to offend or disturb. Another approach is the widely accepted convention of showing programs aimed at adults later in the evening. However, neither of these approaches fully resolves the problems, which remain thorny. In the end, those who are somewhat libertarian must accept that most other people are less so, that the concerns about sex, violence, and profanity are widely felt, and that the availability of television in the home does make it different from other media. This is despite the fact that the long-term effects of television may be no more – or may be even less – than for other media. ('Video nasties' are an extreme case.)

TELEVISION ADVERTISING

Many of the concerns about television in general are reflected in people's concerns about television commercials: their power to influence the viewer, the effects on children, materialism, stereotyping, and so on. Here again there is an implicit presumption that TV advertising must be strongly persuasive.

Our own view is that advertising is a fairly weak force, which is why advertisers have to do so much of it. We believe that people generally do not respond to being told to do something. Most advertisements do not even explicitly say 'Buy Me' let alone 'Buy Now'. As consumers, each of us seldom buys any of the hundreds of brands or services that we see promoted in commercials. This ties in with our low involvement when watching most television and with the apparently weak effects of television in shaping our attitudes more generally.

If television advertising does not persuade people to buy, then why do advertisers do it? The answer would seem to be that advertising in general, and television advertising in particular, has three main features.

1 It generally has little effect on the volume of purchases for a total product category, such as cars or breakfast cereals, and is rarely aimed at that.
2 It is mainly competitive between brands, aiming to encourage people to buy one brand rather than another. Hence it can also help to differentiate otherwise similar brands and make them less sensitive to price competition.
3 It can make people aware of a new or existing brand and perhaps help to lead them to try it. If they then like it, they may become users. On most occasions, however, advertising is defensive, reinforcing the existing preferences of the experienced users of a brand and safeguarding the brand's market share.

Thus advertising, instead of being highly persuasive, is mostly, we believe, a price to pay for staying in the market. We develop this concept more fully in Appendix A.

SUMMARY: IS TELEVISION A GOOD THING?

There are many concerns about television, ranging from inadequate programming, and viewing being a waste of time, to worries about television's portrayals of sex, violence, profanity, political issues, and society's values or prejudices. The striking finding is that there are *no* dramatic findings about television's effects in these areas. There is no reason to suppose that exposure to an hour's broadcast about anything will usually have much effect.

Concern is largely, it seems, triggered by the sheer size of the medium. If everybody watches so much, people feel that it 'must have some effect' and they may even argue that viewers' low involvement makes them more vulnerable to influence. Yet the evidence about effects is not even remotely suggestive, let alone clearcut.

There is also no clear answer to the question of whether television is 'a good thing'. If it is taken to mean 'Are people happier than they would be if television did not exist?' then our answer would be a qualified 'yes'.

People spend nearly half of their free time watching television; they find it fairly to very enjoyable; it is not at all obvious that without television they would be doing something they liked better. When Noel Coward was asked whether he liked being old, he said that it was better than the alternative.

The serious and often strongly felt concerns raised by television must be taken into account, as we have tried to do in this chapter. With television more than with print media, consumers can stumble unwittingly into offensive material, either by switching channels or by watching an apparently harmless program which suddenly becomes embarrassing or disturbing. One counter-argument is that this is rather like real life: in the midst of life we come across death, violence, rape, accidents, illness, none of which is bland or pleasant. Another is that, even although television is a shared, family medium freely available in the home, people do not have to watch programs that they find objectionable nor should they prevent others from watching what they want.

In our view, the debate boils down to a question of where one draws the line. Almost everyone would probably agree that children should be discouraged from watching at least certain kinds of violent or disturbing material. However, ethical standards vary from issue to issue and reflect national morals: to European eyes, American television is somewhat prudish about explicit sex and real-life bad language but is noticeably (even unpleasantly) violent.

The worry that television viewing is too passive is also far from clear cut. Some commentators dislike the idea that people merely sit watching football on the screen without ever kicking a ball around. Others seem to fear the reverse: that suggestive programs might actually lead people to do something. We need entertainment and we need to relax. As long as people are provided with a sufficient range of programs and so can devote, if they wish, a substantial minority of their viewing to their personal choice of somewhat richer, more demanding programming, then major worries about television as a waste of time will be reduced. We believe that broadcasting policy should more explicitly address this aim.

NOTES

More books and papers have been written about the topic of concern than about any other aspect of television. Here we give some general sources and selected specific references. Bower (1985) discusses what US viewers say they want and do not want from television, including trends over the period 1960–80. This covers many of the concerns discussed here.

Range and Quality of Programs

For evidence from group discussions see CPB (1978), Taylor and Mullan (1986). On consumer concerns see NCC (1981). See also UK discussions of the scope for subscription television (page 119).

Time Spent Viewing

Winn's (1977) attack on television is based especially on the time that it wastes. Group discussions in the USA have found some ambivalence about whether watching television is worthwhile (CPB 1978), while Taylor and Mullan (1986) found a clear positive balance of opinion among UK viewers. However, the initial orientation of the two studies was not directly comparable.

Specific Concerns

Two recent reviews of the field are Ball-Rokeach and Cantor (1987) and Oskamp (1987). Earlier reviews include Curran et al. (1977), Comstock et al. (1978), NIMH (1982), and – on the effects of television – Klapper (1960) and Halloran (1970). The issues are also discussed in texts on mass communication theory, e.g. De Fleur and Ball-Rokeach (1982) and McQuail (1987). Shoemaker (1987) lists and classifies 31 mass communication textbooks.

For blanket disapproval of television, see for example Mander (1978). For some people's disapproval of earlier mass media, see Hirsch (1977a).

Violence and Aggression

See the US Surgeon General's Scientific Advisory Committee report (1972) and the detailed research findings given in Rubinstein et al. (1972). Violence was also a main topic in the follow-up review (NIMH 1982). De Fleur and Ball-Rokeach (1982) include a summary of the main theories and debates. Fuller summaries include Baker and Ball (1969), Howitt and Cumberbatch (1975), and BBC (1988). The main analyses of violent content are by Gerbner in the USA and Cumberbatch in Britain and their associates (e.g. Gerbner and Gross 1976, Gerbner et al. 1986, Cumberbatch et al. 1987).

The numerous laboratory and field studies are well summarized in the 1972 and 1982 US Government reports. See also Belson (1978). The two panel studies are by Van Vuuren (1981) and Milavsky et al. (1982). Gerbner's (Gerbner 1967, 1973; Gerbner and Gross 1980; Gerbner et al. 1980) evidence of heavy television viewing leading to exaggerated fear of violence in the real world has been questioned by Newcombe (1978), Wober (1978, 1986), Hughes (1980), Hirsch (1980, 1981) and Rubin et al. (1988).

Bad Language

This issue generates many letters to broadcasting organizations, such as the BBC, but has been almost entirely ignored by social researchers. But see Bower (1985).

Sex

Little research has been done on sex on television as a source of offense or embarrassment (again, see Bower 1985) but there has been some work on the alleged effects of pornography (Commission on Obscenity and Pornography, 1971) and the possible links between sex and aggression in the media and real life (Zillman and Bryant 1982; Zillman 1984). The technical problems are broadly similar to those discussed for violence and aggression more generally. The added complication is that, unlike violence, sex is seen by most people as potentially good as well as bad.

Media Portrayals

This is a heavily researched area, mainly in terms of content analysis rather than the effects. Some studies of child development explore the role of television's picture of the world ('social reality') on socialization, e.g. Greenfield (1984). The quotation on p. 144 is from NIMH (1982), which also gives a good review of the field. Viewers' perceptions of media portrayals are far from straightforward, as shown for example by Vidmar and Rokeach (1974).

Children

See Himmelweit et al. (1958), Schramm et al. (1961), Belson (1967), Liebert et al. (1973), Noble (1975), NIMH (1982), and Dorr (1986). On attention and comprehension, see Bryant and Anderson (1983). On children and commercial television, see Ward et al. (1986). A readable general book on the issues, with advice to parents and teachers, is Greenfield (1984). Some of the qualitative studies in Lindlof (1987) will also be of interest to the general reader.

News and Public Affairs

On this subject much has also been written. The role of television in politics has been extensively examined (e.g. Blumler and McQuail 1968; Seymour-Ure 1974; Lang and Lang 1985), as have the production and content of television news (Schlesinger 1978; Tuchman 1978; Golding and Elliott 1979; Gans 1980). A routine survey of British viewers' perceptions of balance is reported in IBA (1987). Cohen (1987) compares news interviews in the USA, UK, West Germany, and Israel. A lively account of the role of television in the 1968 US presidential election is McGinnis (1969). For the Kennedy-Nixon debates see Brown (1982) and Comstock (1987b). Robinson and Levy's (1986) wide-ranging study suggests that television is not really the public's main source of news, despite the widespread belief that it is.

Societal Values

A recent, well penned polemic is Postman (1986), which argues that television has trivialized modern society. The issues are too broad to be easily amenable to empirical research, although readers of Taylor and Mullan (1986) may find their faith in humanity somewhat restored.

Media Imperialism

See Wells (1972), Tunstall (1977), McBride Commission (1980), and McPhail (1987). Lee (1980) shows the importance of national culture in determining the impact of US media, for example by comparing Taiwan (low impact) and Hong Kong (high impact). The texts on mass communication surveyed by Shoemaker (1987) included little or no discussion of media outside the USA, the only exception being that of McQuail (1987), who is British and based in the Netherlands.

Television Advertising

This is also discussed in Appendix A. See Ehrenberg (1974) for background to our general orientation in this area, and the references in the notes on Chapter 9. Some of the foremost critics of advertising include Packard (1957) and Galbraith (1985), who argued that it had strong psychological and economic effects respectively. (We believe that Packard has inadvertently done more for the advertising business than any other single writer.) An empirical study suggesting that most North American television commercials contain little product information is Pollay et al. (1980). The sales effects of advertising are widely discussed (see, for example, Lambin 1975, Kyle 1982, Waterson 1984 and the detailed case-histories in IPA (1982–8)).

Chapter 12
The Future

Although technological developments may greatly change the ways in which programs reach viewers in the future, what, how, and why people watch is unlikely to change so dramatically. In 2020 we expect television still to be a highly watched but mostly low-involvement mass medium.

As now there will be exceptions: some broadcasts will be of strong interest to certain people and some will be successfully targeted at relatively narrow audiences. However, these will still account for only a relatively small proportion of people's total viewing, even among their target viewers.

NARROWCASTING?

In contrast with this view, some commentators have suggested that the new technologies will lead to the 'disaggregation' of the audience or even to the 'end of mass media'. They predict, in place of a few channels broadcasting programs which have to satisfy large and rather passive audiences, a fundamental shift to 'narrowcasting': many channels transmitting specialized material to appeal to small, interested audiences, rather like print media or radio. This is quite different from our position: we do *not* foresee that narrowcasting will replace mainstream television as we broadly know it today. Our view is based on the features of television and its audience discussed in earlier chapters. Many of these seem to us unlikely to change merely because more television channels become available.

Compared with print media, there is far less scope in television to cater for narrow interests. While having more channels is a prerequisite for narrowcasting, it is not enough: there also has to be the demand for such specialized programming and the money to finance it. To revolutionize viewing, the programming funds for narrowcasting will have to be in multiples of what is spent now, not just fractionally more.

The first and crucial factor is the cost of making watchable, minority-taste programs on a very large scale. The programs would have to be attractive enough to woo audiences day after day from competitive channels carrying high quality entertainment shows, news, and some demanding programs of their own. Minority-taste audiences, and especially connoisseurs, cannot be expected to choose or tolerate programs with lower production values, such as an under-rehearsed *King Lear* shot with a single camera.

The second factor is that no suggestions have yet been made as to who will provide the extra billions needed every year. There is little scope for deriving that much extra revenue from advertisers, since the television audiences for current 'minority-taste' programs typically have a composition similar to those for mass programs; airtime for such programs cannot therefore attract premium rates.

Nor is there much scope for large-scale narrowcasting funded by subscription. As noted in Part Two, viewers watch and enjoy many lower-rating programs but these are mostly of a fairly general and watchable kind. Moreover, the narrowcasting channels are likely to seem expensive in competition with 'free' or almost free mainstream television. As we noted in Chapter 7, half of the households in the USA are now spending quite heavily on cable television – a total of $10 billion in 1986. This is a big change from receiving only 'free' television. However, only about a quarter of this money goes into programming, mostly for movies and other mass entertainment.

The regular collection of a few dollars by means of scrambled DBS from a few hundred thousand opera lovers, say, scattered across the whole of the USA or Europe is an idea that has been mooted for years but has not yet been shown to be viable, especially on a regular basis. We doubt also whether more technical, specialized audiences (from gardening enthusiasts to nuclear physicists) would provide sufficient markets to support narrowcasting channels, since television has not shown itself to be a good medium for passing on detailed information. Illustrated books and magazines are cheaper, faster, and more flexible, and there will be many technological advances with print, such as 'desk top' publishing and cheap fax machines.

There could be some exceptions to these rather gloomy forecasts for the prospects of narrowcasting but they would not amount to a media revolution. It seems to us that the high cost of producing several hours of watchable programs each day, the slowness of the medium for passing on information, and the low cost of mainstream television to the viewer constrain television to being a mass medium. Television audiences in the future will still have to be measured in millions rather than thousands for programs to be viable.

VIDEO TECHNOLOGY IN THE HOME

A more positive development will be the continuing progress of video technology available in the home. The number of television sets per home seems likely to keep on increasing. Most sets will be remote controlled, and will also be slimmer, flatter, and have square-cornered screens.

As and when a world standard is adopted for high definition television, the picture quality will improve dramatically. How quickly HDTV will catch on is partly a matter of costs (at present looking very high, both for viewers and for broadcasters re-equipping themselves) and partly a matter of worldwide agreement on technical standards and the availability of band widths. Demand from viewers for broadcast HDTV could develop faster than some people think if, as seems possible, high-quality pictures become available on normally priced VCRs or on cable. These would contrast with the low-quality pictures on over-air television.

The television screen will also become bigger and especially wider, with an 'aspect ratio' increased from the current 4:3 to perhaps 5:3 as in most cinemas. Sound will be improved, which will be helpful as dialogue is easy to miss, especially when degraded on video recordings. This may involve a switch to stereo, perhaps combined with the re-engineering needed for 'enhanced' or HDTV forms of transmission.

The effective capacity of the television set with a dozen or 15 channels will be further extended by VCR or some other storage technology. This will probably provide homes worldwide with the ability to record and play back programs, using a fixed memory built into the set. A different type of removable read-only storage medium may be used for rented and increasingly for purchased pre-recorded material. These storage facilities will be smaller and have higher density than existing half-inch video tapes. Technically, there are quite a few possibilities here.

With such devices already in a majority of the world's television homes by the year 2020 or so, more programs may be transmitted in the middle of the night, so that they can be recorded in either scrambled (requiring payment) or unscrambled form. For this to work, the 'time-shifting' technology must be widely understood as well as widely installed. Pre-recorded programs, especially the top-selling titles, are also likely to be even more widely available than today. They may be offered for outright purchase at roughly today's price for an audio cassette or long-playing record.

It is also likely that more television sets than now will be used some of the time to display material other than television programs. More homes will conceivably use their sets as monitors for home computers, mostly for playing games. (The personal computers and word processors used by professionals working at home will continue to have their own screens.) By 2020, many homes, more than those today which have 35 mm slide projectors or 8 mm movie cameras and projectors, may have their own video cameras. They will then use their television sets to screen their own home movies. Such usage will still be negligible compared with television viewing, however.

Broadcast videotex, as discussed in Chapter 7, should become cheaper and more widespread. Using a built-in memory chip, it may also become very fast, all the data becoming instantly accessible to the viewer instead of the current delay of up to 20 seconds for a particular 'page' of information to be retransmitted. It will give up-to-the-minute news headlines, weather, television program schedules, sports results, etc. Some sets may also be used for limited *interactive* videotex applications on the screen, especially home shopping, but most of these services will use the traditional narrowband telephone network, rather than needing any wideband two-way cable.

All of these technologies, and many more, are available today but technical availability need imply neither greatly increased extra value to the consumer nor availability at a realistic price. The habitual production-orientated bias of technologists is to try to sell us more capability than we want, e.g. 80-channel interactive cable or high-capacity online videotex. Most people's private needs and uses for information are very small in absolute terms (people send or receive at most a few letters per week, other than junk mail) and relative to our use of television sets for entertainment.

The 'Wired Society'

In the early 1980s, a new future was widely proclaimed, where everyone would use a two-way wideband cable network (the 'motorway of the future') to interact with the outside world in almost all conceivable ways: interactive shopping for groceries, durables, houses, and holidays; financial services such as banking, insurance, and securities; remote meter reading; burglar and fire alarms; computer-aided instruction; electronic delivery of mail and newspapers; as well as an infinite number of specialized and even local access television channels. This was actually a revival of the US cable industry's futuristic 'blue-sky cable' sales pitch of the late 1960s. It led to experiments and test markets in several countries, and in Britain to a less expensive flow of words (sometimes labelled Bakervision after the then Minister for Information Technology) about a society wired together by interactive optical fibre at a cost of billions. This vision was inspired less by market analysis than by an astonishing belief that replacing much of the personal service element in shopping, banking, transport, mail, etc. would actually create more new jobs.

These extravagant predictions have given way to a more pragmatic approach. Wideband cable is now seen mainly as a way of delivering television. Many of the other predicted applications are also being developed and tested but without necessarily being linked to expensive two-way cable technology. Since few applications actually need two-way video, most can be done far more cheaply by using the ordinary telephone network – and possibly by simply picking up and using the telephone itself! This also gives almost universal availability. For each application the technology and its cost must be carefully balanced against market demand. This more evolutionary approach does not mean that there will not be substantial change. For instance, there are likely to be considerable further changes in work habits, with a blurring of home and workplace for a significant minority. But this need have little to do with a fully-switched wideband cable network going into the home of anyone, never mind everyone.

More Channels – More Choice

There will certainly be more channels but what is not clear is how, in 30 years' time, they will be divided in each country between different methods of transmission and payment.

Our own hunch is that, excluding some totally unpredicted new technology, there will be little more cabling, even (or especially) in countries such as Britain where it has not yet developed. This is because of the inherently high cost of cable and the lack of sufficient consumer demand for its unique capabilities. We see little demand from viewers as a whole for local and/or access television, for interactive television, or for television systems with 40 or 80 channels.

If viewers have a large number of channels, the evidence so far is that they typically use fewer than ten, and that these mostly tend to be the same channels. Although younger viewers seem to be more willing to search through many channels to find a program that they like, it is not clear whether they will become less willing to do so as they grow older or whether there is a real and permanent difference between the present generations.

Either way, a system of perhaps ten or twenty channels seems enough to give the viewer plenty of choice within the range of programs available today or likely to be available in the future. Anything beyond about twenty channels makes it harder for viewers to find what they want, while adding virtually nothing to the range of programming that is actually watched. People who want a still wider choice can already use a VCR.

In our view, in 30 years' time most people in developed countries might have ten to twenty television channels delivered by wireless transmission, either terrestrial or DBS. Several factors will determine the penetration of DBS. First is the cost and capacity of the technology itself: within 30 years, DBS may be able to deliver more channels than terrestrial transmission at much the same low cost per home. Second is the amount of good programming available: if much more money goes into original programming, more channels will be justified. Third is the transmission standard. If governments agree on a standard for HDTV, this will involve a great deal of re-engineering of studios, transmission systems, and individual sets. It will also increase the bandwidth of each channel by a factor of up to 4, so that terrestrial transmission would only have capacity for about three to five channels. This would increase the need for DBS, though 'enhanced' or 'extended' formats may be easier to accommodate. However, new technology may greatly expand the capacity of terrestrial transmissions, via compression techniques (in using a given bandwidth) or the use of new parts of the spectrum (e.g. microwaves).

CUTBACKS AND COMPETITION

Recent policy initiatives both of government (as in Britain) and of shareholders or management (as in the US commercial networks) have resulted in cutbacks on spending among broadcasters in order to combat over-staffing, restrictive practices, and inflated salaries, and to get better use of resources.

There has of course been (sometimes substantial) scope for savings, though no-one seems to have spelt out well-defined targets of more than a few percent. Nonetheless, the resulting savings have not been of direct benefit to viewers since they pay either little or nothing (as in the case of television funded by advertising). Viewers' concern is more with programs and choice, and they have shown themselves quite prepared to pay for this (e.g. VCRs, second television sets, cable subscriptions in the USA). Thus the current cult of 'conspicuous austerity' may not last into the future: viewers may not want broadcasters to waste money but they do not want cutting back on programming. There are already some signs of contrary reactions to the recent savings imposed on the US networks: 'Cutting budgets was easy, recruiting top talent is not.'

Because there will be more channels anyway, two related trends have been towards more competition and deregulation, partly as a result of the fashionable if naive belief that competition automatically gives consumers what they want.

Competition has in the past often enlivened what had been dull programming. But, because of marketing and transaction costs, it can actually lead to customers having to pay more. Also, and far more important in the present context, competition for the same source of funds, especially for advertising revenue, can lead to a narrowing of the range of programs offered, as was discussed in Chapter 9. Hence there could in future be a move towards making viewers themselves pay for their television.

VIEWERS PAYING

One of the extraordinary features of television is how widely it is accepted that it should be free (or apparently free) or at least very inexpensive indeed. Nobody seems to think in the same way about the cost of the television set or that of newspapers or holidays. Mainstream television everywhere costs the viewer less, probably far less, than what the market would bear. How much would television have to cost before families stopped watching it, and paying for it, if all programming were supplied by competitive subscription channels? How many people would opt out of subscribing to one or more of the major channels at a time when they actually want more choice for their main leisure activity?

Channel Subscriptions for Mainstream Television?

In the early 1980s, consumers started paying fairly substantially for *add-on* services such as VCRs or cable. This trend is likely to continue. A different change would be some form of charge for *mainstream* television, with viewers paying more directly and selectively for the main national networks, currently available to everyone and funded by license, tax or advertising. As discussed in Chapter 9, this would probably be subscription or 'pay-per-channel' television, since 'pay-per-view' for individual programs would be too expensive to operate, relative to the price of the programs themselves, to make much sense on this scale.

One possible advantage of subscription television in license-fee countries is that viewers would no longer be obliged to choose between either paying one all-in license fee or not having television at all, but could choose to pay selectively. Governments might then allow competitive channel operators to charge prices closer to what the market would bear. These would be substantially higher than now and hence might provide the means in future for viewers to contribute to larger budgets for program-making.

Despite these higher prices, most households would, we think, continue to subscribe to all mainstream channels because: (a) most people want more choice; (b) the savings incurred by opting out of one or two channels would be small in absolute terms; (c) there would be family and social pressures against such noticeable penny-pinching; (d) the channel operators could promote their products very effectively by, say, scrambling the soundtrack only so that non-subscribers could see but not hear the programs. (This would probably also be technically simpler than scrambling the video signal.)

The cost of such mainstream channel subscriptions would, however, be substantially higher than any license fee giving the same net revenue for making programs. Subscribers would have to pay more to cover the collection and marketing costs, and also to make up for the less prosperous if small minority who would be priced out of the market. A more efficient and equitable policy would be simply to increase the license fee but to do this would require political will.

It is fashionable to discuss television largely in economic terms but, given how much we watch, and how little we pay, television is likely to remain of far greater social than economic significance.

PROGRAMMING

Program production standards have been greatly enhanced in the last thirty to forty years: color, more cameras, more outdoor location work, easier and better action replay, instant news, graphics, etc. Creative intangibles in using the medium have also improved so that even the best 'golden oldies' now seem rather stiff or at least dated.

Some development has also occurred within each program category, such as in *All in the Family*, *Monty Python*, *Hill Street Blues*, and occasional shows, such as *Soap*, which span or deliberately mix up types. There has been some growth in international programming, including co-productions. Nevertheless, television still consists mostly of regular series and standardized genres. This kind of steady evolution in programming is expected to continue; no dramatic, major change seems to be foreseen by anyone.

Because of the combative instincts of broadcasters and their tendency to be impressed by audience ratings even in license-fee systems, they may continue to need some encouragement to produce the more demanding programs. There will still be a good deal of consistent demand for such programming from all parts of the audience for a substantial if lesser part of their viewing fare. However, we will seldom watch programs with lower, less professional (and usually less costly) production values when similar but better-resourced programs are available. Thus minority-taste programs might be starved of funds by the very diversity of our own tastes. Improvements in both the range and the quality of programs will require money.

Perhaps governments around the world should not in future be holding down television funding (from the license fee, taxation or other such sources) to artificially low levels. At the time of writing, the French Government has reduced the fee there by some 6 percent, allowing more advertising time instead, while the British Government has pegged the $100 UK license fee to the rate of general retail price inflation. Yet in most countries average earnings tend to grow faster than inflation, and consumer spending on leisure is growing faster still (in the UK it is almost $4000 per household a year).

Governments are not allowing viewers to spend on television, people's main leisure activity, what the market appears to want. Suppose 95% of the population spent on average 25 hours of every week reading books from public and commercial libraries; would governments resist having a greater range of books available?

In less developed countries and small countries generally, the high absolute cost of programming and transmission will continue to constrain programming standards. There will be more imported programs, as their low costs and high production values are inescapable. This will lead to continuing charges of 'cultural imperialism'. Nonetheless, television systems need not expect to be altogether dominated by US imports. The evidence is that people will also watch some domestic programming as long as the production budgets are not too undernourished. The way to combat 'undue' imports may be to let the viewers spend more money on native programming.

American programs are not all-conquering. Game shows do not travel well (although formats certainly do) nor do daytime soap operas. Sport mostly has to be national or truly international to get big audiences, and most news and public affairs programs are of purely domestic interest.

Overall, the number of channels is likely to increase faster than the amount of programming produced in each country. The gap will be filled partly by re-runs but mainly by imports and international co-productions. Probably the main exporter of programs will still be the USA but other countries, perhaps including Japan for the first time, will also be in the market. As long as each country's domestic television production is properly funded, it should still attract the bulk of its people's viewing.

CONCLUSION: THIRTY YEARS ON OR BACK

In this book we have described the basic economics of television and the main viewing patterns of its audience today, especially in the USA and Britain. What does all this tell us about television in the future? Such predictions cannot be made with certainty but the past and present can tell us a great deal about the next thirty years.

We would argue that many of the features of television are fairly fundamental to the nature of the medium, particularly the massive viewing of television, the low-involvement nature of most of that viewing, the high cost of producing watchable programs, and the low cost to each viewer because the audiences are so large. These features are not caused by historical accident, government policies or the limited number of terrestrial channels.

We conclude that the patterns of viewing described earlier are unlikely to change significantly, except that people may watch even more than now in thirty years' time and are likely to spread that viewing over a slightly larger number of channels. Such an apparently low-key conclusion is more widely accepted today than five or six years ago, at the height of excitement about cable and the 'video revolution', but it still seems to be a minority view. To put it into perspective it is helpful to look back briefly at the changes in television over the past thirty or forty years.

About thirty years ago, the USA had three networks and Britain had two. Even in these two leading countries, many homes did not have a television. Most other countries had either no television at all or only one channel. Television sets had poorer picture quality and were black-and-white except in a handful of US homes. Cable was merely what linked the set to its aerial or community antenna. Video tape was used only in studios. 'Cassette' meant either a box for a 35 mm photographic film or the new Philips audio cassette. Computers were beginning to be used for commercial data processing. The Soviets had just astonished the world by launching the first small satellite in space.

Today we have more channels, longer transmission hours, color, multi-set homes, VCRs, cable television, satellites, home computers, videotex, and experiments with home shopping, home banking, and so on. These amount to dramatic changes in technology and in distribution channels.

However, from the viewpoint of this book, with its focus on the audience, these dramatic changes are still peripheral to the two central issues: *programming* and *viewing*. In these two areas, the changes have been less dramatic.

Imagine some American time-travellers from the late 1950s appearing in a well-equipped US home today. They would be very struck by television in color and by the picture quality, the number of channels, the remote switch and the VCR, cable-television movies, and so on. They would also be impressed by the high production quality of the programs and the commercials, if somewhat irritated by the amount of interruption. However, they would find that the people in the home still watched mostly in company, and for far more than half of the time watched the same three network channels as thirty years ago. For virtually all of the rest of the time the family would be watching similar fare on an independent or cable channel, or off the VCR: re-runs, movies or first-run syndications, i.e. US-produced mass entertainment.

The travellers would have no difficulty in recognizing the program types: news, soaps, sitcoms, sport, game and chat shows, cartoons, action-adventure. The main character might be a police detective not a cowboy, maybe black or female, and the 'action' would look much more authentic. They might notice the absence of one-off plays but be struck by several new features, such as the children's programs on PBS and special channels for news, weather, rock music, or 'lifestyle' programs. They might also notice that the family spent relatively little time watching these channels and might perhaps recall that, although some of the one-off plays in the 1950s were highly regarded, they themselves had not actually watched them very often.

Our time-travellers illustrate how the enormous advances in television production and especially distribution have had relatively little effect on the range of programs that people watch. Little is known about the detailed patterns of viewing in the 1950s; more is known from the mid-to-late 1960s. However, the two main features described in this book, much viewing and mostly with low involvement, have become more pronounced over the last thirty years. Certainly people watch much more television today than in the past, partly because they have more leisure time and partly because programs are more watchable. At the same time, there is some evidence that attentiveness has declined, at least in the most developed countries.

Within the next thirty years, DBS might become the normal method of transmitting television. This in itself will be no more important to the viewer than caring about whether electricity is generated from coal or oil. Where DBS may affect the viewer is in the number of channels that it makes available, in the quality of the picture and sound, and in the slight increase in international programming and advertising that it will tend to provide. Even without DBS, we are likely to see at least some more money becoming available for programming and more programming being traded internationally. However, most of what people will watch will be of the same broad types as we watch today, viewed (we think) in pretty much the same way. None of this heralds a revolution in the place of this giant medium within our daily lives.

NOTES

Thirty Years On

Many books and articles discuss the future of television, especially recently in terms of the 'video revolution' (e.g. Hollins 1984; Wenham 1982; Dunkley 1985; CEC 1984; ETTF 1988; Home Affairs Committee 1988). Often they date quickly. The view that the effects of future change may only be gradual and limited started to seep into media commentaries in the later 1980s.

Thirty Years Back

US television effectively started when the FCC decided in 1947 that transmission should be in monochrome on VHF channels (rather than in color and on UHF). Color television started coming in on a significant scale in the early 1960s, initially through NBC and its then-parent RCA. Until 1955 the USA had a fourth network, Du Mont.

In Britain, regular BBC transmissions began in 1936. There were about 25 000 television sets at the outbreak of World War II (now there are some 30 million). A second network (ITV) was started in 1955, and color television in 1968.

Appendix A: Television Advertising

Throughout this book we have noted the functions and effects of television advertising in different countries, especially as a source of funds for making and distributing programs. Here we briefly look at advertising's role in marketing, and how in our view it works. (References are listed on p. 153.)

Commercials are the only type of television program explicitly aimed at changing people's attitudes and behavior. Viewers know that they are 'being got at' (with the significant exception of very young children), but both the greatest fans and the fiercest critics of advertising believe that it has powerful effects. We disagree. We believe that advertisements have only a *weak* influence on consumers. This view parallels the discussion in Chapters 10 and 11 on the chiefly low-involvement nature of most television viewing and on the lack of any clear evidence that television has ever had a significant effect on its viewers, other than helping them to pass a great deal of their time.

A frequent viewpoint is: 'Advertising manipulates consumers, though I'm not affected by it myself.' We believe that it is the latter sentiment which is correct, but for all of us. We note that people see a great many advertisements but rarely buy the items in question, let alone rush out immediately to do so. Seeing an actor or actress pretending to use a brand of instant coffee can marginally encourage someone who sometimes buys the brand to do so again but is unlikely to make someone who usually buys another brand to switch to that one. It is even less likely to persuade a non-coffee drinker to start drinking coffee. We think that advertising will have little chance of doubling the market share of a brand for the simple reason that it has not done so for most brands in the past.

If advertising is really as weak as this, then why do firms continue to do so much of it? The answer is, we believe, that they see most of their advertising for established brands as part of their competitive marketing activities with which they defend their existing market shares. They regard their advertising as necessary and cost effective for this, alongside sales people, promotional deals, merchandizing, point-of-sale displays, and so on. Only occasionally is advertising successfully used to create new or extra sales, as with new brands or products, or *sometimes* to increase an existing market share.

We now consider advertising in the broader context of marketing and then discuss its effects in more detail.

THE ROLE OF ADVERTISING IN MARKETING

Marketing means deciding which products or services to supply to which target markets, how they will be priced or funded, and how they will be made available – and then also making it all happen. *Good* marketing means doing this to your own, your customers', and society's profit or satisfaction – to the satisfaction of almost everyone except your competitors.

The more strategic decisions set the scope and shape of the enterprise: whether to diversify from confectionery into savoury snack foods, say. In a large organization these decisions involve senior managers in finance, R&D, operations and so on, as well as in marketing.

The decisions once made are not set in concrete but typically evolve over many years: a product or service, its price, its target market, or its distribution may be almost continuously modified at the margin. But in broad terms the firm commits itself to supplying the product or service and will begin to invest capital in order to do so.

At this stage, the emphasis shifts towards achieving the goals that have been set. In the case of marketing, the aim is mostly to achieve the sales targets (volumes and profit margins) set for each year. Television advertising is one means towards this end.

Most television advertisements are aimed at consumers who pay for what they buy with their own (or their household's) money. Television is usually too expensive, unsegmented, and slow at conveying information to be cost effective for advertising to be aimed at organizational buyers, such as a purchasing manager or industrial engineer, although there are exceptions.

Depending on the particular product and market, a firm will use a wide range of marketing communication channels: media advertising (television, radio, newspapers, magazines, billboards, cinema), public relations, promotions, direct mail, and face-to-face or telephone selling. Selling stock and display material to the wholesale and retail trade can often be more important than trying directly to persuade the consumer to buy: retail shelf-space may be what matters most. Even for this, current or proposed advertising, especially on television, can greatly aid the sales force in its tasks. The communication mix needs to be determined as a whole.

Media advertising involves paying a media owner for time or space in which to insert advertisements. The advertiser normally buys this via an advertising agency, which also creates and produces the advertisements; the agency then receives a commission from the media owner, traditionally 15%. How much the space or airtime actually costs will depend on the state of the market and on the various players' success at bargaining. In addition, the advertiser has to pay for the costs of making the commercials, which can be substantial. A 30-second typical network television commercial can cost between $50,000 and $500,000 to make because it has to be very brief, and good enough to bear being seen several times.

The amount spent on television advertising is huge, over $25 billion in the USA and $2 billion in Britain. However, these figures should be seen in perspective against the much wider background of marketing and promotion. Television is only one type of advertising medium. In the USA and Britain, total advertising expenditure, including newspapers, magazines, radio, etc., is well over twice that spent on television. In most other countries the ratio of non-television advertising is even higher.

Furthermore, marketing communication includes a great deal besides such 'above the line' media advertising. Most businesses spend more 'below the line': on consumer and trade promotions, direct mail, sales people, and so on. There are a few large firms for whom television is the dominant part of their media expenditure but, even then, they usually spend more on selling and on non-media promotions, such as coupons, price cuts, special offers, free samples, and so on.

Investing in Advertising

An advertising investment has three interrelated aspects. The firm must decide how much to spend, in which medium or media, and with which creative strategy and execution (i.e. what to say and how to say it).

In principle, the firm should decide to spend more on advertising if the value of the extra investment is more than its cost. In theory, this would mean successfully forecasting sales of the brand both with and without the proposed advertising and then comparing the cost of the campaign with the present value of the extra profit contribution. In practice, however, the effectiveness of long-term advertising can rarely be reliably quantified in this way, even after the event, and so firms have instead to use various rules-of-thumb in deciding how much to spend. For an existing brand these typically are mainly financial, such as x percent of sales, or last year's advertising budget plus inflation, or how much expenditure is needed to match the competition, all constrained by how much can be afforded. For a new brand, firms may assess how much is needed to cover the potential market.

The creative and media decisions will depend partly on the budget (national television campaigns are for large budgets only), but also on the objectives of the campaign, i.e. what it will aim to communicate and to whom. If the campaign is aimed at a specific consumer segment, such as high-income families, teenagers, or home computer buffs, or if the message is complex, television is unlikely to be the most cost-effective medium. In these cases better targeted media, such as magazines, radio, or direct-mail, may be chosen. Television excels in covering the whole consumer market very quickly and effectively. It is especially useful where the message is fairly simple and is able to exploit the unique combination of moving color pictures-and-sound and exposure in the home. Radio commercials and/or posters are sometimes used as lower-cost supplements to reinforce the main television campaign.

THE EFFECTS OF ADVERTISING

The details of how advertisements work vary from case to case but in broad terms the effects can be summarized fairly simply. There are, we think, three main stages in consumers' behavior which advertising can affect.

1 Consumers' *awareness* and perhaps their growing interest in the product or brand in question.
2 The first or *trial* purchase of the product or brand.
3 The subsequent *reinforcement* of any feelings of satisfaction or easing of any feelings of doubt.

We call this the ATR model of consumer behavior:

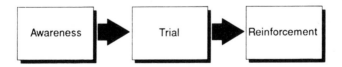

Advertising can act at each stage: to develop, increase or reawaken awareness or interest, to facilitate a first or trial purchase, and to reinforce existing users. The model implies that advertising is a weak force, suggestive rather than strongly persuasive.

The ATR model applies with varying emphases to both new and experienced buyers. But for most products most of the time, advertising is addressing experienced users. One remarkable feature is that the same advertisement usually has to be able to work for both types of buyer, interesting the new without boring or putting off (e.g. overselling) the experienced. We now discuss this model in the context of advertising, firstly for product categories as a whole, secondly for new buyers, and thirdly for established brands.

Promoting the Product Category

Most of the critics of advertising and some of its advocates believe that it creates demand for consumer goods in general. However, very little advertising is for a product class as a whole: 'Buy a car', 'Eat breakfast cereals', 'Go on holiday'. What is more, such generic advertising has only minor effects if any on sales. There are certainly no dramatic claims in the research literature nor any proven cases. Generic advertising cannot have created people's demand for consumer goods.

Most advertisements are for specific brands of a product and are directly competitive. However, brand advertising cannot be credited with creating demand for the total product class on any large scale or for long, for instance the increase in car ownership or in tourism. One brand's advertising does not aim to increase the sales of its competitors nor does it continually increase even its own sales year by year. Obviously in a static market, where competitive brand advertising is often fiercest, it is impossible for every brand to increase sales every year.

Advertising can encourage an initial purchase of a new type of product such as non-stick frying pans some years ago or compact disc players today. However, that does not explain society's continuing demand for more goods or services, which hinges on whether consumers continue to buy something after they, or others, have already used it and liked it. The main inducement for having a car or a washing machine is that it is more convenient than not having one. If one's neighbors already have one, that shows it to be feasible and socially acceptable, as well as perhaps a bit more desirable. But envy and covetousness were among the seven deadly sins long before media advertising was invented.

People's increasing if uneven prosperity, education, mobility, and exposure to mass media (especially magazines, films and now television programs) are four factors which have led to vastly increased expectations. The main factor is prosperity. Eliminating advertising would not, we believe, eliminate the demanding consumer. Manufacturers seldom successfully create major needs but they do attempt to fill them. This results in competition among the different brands of the same product or service, which is where most advertising takes place.

Advertising to New Buyers

Advertisements have a major role to play in communicating with new buyers. This includes new buyers of an established brand, all buyers of a new brand, and buyers of infrequently bought goods or services such as consumer durables or even mortgages. (In the latter cases buyers may already be highly experienced with the product class, e.g. cars, but are 'new' to choosing between current models.)

Advertising can be highly effective in all three cases. Its role here is closer to how people traditionally imagine it to work: making people do something they have not done before. Usually, however, this is only to try a particular brand that they have not yet tried, a new soft drink brand perhaps, rather than be converted to a totally new product category or to consume more of an existing one. It follows that the effects of advertising for new buyers need not depend on its being strongly persuasive.

The first stage in the adoption process is that potential new buyers have to become *aware* of the item. Advertisements can help, together with other factors such as the brand being widely available and already being used by others. It is often difficult for advertising to create such awareness because people who are not in the market for the brand (i.e. not already interested in it) tend to screen out information about it by 'selective perception'. A special effort is therefore needed to attract attention, e.g. by stressing something 'new', by using an unusual creative or media strategy, or simply through repetition to break through the perceptual barrier. (The first time that one is exposed to an advertisement one may notice it only out of the corner of one's eye; the next time it may seem slightly familiar and one may pay it some more attention, such as directly or consciously looking at it; and so on.)

Given growing awareness of the previously unfamiliar item and some degree of interest, the consumer may then decide to buy it. This will be only a *trial* purchase, since the consumer is necessarily unsure about it, not having experienced it yet. A trial purchase can occur for various reasons which often work in combination: because of a neighbor using it, a store stocking or recommending it, seeing it advertised, looking for a change perhaps.

After this initial purchase, the user's scope for evaluating the item may still be limited, especially with infrequently bought goods such as a car or washing machine where one cannot directly compare the purchased item with the brands left in the showroom. Advertisements can then provide some reassurance and may be noticed at least as much *after* as *before* the purchase. They may help the new buyer to feel that the purchase is at least as good as any other that might have been chosen, and that the manufacturer appears to be concerned with maintaining the brand's reputation and after-sales service, since he is 'wasting all that money on advertising'. In the case of more frequently purchased items, the role of advertisements at this *reinforcement* stage is to encourage repeat-buying of the brand.

Advertising for new items aimed at new buyers can therefore work by facilitating first Awareness and interest, then Trial, and finally Reinforcement after use (A-T-R). All three are important but weak functions. While advertising can speed up and ease the launch of a new brand, it cannot by itself create lasting success. In marketing, the saying is that nine out of ten new brands fail. This is not usually thought to be due to bad advertising. The role of advertising for new buyers therefore seems to us at best suggestive or reinforcing rather than strongly persuasive.

Advertising for Established Brands

Advertisements for an established brand are noticed mostly by existing users of that brand and to a lesser extent by users of competitive brands. The advertisements can therefore be reinforcing and reassuring ('That's my brand!') and can also enhance awareness of the brand or at least curtail its erosion. However, these roles are weak, compared for instance with consumers' experience of actually using the item. This explains why:

1 There is often very little information in advertisements (especially television commercials), even for consumer durables. Usually people already know the features of an established brand. They mainly have to be reminded of it.
2 Most advertisements do not look as if they are trying to persuade: they usually do not even say 'Buy me'.
3 Despite heavy advertising, few markets grow much from year to year: most are fairly steady, at least in the short to medium term.

Even market shares are fairly steady for most brands, at least in the medium term. Sales can vary say 10 or 20 percent up or down, which matters greatly to the manufacturer and his profits, but in terms of market share this would typically mean a change of only one or perhaps two percentage points, negligible relative to the structure of the market as a whole. As consumers, we rightly neither know nor greatly care about such changes.

Sophisticated firms do not expect their brand's advertising to pay for itself directly by continually increasing sales, now or later: they know that not every brand can grow in a mature market. This does not mean that advertising for established brands is wasted: it can lead to more sales than would have been achieved without it. However, this effect is mostly defensive, to maintain the brand's existing level of sales. While increased advertising does not generally persuade experienced users to buy more of a brand, *reduced* advertising could be one factor in allowing a brand's sales to erode slowly in the face of a competitors' continuing marketing activities. Brand advertising is therefore a price or insurance to pay for staying in the market, in line with the cost of packaging, quality control, sales people, and so on. Such advertising does not, however, act as any great barrier to the entry into the market of new competitors; the high chance of failure is the main barrier.

Most boardroom discussions about advertising budgets are concerned not so much about how *much* to spend but how *little*: advertising for established brands is something that most company chairmen would like to cut but dare not because the risks are too high. Thus for established brands, advertising and promotional expenditure tend to vary competitively and to move up or down together. In some product categories everybody spends a lot, in others they spend less. There is no inherently correct level of advertising for an established brand: it depends on what the competition is doing.

Despite the economics textbooks, advertising budgets for established brands are not determined by resolving when the marginal dollar of extra advertising expenditure equals the marginal dollar of extra profit contribution from sales. Few advertisers have reliable measures of such marginal returns, especially over the crucial long term. In the shorter term, media advertising for an established brand can rarely be shown to pay for itself directly.

Hidden Persuasion?

Some people interpret the fairly low-key messages in much advertising, especially in Europe, as a sign of 'hidden persuasion'. We believe that this overstates both the sophistication of advertising techniques and the naivety of the consumer. We also think that it misses the point of how advertising works: insofar as (according to the ATR model) there is nothing terribly wicked about its various roles, there seems little point in hiding the message.

However, one exception to the weak functioning of advertising may be when it is aimed at children. There is evidence that many young children do not distinguish between programs and commercials. Although they make few purchases themselves, children can be encouraged by commercials to nag their parents to buy the specific advertised products, even if a stronger influence may be that 'Sally next door has it'. This holds true for older, as well as younger, children. What is not established is how far television advertising makes children much greedier or more materialistic.

A SIDE-EFFECT: PAYING FOR TELEVISION

In Chapter 9 we discussed how the revenue from selling airtime for showing television commercials often pays for all the costs of showing programs on the channel in question. We noted that such television then seemed to be 'free' to the viewer, who did not have to pay directly or out of taxes.

Television funded by advertising is not really free if the costs are passed on to consumers in terms of higher prices for the advertised goods or services. It would be really free only if the advertising paid for itself by leading to higher sales volumes for all competitors or to other economies of scale. Following our discussion of the largely defensive and competitive role and effects of advertising in marketing, we can now see why increased sales for all are unlikely, and that the costs of television advertising are unlikely to be self-liquidating for the market as a whole. Thus, in contrast to common belief, we feel that advertising-induced economies of scale for all competitors are improbable, for several reasons.

1 There is no evidence that per-capita markets are smaller or less efficient in countries such as Germany or Sweden where there is little or no television advertising.

2 If television advertising did greatly increase total sales in all product categories beyond what they would be without it, or if it otherwise reduced prices through economies of scale, far more should be spent on advertising than is now. Yet nobody seriously suggests this. Even if advertising does occasionally increase the total sales of a genuinely new product category, it does so at the expense of other consumer expenditure or investment.

3 If television advertising were no longer possible, its mainly competitive nature makes it unlikely that advertisers' existing budgets would be fully spent on other marketing activities (such as more billboards, more press advertisements, more point-of-sale displays, more sales people, better packaging) to the tune of, say over $25 billion per year in the USA. Some, perhaps as much as half, would instead be used for price cuts. These savings would represent the real cost of television advertising to the consumer now: that is, advertisers now have to charge fractionally more for their products because their competitors' use of the medium forces them to use it as well.

A substantial part, though not all, of the costs of television advertising therefore show up as increased prices to the consumer, which would not arise if this particular form of advertising did not exist. As noted in Chapter 9, the sums involved per viewer are not large, however, and there are attractions in having the payments occur invisibly and in dribs and drabs.

Whether funding televison by advertising is efficient may be open to question. Its efficiency should probably not be the major criterion for judging it. A more telling issue is to what extent the different criteria of advertisers and viewers can be reconciled, as discussed on pages 111–13.

SUMMARY

Television advertising is a major feature in the marketing of many consumer goods and services and, as a by-product, it funds much of the world's television programming and transmission, probably at some small but invisible cost to the consumer. However, even when companies devote most or all of their media advertising to television, it still represents only part of their total promotional expenditure.

As the effectiveness of advertising can seldom be evaluated, there are no clear guidelines on how much should be spent on it. The results are difficult to measure because most advertising is defensive, an insurance policy to keep the market share that one already has. In a static market not all brands can be gaining sales at once.

We regard advertising as a weak influence on people's attitudes and behavior rather than as strongly persuasive. It can help to create awareness and interest in a new brand, possibly help to lead to a first or trial purchase, and (especially for established brands) reawaken awareness and help to reinforce feelings of satisfaction after use.

This is a contentious area but one of the few things known for sure about advertising is that it provides substantial funds for the media. In the context of a book about television and its audience, this is its most important feature.

Appendix B: Who is Viewing?

As noted in Chapter 1, most of the data referred to in this book measure whether people are in a room with the television set on and, if so, which channel or program is showing. A recurrent theme in the book is that television viewing is often at a fairly low level of involvement. We know that we do not always pay attention and sometimes are even asleep. This can all be measured fairly accurately. Four broad levels of people's exposure to a television program can be distinguished: (a) Is the set on? (b) Who is in the room? (c) Is viewing their main, or sole, activity? (d) How much do they like the program?

Here we outline more fully the measurement approaches that are used. (See references listed on page 11.)

IS THE SET ON?

In developed countries, accurate measurement of whether the television set is on is done by electronic meters attached to sets in quite large samples of homes. The samples number several thousand in the USA or the UK, although often only a few hundred in a particular region or market.

If it is reported from this sample that 10 percent of sets are on nationally, this will have been measured within a statistical sampling error of at most a percentage point or so. Thus the true rating for the country may be between 9 and 11 percent but in most instances it would be 10 to the nearest percentage point. There is no instance in this book where this degree of statistical error affects any conclusions.

This type of measurement uses a continuous panel of homes who co-operate in the surveys. There are problems over co-operation rates, updating the composition of the panels, and other technicalities, which can lead to systematic errors or biases that are larger than those associated with sheer sample size. Such biases have been checked experimentally over the years, usually by comparison with other measures of viewing. (For example, there are so-called 'coincidental' surveys by telephone or face-to-face, to establish which if any channel is on and, if so, who is watching, at the moment the questioner calls.) On the whole, agreement has been found to be close. This is especially so in the context of this book, where we are concerned with the broad picture of television viewing rather than the buying and selling of costly advertising time in specific time-slots.

For the selected sample, the meters automatically record, minute by minute (or for even shorter periods), whether the set is on and to which channel it is tuned. The explosive growth of television channels can be coped with fairly easily in this way and so, increasingly, can the measurement of all the sets in a multi-set home. At least on an experimental level, the recording and even the playback of specific programs through VCRs can also be measured, although this requires additional equipment.

The 'set-on' measure is broadly comparable with 'audited circulation figures' in the press (the numbers of copies of a magazine or paper sold) or the number of records sold in shops. These are fairly reliable data but tell us nothing about individual usage (i.e. how many people are watching, reading or listening). In other industries similar sales data arise administratively. Television viewing, however, leaves no trace and the industry therefore has to rely on its special sample-based measuring techniques.

WHO IS IN THE ROOM?

This book is mostly about people, not sets or homes. Therefore a crucial question is who, if anyone, is in the room when the set is on? This has usually been measured by one-week diaries, by means of either one-off surveys or a continuous panel. People record when they start and stop being present or viewing. Time is expressed in quarter-hour units, (often typically defined as 'at least eight minutes during that quarter hour'). Unless the set is also monitored by a meter (as has traditionally been done in Britain), people also have to record which channel is being shown and, as a check, which program is on.

Recently, diary methods have begun to be replaced by so-called 'people-meters'. These are an electronic push-button way of recording the presence of individual viewers, with periodic prompts and the meter itself automatically recording which channel is on at the time. Further technology has also been explored (e.g. infra-red sensing of people in the room).

These methods for measuring the presence of individual viewers with the set switched on are again subject to errors and inaccuracies beyond sheer statistical sample size. However, experimental comparisons of often very different forms of measurement, including 'co-incidental' calls, have shown largely consistent results for how much, what, and when people watch (at least in the sense of being present in the room when the set is tuned to a particular program).

There are inconsistencies which generate some heated debate, because so much money hangs on the precise numbers in television systems funded by advertising, but they are mostly understood and fairly minor – especially for our purposes in this book. A typical problem is to what extent people are supposed to record whether they are actively viewing or merely present in the room when the set is on. Another technical but nasty problem is how to deal with incomplete measurement records from a given household; they are more likely to occur (and hence to affect the overall results) with heavy viewers.

Despite these problems such data are generally more accurate than most social and marketing data. Such accuracy requires much care and expenditure. This tends to be forthcoming, mostly from the advertising industry, when the data provide the only yardstick by which billions of advertising dollars are allocated. In contrast, simple questionnaire methods of asking about people's viewing can lead to greatly inflated and distorted estimates. Unless respondents are carefully led to reconstruct exactly what they did yesterday for instance (as in good quality 'aided recall' interviewing), they tend to say what they *think* they *usually* do.

Both diary and people-meter methods also aim to cope with viewing by guests in the household. This has tended to be under reported (e.g. when compared with 'coincidental' surveys) but apparently is less so by people-meters.

ARE THEY ATTENDING?

In the routine day to day comparative measurement of audience sizes, the advertising industry mainly wants to measure 'Opportunities to See' (OTS): who is in the room with the set tuned to the relevant channel at the time that a commercial is screened. Even just hearing the jingle may have an impact, especially if the commercial has been seen or heard several times before.

But how many of those present are actually paying full attention? How many are alseep or are also doing homework, eating, talking or reading? This has been measured a number of times over the years on an *ad hoc* basis, especially in Britain, using different procedures (e.g. short or longer term recall, coincidental interviewing, diary methods). Studies which photograph or video tape small samples of viewers have graphically illustrated the low-involvement nature of much viewing, although more mundane measurement techniques have gone further in quantifying the incidence of different behaviors.

As mentioned in Chapter 1, during *commercial breaks* in the evening, something like 20 percent of those 'viewing the program' in Britain tend to be momentarily out of the room. This occurs more in breaks between programs than within programs, more for women than men, and more often early in the evening than late. Roughly 40 percent are 'viewing only', 30 percent viewing and otherwise active, and 10 percent are present but not viewing. There is evidence that the breakdown of the US audience during commercials is somewhat similar.

During actual program transmissions, other activities tend to occur less but of those measured as viewing in the evening (i.e. in the room with the set on), some 40 percent are giving the television set less than their full attention. This is a very substantial proportion, reflecting once more the frequent low-involvement nature of television viewing.

In principle, the television industry could routinely measure the number of people viewing actively, with other people in the room being counted as a bonus. In practice, however, it is more economical for the industry to measure presence-in-the-room-with-the-set-on, in order to compare audiences for each channel at different times every day. It is the total number present that mostly varies between different programs. The proportions of these who are fully viewing or asleep/doing something else in particular time-bands (such as prime time versus day-time) tend to be much more stable and hence predictable from just occasional measurements, say every quarter of the year or every few years. It has in any case not been possible to demonstrate a consistent (positive or negative) relationship between the audience's involvement in particular programs and any measure of the 'effectiveness' of commercials within or between those programs.

Presence in the room is the basis of most of the data referred to in this book. For our purposes, the average US or British viewer may spend two or three hours per day actively viewing out of three or four hours in the room with the set on. Either way it is a very large amount.

For print media and radio the problems of what is meant by 'reading' and 'listening' are a good deal worse. We read newspapers and magazines in a mostly casual and haphazard way, while most of our radio listening is now secondary to other activities. The problems of measurement are in both cases considerably more severe than for television.

LIKING WHAT WE WATCH

Beyond measuring how much and what we watch, another major concern is how much we actually like the programs. In Britain the audience's appreciation of programs which they have seen has for many years been routinely measured every week in terms of the degree of interest and/or enjoyment that viewers record when watching. The techniques used are a diary or subsequent interview.

In the USA such assessments of specific episodes seen have been made only occasionally. However, people's reactions to regular programs in general are assessed more routinely, i.e. regardless of whether respondents have seen any episodes that week. The results of such assessments of the audience's appreciation of programs have been discussed in Chapter 5.

References

AA (1987) *Marketing Pocket Book 1988*. London: The Advertising Association.

Allen, C.L. (1965) 'Photographing the TV Audience', *Journal of Advertising Research*, 5: 2–8.

Annan, Lord (1977) *Report of the Committee on the Future of Broadcasting*. London: Her Majesty's Stationery Office (HMSO).

Arbitron (1981) *Description of Methodology*. Laurel, Md: Arbitron Company.

Arbitron (1984) *Audience Estimates in the Arbitron Ratings Market of New York, November*. Laurel, Md: Arbitron Company.

ARF (1987) *Peoplemeters: Evolving a Constructive Industry Course*. New York: Advertising Research Foundation.

Aske Research (1976) *Channel Reach*; (1977) *Watching Television*; (1978a) *Availability to View*; (1978b) *The Welsh-Speaking Minority*; (1980a) *The Effort of Switching Channels*; (1980b) *Channel Reach in 1980*; (1981a) *Alone or in Company*; (1981b) *Repeat Showings*; (1981c) *Some Insights from Canada*; (1984) *Jewel in the Crown: Compelling Viewing?* Reports prepared for the IBA. London: Aske Research Ltd. (Goodhardt et al. 1987, pp. 125–7, list ninety other reports on audiences also prepared for the IBA during 1967–1984.)

Auld, Charles (1987) 'Value for My Television Spend?', *Admap*, November: 33–36.

Baker, R.K. and S. Ball (eds) (1969) *Violence and the Media*. Washington DC: Government Printing Office (GPO).

Ball-Rokeach, Sandra J. and Muriel G. Cantor (eds) (1987) *Media, Audience, and Social Structure*. Beverly Hills and London: SAGE Publications.

BARB/AGB (1987) *BARB Reference Manual*. London: Broadcasters Audience Research Board.

Barnard, N. (1985) 'The Price of Television Airtime', *Admap*, November: 552, 553 and 559.

Barnard, N. and T.P.Barwise (1986) 'TV Advertising: How Big Will the Cake Be?', *Admap*, February: 94–97.

Barwise, T.P. (1980) 'Audience Behaviour: Predictable or Unexpected?'. Presented at 11th Broadcasting Symposium, University of Manchester (19–21 March).

Barwise, T.P. (1985a) 'The BBC – No Rich Prizes for Advertisers?', *Media World*, 17 October, 42.

Barwise, T.P. (1986) 'Repeat-Viewing of Prime-Time Television Series', *Journal of Advertising Research*, 26: 9–14.

Barwise, T.P. and A.S.C. Ehrenberg (1979) 'The Revenue Potential of Channel Four', *Admap*, November: 550–556.

Barwise, T.P., and A.S.C. Ehrenberg (1982) *The Liking and Viewing of Regular TV Programs*. London: London Business School.

Barwise, T.P. and A.S.C. Ehrenberg (1984) 'The Reach of TV Channels' *International Journal of Research in Marketing*, 1: 37–44.

Barwise, T.P. and A.S.C. Ehrenberg (1987) 'The Liking and Viewing of Regular TV Series', *Journal of Consumer Research*, 14 (June): 63–70.

Barwise, T.P., A.S.C. Ehrenberg and G.J. Goodhardt (1977) *Channel Reach and Hours per Viewer*; (1978a) *Strip-Programming: Repeat-Viewing of Episodes on Different Days*; (1978b) *Audience Duplication between Different Programs*; (1978c) *Minority Channels: Hours per Viewer*; (1978d) *Watching TV at the Same Time on Different Days*; (1982a) *Watching Television Alone or in Company*. Reports prepared for the Markle Foundation: London Business School.

Barwise, T.P., A.S.C. Ehrenberg and G.J. Goodhardt (1979) 'Audience Appreciation and Audience Size', *Journal of the Market Research Society*, 21: 269–289.

Barwise, T.P., A.S.C. Ehrenberg and G.J. Goodhardt (1980) 'Viewers' Average Appreciation Scores', *Admap*, March: 137–140.

Barwise, T.P., A.S.C. Ehrenberg and G.J. Goodhardt (1982b) 'Glued to the Box?: Patterns of TV Repeat-Viewing', *Journal of Communication*, 32(4) (Autumn): 22–29.

BBC (1980). *Daily Life in 1980*. London: British Broadcasting Corporation.

BBC (1988) *Violence and the Media*. London: British Broadcasting Corporation.

Bechtel, R.B., C. Achelpohl and R. Akers (1972) 'Correlates between Observed Behavior and Questionnaire Responses on Television Viewing', pp. 274–344 in Rubinstein et al. (1972), Vol. 4.

Belson, W.A. (1967) *The Impact of Television*, London: Crosby Lockwood.

Belson, W.A. (1978) *Television Violence and the Adolescent Boy*. Aldershot, England and Brookfield, Vt: Gower.

Beville, J.M. Jr (1985) *Audience Ratings*. Hillsdale, NJ: Lawrence Erlbaum Associates (new edition forthcoming 1988).

Blumler, J.G. and E. Katz (eds) (1974) *The Uses of Mass Communications*. Sage Annual Reviews of Communication Research, Vol. 3. Beverly Hills and London: SAGE Publications.

Blumler, J.G. and D. McQuail (1968) *Television in Politics: Its Uses and Influence*. London: Faber.

Blumler, J.G. and T.J. Nossiter (eds) (1988) *Broadcasting Finance in Transition: A Comparative Handbook*. New York: Oxford University Press.

Bogart, L. (1972) *The Age of Television*, New York: Frederick Ungar.

Bower, R.T. (1973) *Television and the Public*, New York: Holt, Rinehart and Winston.

Bower, R.T. (1985) *The Changing Television Audience in America*. New York: Columbia University Press.

Broadbent, S.R. and B. Jacobs (1984) *Spending Advertising Money*. London: Business Books (4th edition).

Brown, L. (1982) *Les Brown's Encyclopedia of Television*. New York: Zoetrope.

Bryant, J. and D.R. Anderson, (eds) (1983) *Children's Understanding of Television*. New York: Academic Press.

Bryant, J. and D. Zillman (eds) (1986) *Perspectives on Media Effects*. Hillsdale, NJ: Lawrence Erlbaum.

Budd, A. (1987) 'Give C4 its Liberty', *Broadcast*, 23 October.

CAB (1983) *Cable Audience Methodology Study*. New York: Cabletelevision Advertising Bureau and National Cabletelevision Association.

Cardozo, Richard N. (1965) 'An Experimental Study of Customer Effort, Expectation, and Satisfaction', *Journal of Marketing Research*, 2 (August): 244–249.

CBC (1973) *Dimensions of Audience Response to Television Programs in Canada*. Toronto: Canadian Broadcasting Corporation.

CBC (1977) *A Predictive Code for Television Programs*. Toronto: Canadian Broadcasting Corporation.

CBC (1981) *American Programs as Lead-In to Canadian*. Toronto: Canadian Broadcasting Corporation.

CBC (1982) *Choosing TV Programs: Is it Habit or an Active Choice*. Toronto: Canadian Broadcasting Corporation.

CEC (1984) *Television Without Frontiers*. EC green paper. Brussels: Commission of the European Community.

Cohen, A.A. (1987) *The Television News Interview*. Beverly Hills and London: SAGE Publications.

Cole, B. (1981) *Television Today: A Close-up View*. Oxford and New York: Oxford University Press.

Collett, P. and R. Lamb (1986) 'Watching People Watching Television'. Report prepared for the Independent Broadcasting Authority, London.

Collins, R., N. Garnham and G. Locksley (1987) *The Economics of Television: The UK Case*. London: SAGE Publications.

Commission on Obscenity and Pornography (1971) *Report*. Washington DC: Government Printing Office (GPO).

Comstock, G.A. (1980) *Television in America*. Beverly Hills and London: SAGE Publications.

Comstock, G.A. (1987a) 'Today's Audiences, Tomorrow's Media', in Oskamp (1987).

Comstock, G.A. (1987b) 'Television', in *World Book Encyclopedia*. Chicago, Ill: World Books.

Comstock, G.A., S. Chaffee, N. Katzman, M. McCombs and D. Roberts (1978) *Television and Human Behavior*. New York: Columbia University Press.

CONTAM (1969) 'How Good are Television Ratings?'. Annual ARF Conference. New York: Advertising Research Foundation.

CONTAM (1971) *Television Revisited...A Further Look at TV Audiences*. New York: Television Information Office.

Cook, B. (1988) 'Peoplemeters in the USA: An Historical and Methodological Prospective', *Admap*, January: 32–35.

CPB (1978) *The Effect of Television on People's Lives: A Qualitative Study*. Washington, DC: Corporation for Public Broadcasting.

Crook, David (1984) 'Age of "Narrowcasting" Dawns', *Los Angeles Times*, 10 September:(VI)1.

Csikszentmihalyi, M. and R. Kubey (1981) 'Television and the Rest of Life: A Systematic Comparison of Subjective Experience', *Public Opinion Quarterly*, 45: 317–328.

Cumberbatch, G., M. Lee, G. Hardy, I. Jones (1987) *The Portrayal of Violence on British Television: A Content Analysis*. London: BBC Data.

Curran, J., M. Gurevitch and J. Wollacott (eds) (1977) *Mass Communication and Society*. London: Arnold.

Darke, D. (1986) *Turkey*. London: Michael Haag.

De Fleur, M.L. and S.J. Ball-Rokeach (1982) *Theories of Mass Communication*. New York: Longman (4th edition).

Dorr, A. (1986) *Television and Children*. Beverly Hills and London: SAGE Publications.

Dunkley, Christopher (1985) *Television Today and Tomorrow: Wall-to-Wall Dallas?* Harmondsworth, England: Penguin Books.

Ehrenberg, A.S.C. (1972, 1988a) *Repeat-Buying*. London: Charles Griffin, and New York: Oxford University Press (2nd edition).

Ehrenberg, A.S.C. (1974) 'Repetitive Advertising and the Consumer', *Journal of Advertising Research*, 14(2): 25–34.

Ehrenberg, A.S.C. (1986) *Advertisers or Viewers Paying?* Admap Monograph. London: Admap Publications.

Ehrenberg, A.S.C. (1988b) 'What We Can and Can't Get from Graphs and Why', London Business School: CMaC Working Paper.

Ehrenberg, A.S.C. and T.P. Barwise (1982a) 'Cable Expansion and Broadcasting Policy', *London Business School Journal*, 7: 42–45.

Ehrenberg, A.S.C. and T.P. Barwise (1982b) 'Matters for Assessment in Hunt Report', *The Times*, 15 October: letters page.

Ehrenberg, A.S.C. and T.P. Barwise (1983a) 'Do We Need to Regulate TV Programmes?', *InterMedia*, 11 (July/September): 12–16.

Ehrenberg, A.S.C. and T.P. Barwise (1983b) 'How Much Does UK Television Cost?', *International Journal of Advertising*, 2: 17–32.

Ehrenberg, A.S.C. and T.P. Barwise (1987a) 'What are the Alternatives for Channel 4?', *Broadcast*, 2 October.

Ehrenberg, A.S.C. and T.P. Barwise (1987b) 'The Scope for Subscription TV', *Admap*, December: 10–15.

Ehrenberg, A.S.C. and G.J. Goodhardt (1981) 'Attitudes to Episodes and Programmes', *Journal of the Market Research Society*, 23: 184–208.

Ehrenberg, A.S.C. and G.J. Goodhardt (1982) 'Who Watches Repeats?' *Broadcast*, 1140, 15.

Ehrenberg, A.S.C. and G.J. Goodhardt (1988) 'The Viewing of Different Programme Types', London Business School: CMaC Working Paper.

Ehrenberg, A.S.C. and W.A. Twyman (1967) 'On Measuring Television Audiences', *Journal of the Royal Statistical Society*, A, 1230: 1–59.

Ehrenberg, A.S.C. and J. Wakshlag (1987) 'Repeat-Viewing with People Meters', *Journal of Advertising Research*, 27: 9–13.

Ehrenberg, A.S.C., G.J. Goodhardt and T.P. Barwise (1988) 'Double Jeopardy Revisited', London Business School: CMaC Working Paper.

ETTF (European Television Task Force) (1988) *Europe 2000: What Kind of Television?* Manchester: European Institute for the Media.

Fowler, Mark S. and D.L. Brenner (1982) 'A Marketplace Approach to Broadcast Regulation', *Texas Law Review* 60: 207–257.

Frank, R. and M. Greenberg (1980) *The Public's Use of Television*. Beverly Hills: SAGE Publications.

Galbraith, John K. (1985) *The Affluent Society*. Boston: Houghton Mifflin, and London: Andre Deutsch (4th edition).

Gans, H.J. (1980) *Deciding What's News*. New York: Vintage Books.

Gerbner, G. (1967) 'Mass Media and Human Communication Theory', in F.E.X. Dance (ed.), *Human Communication Theory*. New York: Holt, Rinehart and Winston. (Reprinted in McQuail 1972: 35–58.)

Gerbner, G. (1973) 'Cultural Indicators – The Third Voice', pp. 553–573 in G. Gerbner, L. Gross and W. Melody (eds.), *Communications Technology and Social Policy*. New York: Wiley.

Gerbner, George (1987) Personal communication.

Gerbner, G. and L.P. Gross (1976) 'Living with Television: The Violence Profile', *Journal of Communication*, 26(2): 173–199.

Gerbner, G. and L. Gross (1980) 'The Violent Face of Television and Its Lessons', in Edward Palmer and Aimee Dorr (eds), *Children and the Faces of Television: Teaching, Violence, Selling*. New York: Academic Press.

Gerbner, G., L. Gross, M. Morgan and Nancy Signorielli (1980) 'The Mainstreaming of America: Violence Profile No. 11', *Journal of Communication*, 30: 10–29.

Gerbner, G., L. Gross, M. Morgan and N. Signorielli (1986) 'Living with Television: the Dynamics of the Cultivation Process', in Bryant and Zillman (eds).

Golding, P. and P. Elliott (1979) *Making the News*. London: Longman.

Goodhardt, G.J. and A.S.C. Ehrenberg (1982) 'Viewing Alone or in Company?', *Admap*: 310–11.

Goodhardt, G.J., A.S.C. Ehrenberg and M.A. Collins (1975, 1987) *The Television Audience: Patterns of Viewing*. Farnborough, England: Saxon House, and Lexington, Mass: D.C. Heath. (Updated edition 1987, Aldershot, England and Brookfield, Vt: Gower).

Gorn, G.G. (1982) 'The Effects of Music in Advertising on Choice Behavior: A Classical Conditioning Approach', *Journal of Marketing*, 46 (Winter): 94–101.

Graham, David (1985–6) 'Anti-Public Broadcasting', *Economic Affairs*, Dec.–Jan.: 13–15.

Greene, J.D. (1982) *Consumer Behavior Models for Non-Statisticians*. New York: Praeger.

Greenfield, J. (1987) 'Making TV News Pay', *Gannett Center Journal*, Spring, 21–39.

Greenfield, P.M. (1984) *Mind and Media*. Cambridge, Mass: Harvard University Press; London: Fontana.

Gunter, Barrie and M. Svennevig (1987) *Behind and In Front of the Screen: Television's Involvement with Family Life*. London and Paris: John Libbey.

Gunter, B. and M. Svennevig (1988) *Attitudes to Broadcasting Over the Years*. London: John Libbey and IBA.

Halloran, J.D. (ed.) (1970) *The Effects of Television*. London: Granada.

Harrison, A.A. (1977) 'Mere Exposure' pp. 39–83 in L. Berkowitz (ed.), *Advances in Experimental Social Psychology*, Vol. 10, New York: Academic Press.

Himmelweit, H.T., A.N. Oppenheim and P. Vince (1958) *Television and the Child*. London: Oxford University Press.

Hirsch, P.M. (1977a) 'The Medium is the Motive', *Wall Street Journal*, 28 June.

Hirsch, P.M. (1977b) 'Television Has Entered its Golden Age', *Wall Street Journal*, 4 January.

Hirsch, P.M. (1980) 'The "Scary World" of the Non-Viewer and Other Anomalies – a Reanalysis of Gerbner et al.'s Findings in Cultivation Analysis', Part I, *Communication Research*, 7(4): 403–456.

Hirsch, P.M. (1981) 'On Not Learning from One's Mistakes', Part II, *Communication Research*, 8(1): 3–38.

Hollins, T. (1984) *Beyond Broadcasting: Into the Cable Age*. London: British Film Institute.

Home Affairs Committee (1988) *The Future of Broadcasting*. London: HMSO.

Home Office (1987) *Subscription Television*. London: Her Majesty's Stationery Office.

Hotelling, H. (1929) 'Stability in Competition', *Economic Journal*, 34 (March): 41–57.

Howitt, D. and G. Cumberbatch (1975) *Mass Media Violence*. London: Paul Elek.

Hughes, M. (1980) 'The Fruits of Cultivation Analysis: A Re-examination of Some Effects of TV Viewing', *Public Opinion Quarterly*, 44(3): 287–302.

Hunt, Lord (1982) *Report of the Inquiry into Cable Expansion and Broadcasting Policy*. London: Her Majesty's Stationery Office (HMSO).

IBA (1987) *Attitudes to Broadcasting in 1986*. London: Independent Broadcasting Authority.

IPA (1982–8) *Advertising Works* (Vols 1–4). London: Institute of Practitioners in Advertising.

ITAP (1982) *Cable Systems*. London: Her Majesty's Stationery Office (HMSO).

Jacobs, Brian (1987) 'ITV and the Advertisers', *Admap*, November: 41–43.

Jay, P. (1981) 'The McTaggart Lecture'. Edinburgh International Television Festival.

Kahneman, D. (1973) *Attention and Effort*. Englewood Cliffs, NJ: Prentice-Hall.

Klapper, J. (1960) *The Effects of Mass Communication*. New York: Free Press.

Klein, P. (1971) 'The Television Audience and Program Mediocrity', *New York*, 25 January: 20, 21, 29.

Kleppner, O. (1986) *Otto Kleppner's Advertising Procedure*. Thomas Russell and Glenn Verrill (eds). Englewood Cliffs, NJ: Prentice-Hall (9th edition).

Krugman, H.E. (1965) 'The Impact of Television Advertising: Learning without Involvement', *Public Opinion Quarterly*, 30: 349–356.

Krugman, H.E. (1971) 'Brain Wave Measures of Media Involvement', *Journal of Advertising Research*, 11(1)(February): 3–9.

Krugman, H.E. (1980) 'Sustained Viewing of Television', *Journal of Advertising Research*. 20(3): 65–68.

Krull, R. and W.G. Husson (1979) 'Children's attention: The case of TV viewing', in E. Wartella (ed.), *Children Communicating: Media and Development of Thought, Speech, Understanding*. Beverly Hills and London: SAGE Publications.

Krull, R. and J.H. Watt (1975) 'Television Program Complexity and Ratings'. Paper presented to the American Association for Public Opinion Research, Itasca, Ill.

Krull, R., J.H. Watt and L.W. Lichty (1977) 'Entropy and Structure: Two Measures of Complexity in Television Programs', *Communication Research*, 4(1)(January): 61–86.

Kyle, P.W. (1982) 'The Impact of Advertising on Markets', *International Journal of Advertising*, 1, 4(Oct–Dec): 345–359.

Lambin, J.J. (1975) 'What Is the Real Impact of Advertising?', *Harvard Business Review*, 53, 3 (May–June): 139–147.

Lang, Gladys E. and K. Lang (1985) *Politics and Television Re-Viewed*. Beverly Hills and London: SAGE Publications.

Lee, Chin-Chuan (1980) *Media Imperialism Reconsidered*. Beverly Hills and London: SAGE Publications.

Liebert, R.M., J.M. Neale and E.S. Davidson (1973) *The Early Window*. Oxford and New York: Pergamon Press.

Lindlof, T.R. (ed.) (1987) *National Audiences: Qualitative Research of Media Uses and Effects*. Norwood, NJ: Ablex.

LoSciuto, L. A. (1972) 'A National Inventory of Television Viewing Behavior', pp. 35–86 in Rubinstein et al. (1972).

Lyle, J. (1972) 'Television in Daily Life', in Rubinstein et al., *Television and Social Behavior*. Washington DC: Government Printing Office.

Mander, J. (1978) *Four Arguments for the Elimination of Television*. New York: Quill (1980), Brighton, England: Harvester.

Mayer, M. (1966) *How Good are Television Ratings?* New York: Committee on National Television Audience Measurement.

McBride Commission (1979) *Many Voices, One World*. Report by the International Commission for the Study of Communication Problems. Paris: Unesco, and (1980) London: Kogan Page.

McCarney, L.J. (1984) 'Social and Economic Aspects of Monopoly and Pluralism in Television Broadcasting – A South African Perspective'. Doctoral Thesis: University of Cape Town.

McGinnis, J. (1969) *The Selling of the President*. New York: Trident Press.

McPhail, T.L. (1987) *Electronic Colonialism*. (2nd edition). Beverly Hills and London: SAGE Publications.

McPhee, W.N. (1963) *Formal Theories of Mass Behavior*. New York: Free Press.

McQuail, D. (ed.) (1972) *Sociology of Mass Communications*. Harmondsworth, UK: Penguin.

McQuail, D. (1987) *Mass Communication Theory*. (2nd edition). Beverly Hills and London: SAGE Publications.

Media World (1982) 'The Reality of Second Set Viewing', *Media World*, May 1982: 44 and 50.

Meneer, P. (1987) 'Audience Appreciation – A Different Story from Audience Numbers', *Journal of the Market Research Society*, 29: 241–264.

Milavsky, J.R., H.H. Stipp, R.C. Kessler and W.S. Rubens (1982) *Television and Aggression: A Panel Study*. New York: Academic Press.

Mink, E. (1983) 'Why the Networks Will Survive', *The Atlantic Monthly*, December: 63–68.

NCC (1981) *Consumer Concerns Survey*. London: National Consumer Council.

Newcombe, H. (1978) 'Assessing the Violence Profile of Gerbner and Gross: A Humanistic Critique and Suggestion', *Communication Research*, 5: 264–282.

Nielsen (1974, 1976, 1978, 1981, 1987) *The Television Audience*. Northbrook, Ill: A.C. Nielsen Company (Published annually).

Nielsen (1983) 'Before-and-after Pay-cable Tracking Study', in *Summary of 1983 Client Meetings*. Northbrook, Ill: A.C. Nielsen Company.

Nielson (1985) *Video Cassette Recorder Usage Report*. New York: Nielsen HomeVideo Index.

NIMH (1982) *Television and Behavior: Ten Years of Scientific Progress and Implications for the Eighties*. Vol. 1: Summary Report and Vol. 2: Technical Reviews. Washington, DC: National Institute of Mental Health.

Noble, G. (1975) *Children in Front of the Small Screen*. London: Constable.

Onoe, Hisao and Yasuo Sakamoto (1979) *The Social Benefit of TV*. Research Report of the Cost-benefit Analysis Working Group. Tokyo: NHK Hoso Bunka Foundation.

Oskamp, S. (ed.) (1987) *Television as a Social Issue*. Applied Social Psychology Annual, Vol. 8. Beverly Hills and London: SAGE Publications.

Owen, B.M., J.H. Beebe and W.G. Manning Jr (1974) *Television Economics*. Lexington, Mass: Lexington Books.

Packard, V. (1957) *The Hidden Persuaders*. New York: David McKay, and London: Longman (reissued 1960 by Harmondsworth, England: Penguin).

Peacock, A. (1986) *Committee on Financing the BBC*. London: HMSO.

Phillips, W. (1988) 'The Real Cost of Television, 1966–87', *Admap*, January: 10–19.

PMM (1985) *BBC: Value for Money*. London: Peat, Marwick, and Mitchell.

Pollay, R.W., J. Zaichkowsky, and C. Fryer (1980) 'Regulation Hasn't Changed TV Ads Much!', *Journalism Quarterly*, 57(3): 438–446.

Poltrack, D. (1983) *Television Marketing: Network, Local and Cable*. New York: McGraw-Hill.

Postman, N. (1986) *Amusing Ourselves to Death*. London: Heinemann.

Pragnall, A. (1985) *Television in Europe*. Manchester: European Institute for the Media.

Pretorius, D.J.L. (1984) Personal communication.

Reiss, Pamela (1987) 'TV Audiences: VCRs as the fifth dimension', *Admap*, November: 44–49.

Research Services (1962) *Television Attention Research 1961*. London: Research Services Ltd.

Robinson, J.P. (1969) 'Television and Leisure Time: Yesterday, Today and (Maybe) Tomorrow', *Public Opinion Quarterly*, 33: 210–222.

Robinson, J.P. and M.R. Levy (1986) *The Main Source: Learning from Television News*. Beverly Hills and London: SAGE Publications.

Roper Organization (1979) *Public Perception of Television and Other Mass Media: A Twenty Year Review, 1959–78*. New York: Television Information Office.

Rosengren, K.E., L.A. Wenner and P. Palmgreen (eds.) (1985) *Media Gratifications Research*. Beverly Hills and London: SAGE Publications.

Rubin, A.M., E.M. Perse, and D.S. Taylor (1988) 'A Methodological Examination of Cultivation', *Communication Research*, 15, 2 (April): 107–134.

Rubinstein, E.A., G.A. Comstock and J.P. Murray (1972) *Television and Social Behavior*. Vols. 1–5. Washington DC: Government Printing Office. (Summarised in Surgeon General's Scientific Advisory Committee, 1972.)

Rust, R. (1986) *Advertising Media Models*. Lexington, Mass: Lexington Books.

Schlesinger, P. (1978) *Putting 'Reality' Together: BBC News*. London: Constable.

Schramm, W., J. Lyle and E. Parker (1961) *Television in the Lives of Our Children*. Stanford: Stanford University Press.

Seymour-Ure, C. (1974) *The Political Impact of Mass Media*. London: Constable and Beverly Hills: SAGE Publications.

Shoemaker, Pamela J. (1987) 'Mass Communication by the Book: A Review of 31 Texts', *Journal of Communication*, 37(3)(Summer): 109–131.

Sluckin, W., D.J. Hargreaves and A.M. Colman (1982) 'Some Experimental Studies of Familiarity and Liking', *Bulletin of the British Psychological Society*, 35: 189–194.

Smith, A. (1776) *An Inquiry into the Sources and Causes of the Wealth of Nations*. London: W. Strahan; Dublin: Whitstone.

Soong, R. (1988) 'The Statistical Reliability of People Meter Ratings', *Journal of Advertising Research*, 28: 50–56.

Spaeth, J. (1988) 'Single Source Data: When Peoplemeters Aren't Enough', *Admap*, January 36–41.

Steiner, G.A. (1963) *The People Look at Television*. New York: Alfred A. Knopf.

Stewart, W.B. (1970) 'CBC Television and the Faithful', *Public Opinion Quarterly*, 34: 92–100.

Stewart, W.B. (1981) 'The Audience Size of TV Programs'. Canadian Broadcasting Corporation: Working Paper.

Surgeon General's Scientific Advisory Committee (1972) *Television and Growing Up: The Impact of Televised Violence*. Washington DC: Government Printing Office. (Contains summary of Rubinstein et al., 1972.)

TAA (1983a) *The Audience Rates Television*. Boston, Mass: Television Audience Assessment.

TAA (1983b) *Appeal and Impact: A Program Ratings Book*. Boston, Mass: Television Audience Assessment.

TAA (1983c) *The Multichannel Environment*. Boston, Mass: Television Audience Assessment.

TAA (1984) *A Summary of Television Audience Assessment's Research and Development Activities 1981–1984*. Boston, Mass: Television Audience Assessment.

TAM (1961) *Comparison Survey of Audience Composition Techniques*. London: Television Audience Measurement.

Tannenbaum, P. (ed.) (1980) *Entertainment Functions of Television*. Hillsdale, NJ: Lawrence Erlbaum.

Taylor, L. and R.G. Mullan (1986) *Uninvited Guests: The Intimate Secrets of Television and Radio*. London: Chatto & Windus.

Tiedge, J. and K. Ksobiech (1986) 'The Lead-In Strategy for Prime-Time TV: Does It Increase the Audience?' *Journal of Communication*, 36(3): 51–63.

Tuchman, G. (1978) *Making News: A Study in the Construction of Reality*. New York: Free Press.

Tunstall, J. (1977) *The Media Are American*. London: Constable.

Twyman, W.A. (1986a) 'Television Media Research', in R. Worcester and J. Downham (eds), *Consumer Market Research Handbook*. Amsterdam: ESOMAR (3rd edition).

Twyman, W.A. (1986b) 'Attention and the Measurement of Media Exposure for Press and Television', pp. 689–743 in *Media Research and Planning*. Amsterdam: ESOMAR.

Twyman, W.A. (1988) 'Which Peoplemeter?', *Admap*, January: 27–31.

Van Vuuren, Daan P. (1981) 'The Impact of Television on Adolescents in South Africa'. Paper presented at the Fourth International Conference on Experimental Research in TV Instruction, St. John's, Newfoundland.

Vidmar, N. and M. Rokeach (1974) 'Archie Bunker's Bigotry: A Study in Selective Perception', *Journal of Communication*, 24: 36–47.

Vogel, H.L. (1986) *Entertainment Industry Economics*. Cambridge: Cambridge University Press.

Wakshlag, J. (1985) *A Content Analysis of American and Canadian Broadcasting*. Prepared for Aske Research Ltd.

Wand, B. (1968) 'Television Viewing and Family Differences', *Public Opinion Quarterly*, 32: 84–94.

Ward, Scott, T. Robertson and R. Brown (eds) (1986) *Commercial Television and European Children*. Aldershot, England and Brookfield, Vt: Gower.

Waterson, M.J. (1984) *Advertising, Brands, and Markets*. London: Advertising Association.

Watt, J.H. and R. Krull (1974) 'An Information Theory Measure for Television Programming', *Communication Research*, 1(1)(January): 44–68.

Webster, J. (1985) 'Program Audience Duplication: A Study of Television Inheritance Effects', *Journal of Broadcasting and Electronic Media*, 29: 121–133.

Webster, J. (1986) 'Audience Behavior in the New Media Environment', *Journal of Communication*, 36(3): 77–91.

Webster, J. and J. Wakshlag (1983) 'A Theory of Television Program Choice', *Communication Research*, 10: 430–446.

Webster, J., A.S.C. Ehrenberg and T.P. Barwise (1988) 'A Comparison of US and British TV Industry Costs', London Business School: Working Paper.

Webster, L.L. (1980) 'Who'll Watch at Breakfast?', *Broadcast*, 24 November: 17–20.

Wells, A. (1972) *Picture-Tube Imperialism? The Impact of US TV in Latin America*. New York: Orbis.

Wenham, Brian (ed) (1982) *The Third Age of Broadcasting*. London: Faber and Faber.

Wheen, Francis (1985) *Television: A History*. London: Century.

Wightman, D. (1982) Personal Communication.

Williams, R. (1974) *Television: Technology and Cultural Form*. London: Fontana.

Willman, P. (1986) *Technological Change, Collective Bargaining and Industrial Efficiency*. Oxford: Clarendon Press.

Wilson, C.C. II and F. Gutierrez (1985) *Minorities and Media: Diversity and the End of Mass Communication*. Beverly Hills and London: SAGE Publications.

Winn, Marie (1977) *The Plug-In Drug*. New York: Viking.

Wober, J.M. (1978) 'Televised Violence and Paranoid Perception: The View from Gt. Britain', *Public Opinion Quarterly*, 42: 315–321.

Wober, J.M. (1986) 'The Lens of Television and the Prism of Personality', pp. 205–231 in Bryant and Zillman, *Perspectives on Media Effects*. Hillside, NJ: Lawrence Erlbaum.

Zajonc, R.B. (1968) 'The Attitudinal Effects of Mere Exposure', *Journal of Personality and Social Psychology*, 9 (Monograph Supplement 2), Part 2: 1–27.

Zenaty, Jayne W. (1984) 'New Communications Technology in the Year 2000'. AAA/ANA presentation to the Federal Trade Commission (October). Chicago, Ill: Leo Burnett USA.

Zillman, Dolf (1984) *Connections Between Sex and Aggression*. Hillsdale, NJ: Lawrence Erlbaum.

Zillman, Dolf and Jennings Bryant (1982) 'Pornography, Sexual Callousness, and the Trivialization of Rape', *Journal of Communication*, 32(4)(Autumn): 10–21.

Zillman, Dolf and Jennings Bryant (eds) (1985) *Selective Exposure to Communication*. Hillsdale, NJ: Lawrence Erlbaum.

Glossary

Above-the-line: In *advertising*, the amount spent on placing advertisements in media where the advertiser pays for the airtime or space (television, print, radio, billboards, cinema); all other promotional and publicity expenditures are 'below-the-line' (consumer promotions, trade deals, price cuts, direct mail, telephone selling, brochures, PR, etc.). In *TV production*, creative costs are above-the-line (writers, directors, producers, and main cast) as opposed to 'below-the-line' technical and promotional expenses.

Added value: A quality, often fairly intangible, which distinguishes one brand from others in its product group.

Add-on services: Television services such as pay-TV or VCRs, which are bought by some homes to give program choices that are additional to the 'mainstream' broadcast channels which are available in all television homes in the area and which people watch most of the time.

Addressability: Technical interaction between the transmitting station (or cable head-end) and each receiving household, e.g. to permit and/or to measure the viewing of specific programs or channels.

Advertising: Loosely describes all publicity activities but strictly refers only to 'above-the-line' media advertising, which is paid for.

Aerial, antenna: Electrical conductor used to transmit or receive broadcast signals.

Affiliates: Television stations which by contract receive most of their broadcast material from a particular network but are not owned by that network.

Aspect ratio: The ratio of the width of a screen to its height, currently 4:3 for television. Cinema and HDTV have an aspect ratio of about 5:3.

Audience availability: Able to watch television, often measured as 'being at home but not asleep in bed'.

Audience duplication, Audience overlap: The viewers that two broadcasts have in common.

Audience inheritance, lead-in-effect: The tendency for a program to have extra audience overlap with the adjacent programs on the same channel.

Audience ratings, Ratings: The percentage of a particular population watching a television program, commercial or channel at a specific time. Usually measures the people who are in the room with the television set switched on. 'Household ratings' or 'set ratings' refer to the percentage of households with a set on that is tuned to the program.

Audited circulation figures: The number of copies *sold* (not given away) by a magazine or newspaper, as checked by independent auditors.

Bandwidth: A measure of the capacity of a communication channel, especially the amount of electromagnetic frequency spectrum needed for a television or radio channel. A color television channel has a bandwidth of about 6 million cycles per second (6 Megahertz or MHz).

Barter: Arrangements, usually in the USA, by which stations pay production companies with advertising time on their stations (rather than with money) in exchange for the right to broadcast a program.

Basic cable: Normally refers to cable-only channels with advertising, supplied to subscribers at no extra cost to the basic monthly connection charge. Cable operators pay the basic cable networks a small fee per subscriber. Pay cable refers to premium channels (without advertising), for which subscribers pay extra for a channel or group of channels.

Below-the-line: See Above-the-line.

Broadcast channel: Technically, a section of the frequency spectrum which can be allocated to a particular station for over-air transmissions. In practice, often refers to the station itself or its programs.

Television which is 'broadcast' is available to anyone in the region with suitable receiving equipment. The term 'broadcast' is also used for programs which are of broad audience appeal (cf. narrowcast).

Cable television: A system by which television signals are transmitted via over- or underground cables, rather than over-air.

Camcorder: Short for camera/recorder, i.e. a light, portable unit combining the functions of video camera and (video and sound) recorder.

CATV, Community Antenna Television: Homes in an area of poor over-air reception are cabled to a large, shared aerial.

Channel: The means through which a product or service (e.g. television programs) is physically moved from producer to consumer. Also used to refer to the broadcaster (e.g. NBC, BBC1, Channel 4) who transmits through that channel (see Broadcast channel).

Chat show, talk show: A host and guests chatting in front of a studio audience. Sometimes interspersed with music and variety.

Coincidental calls: Carefully timed survey interviews (face-to-face or by phone) asking whether and what channel the informant and/or others in the household are watching at the moment the interviewer calls.

Commercial break: When program broadcasts are interrupted to transmit one or more paid advertisements.

Commercials: The usual term for television or radio advertisements.

Complementary programming: When one TV station transmits a very different type of program from another at a given time, to give viewers a wider choice of program types at that time.

Co-productions: Programs whose production costs are shared by two or more broadcasting organizations, usually in different countries.

Correlation: When two things tend to vary together (e.g. that taller children tend also to be heavier). A correlation is *low* if there are quite a few exceptions (e.g. tall light children).

Cultural imperialism: The tendency for one country's mass culture to be dominated by that of another country.

Cume: The percentage of people who, cumulatively over a period of time, see at least one episode of a series or set of similar broadcasts (e.g. early evening CBS News).

Current affairs: See Public affairs.

DBS, Direct Broadcasting by Satellite: Using a high-powered satellite to transmit up to a dozen or so channels directly to dwellings. The relatively high power means that DBS can be received via a small dish aerial. In the 1990s, DBS dish aerials may be replaced by small flat plates. Also called Direct to Home (DTH) satellite broadcasting.

Demandingness: The degree to which a program requires intellectual and/or emotional effort or involvement from its viewers.

Deregulation: Freeing broadcasters from governmental restrictions concerning say, station ownership or program content. Based on a belief in market forces getting it right, or at least better.

Desk-top publishing: Design and production of text and graphics by amateurs or small publishers, using a micro-computer and non-impact (e.g. laser) printer, thus sidestepping the need for expensive outside design and typesetting.

Diary methods: People recording their television viewing, usually quarter-hour by quarter-hour in a pre-structured 7-day 'diary'.

Dish aerial: Aerials that allow reception of satellite transmissions: small dishes for DBS; large dishes for medium or low-powered satellite transmissions, e.g. for retransmission by a broadcaster or cable operator.

Duplication: See Audience duplication.

Encryption: See Scrambling.

Enhanced or Extended Definition TV: Less ambitious than HDTV, but compatible with present equipment and potentially cost-effective.

Fax: Short for 'facsimile'. A system for transmitting a print-on-paper image via an ordinary telephone line. Normally, the sender's fax machine scans the paper and the receiver's machine reproduces it. Fax messages can also be generated by computer.

FCC, Federal Communications Commission: The government-appointed but 'arms-length' agency in the USA which regulates all communication media (broadcasting, telephones, newspapers etc.) within US territories.

Features: Special attraction, one-off television programs which often focus on a particular subject, person, event or type of entertainment.

First-run: The first showing of a program or series.

Fully-Switched Cable: A system with two-way cable such that a video-signal can be sent from any subscriber to any other (rather than just from and to the head-end); the video equivalent of the telephone system.

GDP, Gross Domestic Product: A measure of the size of a country's economy.

Generic: Relating to a product class as a whole rather than to a particular brand. Also refers to a product sold in plain unbranded packaging.

Guest-viewing: Television viewing by visitors to a household.

HDTV, High Definition Television: The use of more 'lines' and higher resolution in transmitting the television signal, in order to produce clearer pictures.

Head-end: The physical hub of a local cable system transmitting television programs to subscribing households which are connected to it by cable.

Heavy viewers: People who tend to watch well over the average amount of television (e.g. more than 35 or 40 hours per week in the USA, UK or Japan compared with an average of about 25 hours). Typically includes a quarter to a third of a nation's population of television viewers.

IBA, Independent Broadcasting Authority: The government-appointed but 'arms-length' agency in the UK which has been regulating independent Television (ITV) and (at time of writing) commercial radio companies there.

Independents ('indies'): In the USA, local stations that function independently of the networks. Often the stations are linked in chains across several cities, forming co-operative 'mini-networks', or are grouped under the same ownership.

The term 'independents' is also used to describe television production companies which are not owned by a broadcaster or a major film studio.

Independent Television (ITV): The service provided in Britain by (large) regional 'independent television companies' which are privately owned, funded by advertising, and independent of the license fee.

In-house: Television productions by the broadcasting organization itself instead of being bought in from outside producers or other broadcasters.

Interactive (or 'two-way') cable: Cables with capacity to transmit signals both ways between cable subscribers and the head-end, so that viewers can send or request information via the system instead of, say, by telephone.

Involvement: Broadly, the degree of viewers' commitment or attention to what they are viewing.

Keypads: Remote switch with extra buttons for controlling videotex or interactive cable.

Lead-in effect: See Audience inheritance.

License, License fees: An arrangement for funding broadcasting under which each household using a television is obliged to have a license and to pay an annual fee for it, with the level usually set by the government. Used to fund some or all of broadcasting in many countries.

Light viewers: People who tend to watch relatively little television (less than 10 or 15 hours per week compared with an average of 25 hours). Typically a quarter to a third of a nation's population of television viewers.

LPTV, Low Power Television: A type of local broadcast station with a limit on its licensed power output, to avoid interference with other stations' signals.

Mainstream television: The broadcast channels which are available in all homes with a television set in the area and which people watch most of the time.

Market forces: The forces controlling supply and demand, especially in an unregulated, free market. Returning to the ideas of Adam Smith (1776), liberal market economists believe that, as long as market forces are given free play, the price, quality, and quantity of products or services supplied will *automatically* produce the best possible reflection of customers' preferences as if 'led by an invisible hand'. Modern economists put more stress on competition as a spur for efficiency and innovation. Although few economists are wholly starry-eyed about market forces, most believe that competition is good in almost all practical cases.

Markets: Used in the USA to describe limited urban or rural regions reached by a television or radio station. More generally used to describe the customers for a product or service (usually one that is paid for).

Mass media: Those communication media that are directed at and/or used by the general population rather than a particular (and usually rather small) subgroup, minority or segment.

Mass programs: See Minority programs.

Media imperialism: Cultural imperialism applied specifically to mass media, especially television.

Megahertz, MHz: Million cycles per second. See Bandwidth.

Mini-series: A limited-length drama serial with up to about half a dozen episodes. Usually based on a novel, made with high production values, and heavily promoted.

Minority programs: (As opposed to 'mass programs'). This and related terms are used differently by different commentators. Some merely mean low-rating programs. Some mean programs on specific topics that usually interest or are thought to interest a relatively small and defined proportion (or 'segment') of the population, e.g. people interested in opera, gardening, psychology, a particular sport, or a specific ethnic interest. Others go further, assuming that viewers of a minority program are identifiable in other respects (e.g. that the audience profile of an opera on television is similar to, or only a little broader than, that of the audience in an opera house). In practice, television audiences are not markedly 'segmented' in this way, quite unlike the press.

We use the term 'minority-taste' programs to reflect the fact that some programs appeal to or tend to be watched by relatively few people who have a taste for that particular type of program but who, in practice, are not clearly identifiable in any other way.

Multi-channel cable: A cable television system supplying many channels including basic cable and pay cable channels, superstations, and other non-local channels, as well as the local broadcast stations which could have been distributed by CATV.

Multi-set homes: Households that have more than one television set.

MVDS, MMDS, (Multi-channel) Multi-point (Video) Distribution Service: A type of pay-TV using line-of-sight microwave transmission (Super High Frequency – even higher than UHF).

Narrowband: A telephone (cable or over-air microwave) link with enough capacity (bandwidth) for voice and medium-rate data traffic but not for a full video signal (cf. wideband cable).

Narrowcast channel: A somewhat confused term used in various ways, all in contrast to broadcasting. Usually, narrowcasting refers to a channel and means that it shows programs of a specific type and/or programs which are aimed at (but not necessarily viewed by) a specific minority or segment of the population. This raises various assumptions and ambiguities: see Minority programs, segmentation.

Networks: A group of television or radio stations, operating in different localities, which are owned by or affiliated to the same company. The stations usually transmit the same program material at more or less the same time, especially during prime time.

The term 'networking' is also used when programs (or commercials) are broadcast at the same time by stations which are independent of each other.

Opportunities to see, OTS: The number of times when a viewer will be present with the television set tuned to the relevant channel while the commercials of a particular advertising campaign are being shown.

Over-air transmissions: The traditional system in which television signals are sent ('broadcast') via the air waves rather than by wire.

Panel: In audience research, a group of households who take part continuously (or over a set time period of time) in survey measurements of television and radio audiences. Allows analyses of the 'flow' of audiences between programs, etc. rather than just producing audience size ratings.

Pay cable: See Basic cable.

Pay-per-view: A special version of pay-TV which charges program by program or by the amount viewed.

Pay-TV: Any system in which viewers pay on an individual household basis for the right to watch a particular channel, possibly just for specific times (pay-per-view).

Peak viewing: Times when the largest number of people tend to be viewing television; from about 7.00 pm to 10.00 pm in most countries. (See also Prime Time.)

People-meters: Electronic push-button ways of recording the presence of individual viewers when measuring audience ratings. Employed with panels of homes, often to replace diary methods.

Phone-ins: Inexpensive programs that are based around a presenter and guests and/or a small panel of commentators in a studio receiving telephone calls from the public and discussing the subjects that they raise.

Pre-recorded material: Programs or films retailed on video cassette for rental or sale to VCR owners, in contrast to the programs they themselves record off-air.

Prime time: Those hours when the television ratings are highest. Used with very specific time-limits in connection with costs of airtime for commercials.

Production values: Aspects of the amount of effort and money invested in making a television program (e.g. high quality actors, writers, producers, number of cameras, degree of rehearsal, location work, special effects).

Public affairs/Current affairs: Programs dealing with topical issues of public concern (political, economic, social, etc.).

Public Relations, PR: Usually refers to deliberate attempts by persons or organizations to create a good relationship with the public (e.g. customers, voters). People working in Public Relations provide specialist assistance in achieving this especially in seeking to gain favorable media coverage.

Public Service Channels: Broadcasters concerned with the range and quality of program (especially cultural, informative, or minority-interest) that they offer to the public as well as with the number of viewers or income that they attract.

Ratings: See Audience ratings.

Ratings war: Competition between television channels (stations, networks, etc.) in which each strives at each time for the largest possible audience (within the restrictions of its programming budgets).

Reach: See Cume.
'Channel reach' is the proportion of people who tune into the channel at least once (for say a minimum of 15 minutes) over a period such as a day or a week.

Read-write video disks: Video disk on to which the user can record information (either once or, on some systems, repeatedly) as well as being able to retrieve it. Most video disks sold to date are 'read-only', unlike VCRs.

Repeat-viewing: When a viewer of one episode of a regular program watches a following episode. (Usually does *not* refer to seeing the same episode again on a re-run or on a VCR.)

Re-runs, Repeats: When a program or series is shown for a second (or subsequent) time.

Residuals: Contractual payments over and above an initial fee, made to actors, writers, etc. when a program is re-run or sold to another market.

Royalty: Contractual payments made to actors, writers, etc. at intervals and based on a proportion of sales or revenues to date (rather than a one-off fee).

Satellite: A space vehicle orbiting the earth. In the context of television, one that is able to receive and re-transmit television signals.

Scheduling: The timetabling of each channel's programming.

Scrambling, Encryption: Deliberate distortion of a signal to prevent unauthorised viewers (e.g. non-subscribers) from viewing and/or hearing it. Subscribers' descrambling or decryption equipment can be produced at various levels of sophistication to prevent pirating.

Segmentation: Any marked tendency for a separately identifiable subgroup of the population to have similar tastes or behavior (e.g. viewing a particular television program, buying a particular brand or product), especially when they can also be identified in some other way as reachable targets for advertising purposes (e.g. young mothers, owners of hi-fi equipment, etc.) See Minority programs.

Serials: Narrative drama programs that have a continuing story-line over a sequence of episodes. Applies particularly to soap-operas.

Series: Continuing drama programs where individual episodes have a self-contained plot but use more or less the same cast of main characters. Also used to describe non-drama programs spread over many episodes or editions. Most sitcoms and action-adventure programs are series.

Sitcom, Situation comedy: Comedy drama based on the humor of character and situation – the plot is usually resolved at the end of each self-contained episode.

Smart card: A plastic card that contains a printed electronic circuit which is programmed (smart) to allow the user to unscramble transmitted signals and to note how much the card has been used (as with telephone cards).

SMATV, Satellite Master Antenna Television: A private multi-channel cable system for an hotel or apartment block.

Soap opera: A type of program series with a continuing human interest or even melodramatic plot. So named because such drama serials on US radio were originally sponsored by a soap manufacturer.

Stripped programming: When a program is shown in the same time-slot on several days each week. Often done in the US for re-runs of old successful series for which there is a big backlog of available episodes.

STV, Subscription Television: Usually refers to a terrestrial television service funded by monthly payments by subscribing households on a 'pay-per-channel' basis (as opposed to 'pay-per-view'). The signal is scrambled to stop non-subscribers from viewing.

Superstation: An independent broadcast station which is also distributed via satellite to cable operators across the whole USA. Outside its local broadcast market, a superstation is like a basic cable channel.

Syndication: Where a television series is sold (syndicated) to different broadcasting organizations in different parts of the same country (especially in the USA). Programs are usually syndicated after a successful network run but there is now also a growing trade in 'first-run syndication'.

Talking heads: Discussion program with two or more named participants in a studio, where the camera mostly focuses on the head of the person speaking.

Teletext: A broadcasting system which transmits text, data, and graphics at the same time as ('on the back of') an ordinary television program signal, for reception on specially equipped television sets. By definition, this can be one way only, from transmitter to individual viewer.

Television schedulers: Those who determine the day and time that programs and advertisements are broadcast.

Time-shift: Using a VCR to record a program off-air for playback at a preferred later time.

Tracking: Monitoring a market over a period of time, continuously or via repeated surveys at intervals of either the same sample (a panel survey) or a different sample each time. The aim is to measure trends and the process of change.

Trailer: An announcement or promotion about a program or its next episode, transmitted by the broadcaster (not a 'paid-for' advertisement).

UHF, Ultra-High Frequency: Higher frequency than VHF, the UHF band enables more channels to be broadcast (e.g. channels 14 through 83 in the USA, 21 through 68 in Britain). But, for the same transmitter power, the UHF signal has lower effective range. This and tuning difficulties put early UHF stations at a severe disadvantage versus VHF.

VCR, Video Cassette Recorder: A machine that enables one to record a television program for subsequent viewing at a different time. Usually can also show material (films, television programs, and home-movies) pre-recorded on video tape.

VHF, Very High Frequency: The band from 30 to 300 MHz, including television channels 1 through 13. See Bandwidth, UHF.

Video disks: A laser-based form of audio-visual recording. Gives much better quality than video tapes, much quicker access to specific items recorded on the disk, and is cheaper to reproduce than video tapes. However, so far incapable of being used for in-home time-shift recording.

Videotex, Videotext: The generic term for various systems which display text, data, or simple graphics on ordinary television screens. The signal can be transmitted by one-way broadcast (teletext) or by cable or telephone line (on-line videotex). The latter can also allow signals to go from the viewer to the transmitter, to provide access to a large data base or to initiate transactions (e.g. in-home shopping, or banking).

Viewdata: British term for on-line (i.e. non-broadcast) video text.

Watchmen: Miniature portable television sets that can be used with headphones.

Wideband Cable: Forms of cable that can carry enough bandwidth to transmit full video signals (i.e. television pictures and sound).

Author Index

Subject Index

About the Authors

Patrick Barwise is Senior Lecturer in Marketing at the London Business School, and Director of its London Executive Programme. He previously worked for IBM. Apart from television, his interests include strategic investment decisions, marketing planning, management development, consumer behavior, and the use of information.

Andrew Ehrenberg has been Professor of Marketing at the London Business School since 1970, is Director of its Centre for Marketing and Communication, and has also worked in industry for 15 years. He has published many papers on marketing, media, and statistical topics. His other books include *Data Reduction*, *Repeat Buying*, and *The Television Audience*.